ATTACHMENT THERAPY ON TRIAL

Recent Titles in Child Psychology and Mental Health

Children's Imaginative Play: A Visit to Wonderland
Shlomo Ariel

ATTACHMENT THERAPY ON TRIAL

The Torture and Death of Candace Newmaker

Jean Mercer, Larry Sarner, and Linda Rosa
with a chapter by Gerard Costa

Child Psychology and Mental Health
Hiram E. Fitzgerald and Susanne Ayres Denham, Series Editors

PRAEGER

Westport, Connecticut
London

Library of Congress Cataloging-in-Publication Data

Mercer, Jean.
    Attachment therapy on trial: the torture and death of Candace Newmaker / Jean Mercer, Larry Sarner, and Linda Rosa ; with a chapter by Gerard Costa.
       p.   cm.—(Child psychology and mental health, ISSN 1538–8883)
    Includes bibliographical references and index.
    ISBN 0–275–97675–0 (alk. paper)
    1. Newmaker, Candace, 1989–2000—Mental health. 2. Newmaker, Candace, 1989–2000—Death and burial. 3. Attachment disorder in children—Treatment—United States—Case studies. 4. Social workers—Malpractice—United States. I. Sarner, Larry. II. Rosa, Linda. III. Title. IV. Series.
RJ507.A77N495   2003
618.92′89—dc21   2002044991

British Library Cataloguing in Publication Data is available.

Library of Congress Catalog Card Number: 2002044991
ISBN: 0–275–97675–0
ISSN: 1538–8883

First published in 2003

Praeger Publishers, 88 Post Road West, Westport, CT 06881
An imprint of Greenwood Publishing Group, Inc.
www.praeger.com

Printed in the United States of America

The paper used in this book complies with the Permanent Paper Standard issued by the National Information Standards Organization (Z39.48–1984).

10 9 8 7 6 5 4 3 2 1

To the children, and to the brave adult survivors
who came forward to tell us their stories.

Contents

Series Foreword *by Hiram E. Fitzgerald and Susanne Ayres Denham*   ix

Acknowledgments   xi

Introduction: Attachment Therapy and Its Victims   1

PART I   THE CASE OF CANDACE NEWMAKER

1. Candace's Adoption and Death: How a Second Chance Became
   the Last Chance   15

2. The Backstory: People and Systems Behind Candace's Death   37

3. Candace's Treatment: What They Did and Why They Did It   57

PART II   THE FACTS BEHIND CANDACE'S CASE: REALITIES OF EMOTIONAL
   DEVELOPMENT AND CHILDHOOD MENTAL ILLNESS

4. Some Facts About Normal Emotional Development (and What
   the Attachment Therapists Believed)   85

5. When Emotional Life Goes Wrong: Some Facts About Childhood
   Mental Illness versus the Attachment Therapists' Beliefs   109

6. Better Treatment for Candace: How Trained Psychotherapists
   Would Have Approached This Case   135
   Gerard Costa

PART III   PREVENTING MORE CASES LIKE CANDACE'S: PROBLEMS AND
            SOME POSSIBLE SOLUTIONS

7. Science and Psychotherapy: Is There Evidence That Attachment
   Therapy Is a Valid Treatment?   163
8. The Deceivers and the Deceived: Factors That Made Attachment
   Therapy Acceptable to Parents and to Practitioners   187

9. The Law and the Child: How Our Legal System Affected
   Candace Newmaker's Life and Death   211

   Conclusion
   Lawsuits and Legislation: Where Do We Go from Here?   235

   Bibliography of Materials Relevant to Attachment Therapy   249

   Index   255

Series Foreword

The twentieth century closed with a decade devoted to the study of brain structure, function, and development that—in parallel with studies of the human genome—has revealed the extraordinary plasticity of biobehavioral organization and development. The twenty-first century opens with a decade focusing on behavior, but the linkages between brains and behavior are as dynamic as the linkages between parents and children and between children and environment.

The Child Psychology and Mental Health Series is designed to capture much of this dynamic interplay by advocating for strengthening the science of child development and linking that science to issues related to mental health, child care, parenting, and public policy.

The series consists of individual monographs, each dealing with a subject that advances knowledge related to the interplay between normal developmental process and developmental psychopathology. The books are intended to reflect the diverse methodologies and content areas encompassed by an age period ranging from conception to late adolescence. Topics of contemporary interest include studies of socioemotional development, behavioral undercontrol, aggression, attachment disorders, and substance abuse.

Investigators involved with prospective longitudinal studies, large epidemiologic cross-sectional samples, or intensely followed clinical cases or those wishing to report a systematic sequence of connected experiments are invited to submit manuscripts. Investigators from all fields in social and behavioral sciences, neurobiological sciences, medical and clinical sciences, and education are invited to submit manuscripts with implications for child and adolescent mental health.

Hiram E. Fitzgerald
Susanne Ayres Denham
Series Editors

Acknowledgments

We want to express our gratitude to a number of people whose help and support made this book possible. Above all, we thank Steve Jensen and Laura Dunbar of the Jefferson County, Colorado, Prosecutor's Office, who understood the role of the Attachment Therapy philosophy in the death of Candace Newmaker. We are grateful also to Detective Diane Obbema, whose special contribution was her careful analysis of the videotapes documenting Candace's treatment and death. Additional thanks go to Peggy Lowe and Carla Crowder, whose investigative reporting provided helpful details about Candace's family background. Pat Curry and Patricia Crossman contributed invaluable background information. Finally, we thank for their very concrete assistance the library staff of Richard Stockton College, who helped in locating some rather obscure material.

For their support and encouragement, we thank Scott Lilienfield, editor of *Scientific Review of Mental Health Practice,* and the board of directors of the New Jersey Association for Infant Mental Health, who reminded us that we were not alone in our concern about Attachment Therapy.

Introduction: Attachment Therapy and Its Victims

Like all stories of the death of children, this book is a sad one. The tale it tells may make the reader feel rage and outrage, contempt, fear, pity, and nausea, and underneath all these feelings will lie a profound sense of mourning for the unnecessary death of one who had no real chance to live.

Most of the people involved in this story had good intentions. They meant well and they wanted to be good human beings. Their plans for good resulted in catastrophe, not because of their own evil natures but because of ignorance, confusion, gullibility, and a desire for personal importance.

Candace Newmaker, a 10-year-old from North Carolina, died in Colorado in April 2000. She died in the course of a treatment given her by two unlicensed social workers attempting to make her more satisfactory to her adoptive mother, Jeane Newmaker, a pediatric nurse at Duke University Hospital.

Jeane Newmaker was present at Candace's death and made no move to stop what happened. She had told Candace that the treatment was "your very last chance"—a last chance to cooperate and become the daughter Jeane Newmaker wanted, a last chance to avoid abandonment and institutionalization. Whether there was anything Candace could have done to take this chance and escape with her life, we will never know. Candace's last chance became her last breath, as she suffocated inside a tightly wrapped sheet while adults pressed their weight against her body.

Newspaper readers and television watchers who saw reports of Candace's death had far more questions than the reports could answer. How could this have happened? Why were social workers carrying out a potentially fatal physical treatment? Aren't physical treatments normally done by physicians, nurses, physical or occupational therapists, even dentists or dental hygienists—people who have some training in the functioning of the human body?

What made the practitioners continue their actions until the child was dead? How did they learn or create such techniques to begin with? And how—one of the most serious questions of all—did a mother with advanced nursing training sit by while her child died at the hands of those who were meant to help her?

The answers to these questions make up several fascinating, distressing stories. One, of course, is the life story of Candace herself: her separation from her birth mother, her adoption by Jeane Newmaker, and her adoptive mother's concerns about her. Another story is the history of the treatment Candace received and its links with charlatanism for decades in the past. And a third story has to do with what we might call incidental risk factors: how law, custom, and human thought processes have made it easier for harmful fringe therapies to survive than for them to be regulated.

A fourth, less dramatic, but most important story forms the foundation for this book's analysis of Candace's treatment. This is the story of human development in childhood as learned through the meticulous, time-consuming, tedious scientific investigation of scholars such as Sir Michael Rutter and clinicians such as Charles Zeanah. As we will point out in a later section, our assessment of the events that caused Candace Newmaker's death is based on well-established evidence about child development, not on unverified assumptions. Information from the modern multidisciplinary study of early development provides a solid basis for the evaluation of the treatment Candace received. The whole story could not be told without discussion of the many ways in which Candace's therapists' beliefs contradicted an entire body of well-substantiated information.

This book recounts these stories and discusses ways in which we can change the endings of tales similar to Candace's that are even now being enacted in the United States. It is our hope as the authors of this book that an understanding of what happened to Candace Newmaker can prevent other children from being doomed to repeat her history.

FRINGE THERAPIES AND ATTACHMENT THERAPY

The treatment that culminated in Candace's suffocation is called Attachment Therapy, abbreviated as AT in this book. Although AT practitioners call themselves psychotherapists, the term AT includes several techniques that use physical restraint and painful physical stimulation. AT is almost always applied to children rather than to adults, and these children are often adoptees or have previously experienced abuse, neglect, or painful medical treatment. AT practitioners claim that emotional disturbances are an inevitable result of such experiences. These therapists are convinced that the children suffer from problems in their ability to connect emotionally with adult caregivers—attachment disorders—and are thus in need of Attachment Therapy. Advocates of AT state that their techniques cure children of such problems, making them pleasant, affectionate, helpful, and obedient rather than hostile and even dangerous. As the reader will see in the course of this book, it is rather more likely that AT is a cure without a disease.

The practices of AT will be described in detail in later chapters. We will show that AT is not unique in its techniques but that a number of other treatment forms share its assumptions and techniques. AT is in fact only one of many fringe therapies.

"Fringe therapies" are treatments offered outside the usual boundaries of psychology and medicine. They are rarely, if ever, used in public hospitals or clinics, are not taught in universities with accredited programs, and may be rejected by private insurance. Practitioners of fringe therapies refer to them as alternative, unorthodox, unconventional, or controversial. In fact, there is little controversy about these treatments: they are rejected by most well-credentialed members of the helping professions.

Fringe Therapies as Unvalidated Treatments

It would probably be more accurate to call fringe therapies *unvalidated treatments*. Validation of the efficacy of a medical or psychological treatment must come from clear-cut experimental evidence. For the therapies we call unvalidated treatments, however, any evidence claimed for their effectiveness usually comes from anecdotes told by their practitioners or from poorly designed research such as that critiqued in chapter 7. Nonetheless, a large proportion of parents, perhaps 50%, seek such therapies as an adjunct to conventional treatment for children with chronic illnesses such as autism. It is impossible to say how many such parents rely exclusively on unvalidated fringe therapies.

Many unvalidated treatments for children have physical elements, even when the problem is an emotional or behavioral disturbance. Such treatments also have a shared foundation in the belief in *recapitulation*, or the possibility of regressing in development to an earlier period of life and working forward to a more desirable outcome. One fringe therapy, patterning, forces brain-damaged children through the movement patterns characteristic of infants in the belief that this technique will cause the brain to develop anew along a normal pathway. (The American Academy of Pediatrics has twice advised against the practice of patterning, but patterning advocates continue to sell their treatment.) AT assumes recapitulation of a child's emotional connection with parents, using a line of thought completely parallel to the assumptions of patterning.

Warning Signals

Unvalidated treatments can generally be recognized because of certain associated *warning signals*. As we show in this book, AT has all the red flags that go with any fringe therapy.

1. Unvalidated treatments tend to have harmful side effects. These may range from physical injury or death to the consumption of a family's resources of time and money.

2. Unvalidated treatments lack empirical evidence confirming their claims of effectiveness. When practitioners attempt to present such evidence, it does not meet research criteria established by professional groups.

3. Unvalidated treatments are based on ideas that fail to mesh with currently accepted theory. (This signal alone is not claimed as evidence for fringe status, of course, because theories do change; in combination with other factors, however, it shows that the treatment is much out of step with most professionals' thinking.)

4. Unvalidated treatments fail to comply with standards of practice such as those concerned with physical contact or the use of restraint.

5. Unvalidated treatments are not discussed in professional publications such as peer-reviewed journals. Such publications have high standards and accept only a fraction of the articles submitted to them. Publication of articles in professional journals usually occurs only when several respected persons, experts in the subject area, have reviewed the submitted paper and suggested revisions.

6. Unvalidated treatments make excessively broad claims of effectiveness. One of the early practitioners of AT, Robert Zaslow, claimed that his techniques cured acne, eczema, asthma, and allergies as well as emotional disturbances (Zaslow & Menta, 1975, p. 115).

7. Unvalidated treatments tend to be associated with other unvalidated treatments. Fringe practitioners use several fringe approaches rather than a conventional approach with a side order of fringe treatment.

8. Unvalidated treatments tend to have advocates who respond to criticism with cult-like defensiveness rather than professional concern. For example, Candace Newmaker's death was followed by explanations blaming every possible cause except the treatment and the therapists. This was in marked contrast to the normal professional tendency to examine with care any adverse event that follows a treatment.

PARENTS, CHILDREN, AND FRINGE THERAPIES

The red flags of unvalidated treatments look fairly obvious when they are neatly listed. Detecting them in practice may be a good deal more difficult. For instance, the average person is not likely to know what constitutes adequate research evidence, and even an individual highly trained in one field may have no idea what is well-accepted theory in another.

Uninformed Choices

When fringe therapies are suggested for children, an additional problem appears. Children do not choose or even consent to unvalidated treatments on their own. These choices are the privilege and the responsibility of their parents. To do a good job on such decisions, parents need to be aware not only of the red flags but also of the facts of child development. Even a treatment that would be acceptable for adults may be distinctly at odds with child development as research has shown it to be.

Unfortunately, many parents appear to be even less versed in the facts of child development than aware of the red flags associated with fringe therapies. A national survey (Park, "What grownups understand," 2001) by the child advocacy and research organization Zero to Three in 2001 showed that parents knew especially little about emotional development—although they believed themselves quite knowledgeable. In the same year, a group of participants in a workshop on foster care gave many incorrect answers to a questionnaire about early development and were especially confused about emotional development. Though these people had above-average educations and a sincere interest in children, they held beliefs that would make it easy for an advocate to "sell" AT to them.

It appears that many parents who exercise their rights to choose treatment for their children may be doing so without adequate information. Unfortunately, they may be especially vulnerable to the disinformation often presented with respect to fringe therapies.

MORE THAN ONE DEATH: THE RECORD OF ATTACHMENT THERAPY

Why is it so important to consider whether parents can make good choices of treatments for their children? Surely a single death, however sad, should not be adequate to condemn an entire therapy such as AT out of hand. Freak deaths occur in elevators, but we do not try to educate the public never to take an elevator. So why should Candace Newmaker's death imply anything but the profound fragility of all our lives?

Perhaps a sufficient answer to this question would be that any unnecessary deaths of children are too many. Beyond that, however, Candace's death is not the only one associated with AT, although it received the greatest national publicity. Krystal Tibbets, a 4-year-old Utah child, died in 1996 during an AT-related treatment carried out by her adoptive father. The father, Donald Tibbets, was sent to prison; he testified that he had been advised to use physical restraint on Krystal by her therapist, Larry van Bloem, who still practices in Utah and has opposed legislation to regulate AT. According to Tibbets, he had questioned van Bloem because Krystal sometimes stopped breathing during physical restraint. Van Bloem advised Tibbets to continue the practice. On a subsequent occasion, however, Krystal did not begin to breathe again when released.

Two-year-old David Polreis, a child adopted from Russia, had been treated by AT practitioners. He was found battered, and his adoptive mother, who went to prison, initially claimed he had beaten himself to death with a wooden spoon.

In addition to potentially dangerous physical restraint and painful stimulation, AT practices include "parenting techniques" such as withholding food, demanding physical work, and requiring maintenance of physical postures for long periods of time. One seven-year-old Texas girl, whose teachers called child protective services because the child was emaciated and eating from garbage cans, had been required to hold weights over her head for many minutes to earn her dinner. Such practices are not likely to kill a previously healthy child but are injurious to both physical and emotional health and provide no known benefit.

A final concern about AT is its impact on the education of the treated children. Part of the AT philosophy is the idea that school is a privilege, not a right. Some children spend many years in AT treatment, and as time passes they become increasingly educationally handicapped. This of course limits their ability to tell their own stories in later life or to find redress for the treatment they have received.

GOALS AND METHODS OF THIS BOOK

It will already be clear to the reader that the authors of this book feel a deep concern about the practice of AT. We believe it is the responsibility of professionals and the public alike to put a stop to the use of this unvalidated treatment. AT needs to be identified publicly as the fringe therapy it is. Although legislation to regulate AT is essential, public education is even more important. Unless there is public awareness of the dangers of AT, legislative regulation will simply make AT practitioners go underground, where many of them are already practicing without licensing or supervision. Indeed, as former Surgeon General Everett Koop (2002) pointed out in a *Science* editorial, their underground status may even make them more attractive to some members of an unsophisticated public.

Our goal in this book is to inform the reader about AT, its history, the realities of current practices, and the validity of the research claims made by its advocates. We believe that informed readers will be persuaded that AT is a fringe therapy and a harmful one even in its most innocent manifestations. We will argue that public education and legislation are needed to fight the use of AT.

As the reader will see, much of the advocacy offered for AT is in the form of proof by assertion. Writers who favor AT tend to make simple statements rather than to offer corroborating evidence for their claims. We do not need to do this in this book because we have overwhelming evidence that AT is an inappropriate and potentially harmful treatment for children. We do not want to enter into unsupported exchanges of claims in any case, because the obvious outcome would be along the familiar lines of "is not"—"is too!"

We do not intend to follow the journalistic practice that has been called *pseudosymmetry* by Robert Park (2000). Pseudosymmetry involves choosing equal amounts of information to represent each of two points of view, even though there is much more evidence on one side than on the other. A pseudosymmetrical approach gives the illusion of objectivity but in fact involves a rather subjective choice of evidence. In the present case, it would be extremely deceptive to give such an appearance of balance. In fact, there is no balance between pro-AT and anti-AT evidence. The claims of therapeutic efficacy made by AT proponents are exceedingly weak, and the evidence that AT practices can be harmful is exceedingly strong. Our presentation will be heavily weighted against AT because that is the conclusion the evidence produces. We recognize, however, the extreme difficulty of demonstrating a negative conclusion and supporting the statement that AT does not benefit children.

Organization of the Book

Our presentation will involve several different formats. The first part will be a *case study*, a description of Candace Newmaker's life and death using information from a variety of sources. The second part will be a *comparative* discussion, analyzing the connections and disconnections between the AT viewpoints on emotional development and the research-based views more usually held in the helping professions. The final part of our presentation will be an analysis of events in Candace Newmaker's life in terms of specific causal factors such as common thinking patterns. We will conclude with a discussion of existing legislation and some recommendations for change.

Sources of Information

All of the evidence we have used comes from sources that could be obtained by a highly motivated reader, but the material is not easily available from the nearest newsstand. For example, much of the information about Candace Newmaker's treatment comes from our attendance at the trial of Candace's therapists a year after her death. The therapists had videotaped the treatment, and those videotapes were shown in the courtroom. Transcripts of the trial can be obtained or read at the courthouse in Colorado, so sufficiently interested readers can check those accounts against the ones given in this book.

We have never seen a live AT session, having neither the theatrical skills nor the nerve to pass ourselves off as people seeking training in AT techniques. Information about past and present AT practices was obtained from material published by AT advocates and from statements on AT practitioners' Internet sites. We have provided a reference list of such materials at the end of each chapter where they have been used. A few obscure papers are in German-language publications, but we did not depend on these unless they seemed congruent with those published in English. Our job was made easier by the existence of a number of training videos made by AT practitioners and their associates, as well as by instructional books that gave specific directions for certain practices. We append a comprehensive bibliography of materials about AT.

We had little opportunity for direct interviews with the major protagonists of the Candace Newmaker story. Candace, of course, was dead; her adoptive mother and the two AT therapists had obvious reasons not to talk to us, and we had obvious reasons not to believe them if they had done so. We relied on newspaper accounts for basic background and did not use our small amount of personal interview information unless it was confirmed by a journalistic source.

Part of our involvement in this project emerged from a general interest in the use of restraint and seclusion with psychiatric patients. We availed ourselves of the work of the National Alliance for the Mentally Ill on guidelines for use of restraint and seclusion. The Federal Register supplied the 2001 guidelines for the use of restraint with children in psychiatric facilities funded by Medicaid.

As some readers will be aware, it is possible to use publications such as *Dissertation Abstracts* to find information about the training and background of some practitioners. We were able to find out in this way when an AT advocate had an advanced degree from a nonaccredited university and when one had written a doctoral dissertation in a nonclinical area of psychology rather than the clinical area claimed. We are still searching for evidence of the doctoral degree claimed by one AT practitioner.

Our understanding and interpretation of the AT literature was based on training in child development and in appropriate research and statistical methods. We have provided explanations of and references for relevant ideas so readers can check our accuracy, although obviously a book of this size cannot take the place of the several lengthy textbooks actually needed. We asked an experienced child psychotherapist to write chapter 6 and to provide references for further reading on this subject.

AT: GROWING UNCHALLENGED

As we will see in this book, AT seems to be increasingly available. Although it is impossible to tell how many children have received AT treatment, currently more than 80 separate Internet sites either offer or advocate AT. AT support groups are found in connection with a number of adoption organizations.

There is evidence that AT practitioners are attempting to develop records that will give them credibility in the professional mainstream. AT authors have had a book published by the Child Welfare League of America Press—a well-known professional publisher—and another by Academic Press, an otherwise respectable scholarly publishing house.

Frighteningly, AT advocates have in several cases presented workshops that were approved for continuing education credit by groups such as the National Association of Social Workers (NASW) and the American Psychological Association (APA). Such workshops are attended by clinicians who must show evidence of continuing professional training to keep their professional licenses. Approval of a workshop by NASW or APA seems to imply that those organizations approve the content being offered. It is more likely, though, that the approval signifies inattention and bureaucratic inefficiency. Organizations such as NASW and APA do not directly monitor the quality of continuing professional education, delegating their responsibility to approved providers, usually universities or agencies that provide services. One approved workshop in October 2001 taught its audience a number of AT concepts and tenets and summarily contradicted well-validated ideas about emotion and about child development. The approved provider responded to a written complaint by describing the lecturer as provocative; NASW and APA failed to respond at all. Professional organizations, despite their claims of concern for the public, appear to be indifferent to the quality of continuing professional education.

An additional concern about the growth of AT has to do with its possible connection with so-called wilderness therapy and wilderness camps for teenagers. Periodically, distressing news reports come out of some wilderness facilities, describing the deaths of adolescents. These deaths have often involved physical restraint and suffocation, sometimes while the young man or woman lay face down in the dirt. The beliefs behind wilderness therapy and behind AT may be connected.

A BROADER CONTEXT FOR CONCERNS ABOUT AT

AT may be only one symptom of attitudes about children that need to change. Adults in the United States are not only lacking in information about children, but according to a national survey a few years ago, they do not even like children very much (Applebome, 1997).

Children have historically enjoyed only a few rights. Under American law, for instance, children receive the protection of the government only at one remove. The family is expected to do the job of child-rearing, and the job it does is normally hidden behind the legal barrier of "the family veil." Only after a child has been harmed is the family veil drawn aside and the child's real life experience examined. The family veil, of course, can cover the use of fringe therapies as well as more obviously harmful practices.

In many cultures, children are considered to be the property of their families, property that can be used as desired within extremely broad limits. Bill Cosby's old line—"I brought you into this world, I can take you out of it"—is a succinct statement of this viewpoint. Families in parts of the world can and do sell their children, as child prostitutes and as slaves. Outsiders take boys and girls to be child soldiers, sometimes with the approval of the parents. We will recognize a similar denial of children's rights as human beings when we look at AT beliefs and practices.

The United Nations Convention on the Rights of Children is an ongoing attempt to define children as human beings, not as property. Citizens of the United States (which, incidentally, has never ratified the Convention) may feel smugly that we don't need such rules here. But our examination of AT will show that we do have such a need. Although no law can completely prevent willful mistreatment of children, the provisions of the Convention on the Rights of Children include several points that might have made Candace Newmaker's death less likely if they had applied in Colorado.

For example, Article 10 of the Convention declares that States that are parties to the Convention "shall take all measures to protect the child from all forms of physical or mental violence, injury or abuse, neglect or negligent treatment, maltreatment or exploitation, including sexual abuse, while in the care of parent(s), legal guardian(s) or any other person who has the care of the child." Article 25 recognizes "the right of a child who has been placed by competent authorities for the purposes of care, protection, or treatment of his or her physical or mental health, to a periodic review of the treatment provided to the child and all other circumstances relevant to his or her placement." As we will see in chapters 1 and 2, Candace's case did not receive a careful review even at the beginning of her treatment.

Article 37 requires that "a) No child shall be subjected to torture or other cruel, inhuman, or degrading treatment or punishment," "b) No child shall be deprived of his or her liberty unlawfully or arbitrarily," and "c) Every child deprived of liberty shall be treated with humanity and respect for the inherent dignity of the human person, and in a manner that takes into account the needs of persons of his or her age. ... Every child deprived of liberty ... shall have the right to maintain contact with his or her family through contact or visits." As we will see, Candace Newmaker was deliberately treated in a cruel and degrading manner because this was the intention of the therapists, who considered such treatment the key to emotional change. Under this belief system, respect for Candace's inherent human dignity would be seen as counterproductive.

A change in national attitude, to acceptance of the ideas represented in the Convention on the Rights of Children, might make it unnecessary to work toward public awareness and legislation to counter AT. However, such an attitude change does not seem likely to happen in our lifetimes.

REFERENCES

Applebome, P. (1997, June 26). Children score low in adults' esteem. *New York Times,*
p. A25.
Koop, E. (2002). The future of medicine. *Science, 295,* 233.
Nickel, R. E., & Gerlach, E. K. (2001). The use of complementary and alternative therapies by the families of children with chronic conditions and disabilities. *Infants and Young Children, 14*(1), 67–78.

Park, R. (2000). *Voodoo science.* New York: Oxford University Press.

———. "What grownups understand about child development: A benchmark survey." Retrieved January 20, 2001 from zerotothree.org/executive summary.pdf

Zaslow, R., & Menta, M. (1975). *The psychology of the Z-process: Attachment and activity.* San Jose, CA: San Jose State University Press.

Part I

The Case of Candace Newmaker

Chapter 1

Candace's Adoption and Death: How a Second Chance Became the Last Chance

Life stories are usually told chronologically. Birth is not only a beginning, but the beginning of the stories we tell about ourselves. In the case of Candace Newmaker, the fact of her adoption at 6 years of age splits her life story into two roughly equal parts, with the later part directly and causally linked to her death. We would argue that the earlier part of Candace's life was the back story to the later drama and violence she experienced. In this we disagree with the AT practitioners, some of whom believed that Candace's death was caused by her earlier life rather than the later events.

Because we are convinced that the explanation of Candace's death lies in her life with her adoptive mother, we will begin our story with an account of her adoption in 1996 by Jeane Newmaker, an unmarried nurse-practitioner in her late 30s. The present chapter describes the lives of the small adoptive family, including Candace's school experiences. We will see how Jeane Newmaker, dissatisfied with the progress of her life with Candace, looked for advice and found it in the wrong places. We will see how various forms of therapy became the center of the Newmakers' lives and how a trip to Colorado for intensive treatment culminated in Candace's death and prison sentences for her therapists.

THE ADOPTION

Candace Tiara Elmore, soon to become Candace Elizabeth Newmaker, was free for adoption in 1996. Her birth mother's parental rights were terminated legally, and North Carolina social services workers began to look for a potential adoptive family. Evaluated as unlikely to do well if left with her birth family, Candace was to be offered a second chance for a productive, successful life under the loving care of an adoptive parent who really wanted her.

Cute young babies are much in demand by would-be adoptive parents. For a child such as Candace, however, the brutal truth was that few if any adoptive parents were likely to offer themselves. She was too big and too old, no longer cute or infantile, just a person in need of a loving home rather than a baby to tug at the heartstrings. Not an unattractive child, she nevertheless must have had the behavioral marks left by a roughly functioning birth family and a series of foster homes. Such children are not adorable. (One foster mother had even claimed that Candace's behavior gave the foster mother asthma attacks.)

Chances were poor, then, that Candace would be adopted by a "blue-chip" family such as a married couple who already had two children, who were experienced, sensible, sensitive parents, and who wanted to combine a good deed with the fun of a larger family. Candace would be a leftover child after such families chose the babies they wanted and, if adopted at all, would go to a gay couple or an unmarried woman like Jeane Newmaker. These might prove to be excellent adoptive placements, but everybody involved would know they had somehow been judged second-best.

The Home Study

As she sought to adopt 6-year-old Candace, Jeane Newmaker went through a series of steps mandated by the state of North Carolina. With the help of an adoption agency, Newmaker participated in a home study or preplacement assessment. She was told that the main requirement of her as a potential adoptive parent was to provide a healthy, loving, and nurturing home for a child. Agencies sometimes require adoptive parents to take preparation classes to develop the skills for dealing with a child who has experienced losses, but it is not clear whether Jeane Newmaker took these. An agency may have decided that her training and position as a pediatric nurse-practitioner at Duke University Medical Center were sufficient evidence that Newmaker could handle a child's problems.

The Match and the Early Relationship

A social services caseworker suggested Candace as a possible good match for Jeane Newmaker, who was unsure whether she could handle a toddler and did not ask for an infant. A visitation plan was arranged so the two could have some meetings and weekends together. Jean's decision to adopt was soon made, and Candace moved in during June of 1996. Jeane took off two months from her work at Duke to be with Candace constantly that summer. They traveled and got along well.

Enrolled in the first grade that fall, Candace was an indifferent student, and Jeane tried to help with her homework. As is common in adoptions, they continued to have a honeymoon period through Christmas, which was about the point when the legal adoption process was concluding. Soon after this point, the honeymoon was over and Jeane felt that Candace began to behave in negative ways. Jeane was concerned that Candace was depressed and within two months had a psychiatrist see the child.

Adjustment

Difficult moods and behavior are to be expected in such a situation. As the North Carolina Adoption and Foster Care Network Website points out, "All children, even infants, will have some adjustment problems. A child requires much patience, tolerance, and love." In a case like Candace's, there were some unusually serious changes to be made. Jeane Newmaker arranged for Candace's name to be changed on her birth certificate, not only altering the family name, as is customary, but also changing Candace's middle name, Tiara, to Jeane's own middle name, Elizabeth. Candace, whose birth family had been Protestant fundamentalists, began to receive instruction in Jeane's Roman Catholic faith.

Adoptive families in North Carolina are advised that "some children may have an emotional bond with their birth parents and should stay in contact with them," but no one arranged such contact for Candace. It is possible that Jeane Newmaker could not have done so even if she had wished to, because she was not to be given any identifying information about the birth parents nor was any later to be available to Candace.

Diagnosis and Psychiatric Treatment

According to Jeane Newmaker, when the honeymoon was over, Candace turned into a "really negative, disruptive, enraged child." Jeane was ready to love a child but not prepared to fight with one. The fights escalated at home, although the neighbors noticed nothing but Candace's charming ways. Jeane began to look for professional help, starting where she worked at Duke University Medical Center.

At Duke, Candace was seen by a psychiatrist, Dr. Jean Spaulding, and then by Mai Mai Ginsburg. Candace was said to be doing poorly in school, supposedly having problems sustaining attention long enough to do her schoolwork. She would lose focus when working. Spaulding and Ginsburg diagnosed Attention Deficit Disorder (ADD), a syndrome that involves difficulties with paying attention to a task and completing it. Some individuals with ADD are also impulsive, fidgety, or overactive, all characteristics that would interfere with successful school performance. Like many other children diagnosed with this syndrome, Candace was treated with medication, the central-nervous-system-stimulant Ritalin. Although we might expect Ritalin and other stimulants to make a child less manageable and more distractible, these drugs are thought to have a paradoxical effect on individuals with attention problems and to make them calmer and more attentive.

By the following spring, educational testing done at school was described by Jeane Newmaker as "really negative." Because Candace was experiencing side effects from the Ritalin, such as insomnia, she was switched over to Dexedrine, another stimulant sometimes used to treat ADD. It is notable that Dexedrine carries a specific warning against its use with children who have psychotic disorders that produce inattentiveness, so presumably Candace's psychiatrist felt that psychosis—serious emotional disturbance—had been ruled out in Candace's case. For a brief period, Candace was also given Prozac, an antidepressant medication.

Candace had been on Dexedrine for some time when Jeane Newmaker began to see other behavior problems. Jeane described these in terms of lovability. Candace was no longer a lovable child to Jeane. The more Jeane tried to deal with Candace's lack of loving behavior, the worse she thought it became.

Because ADD had been Candace's diagnosis, Jeane took her to a Duke researcher who was studying the disorder. Dr. Ave Lachiewicz agreed that Candace didn't seem to be "a normal happy kid. It was like having the average 18-year-old adolescent in your house." But with Candace's foster care history, it wasn't surprising that she was emotionally reserved at times. Dr. Lachiewicz saw this as "her defense mechanism for being through so many placements." Jeane Newmaker gave Candace drug holidays in the summer, taking her off medications so she could catch up with her eating and weight without having her appetite diminished by the stimulant drug, and this may have made some difference in her moods and behavior.

Dr. Lachiewicz also met with Candace's second-grade teacher, who said that Candace tried hard in class and considered her to be truly invested in herself. Jeane, meanwhile, reported fights over homework. As another Christmas passed and the relationship between Jeane and Candace apparently deteriorated, Jeane added attendance at a support group to her efforts. She later reported that in group sessions "parents say, 'I wouldn't take that kind of behavior.' And I thought, what would you do? Come to my home and show me what you will do on a day-to-day basis. I'll show you what I'm dealing with, and then you tell me how I'm supposed to deal with this, instead of saying, 'I wouldn't take it, I wouldn't do it, she's letting her get away with that', or whatever."

Throughout 1998, Candace continued to be treated for ADD by Dr. Lachiewicz. Jeane Newmaker was dissatisfied with the results. No one else was seeing a problem outside the home, but Jeane said she saw Candace's behavior deteriorate "before my eyes." Candace's catechism teacher saw her as "a little angel," but Jeane saw a whole constellation of evil behavior. Dr. Lachiewicz agreed that it was time for a second opinion and referred Candace to a Duke colleague, Dr. John March, for an evaluation.

New Psychiatrists, New Diagnoses

Dr. March met with Candace and Jeane on May 26, 1999, and agreed with the diagnosis of ADD. He felt, in addition, that Candace's condition included Oppositional Defiant Disorder (ODD), a syndrome with symptoms such as excessive arguing, active refusal, and noncompliance with adults, deliberate attempts to annoy and upset people, and mean and hateful talking when upset. Jeane New-maker later reported, "I've felt that [the diagnosis] was given to her by the con-stellation of negative behaviors that I had described to him—impulsivity, stealing, lying—couldn't gain trustful relationships and work with people."

March also diagnosed post-traumatic stress disorder (PTSD), a syndrome in-volving anxiety and behavioral symptoms following emotionally traumatic ex-periences. According to Jeane Newmaker's later comments, this "came as a response to Candace's early life experiences when she was abandoned and ne-glected. And we don't know, abused to what extent." March noted, "Much of the functional impairment Candace experiences that appears as a result of PTSD is associated with avoidance, which in turn is most powerfully predicted by a set of traumatic reminders that include people who look like old family members, commands that appear to Candace as coercive and most importantly, implicit abandonment, separation threat cues." (As we will see later, coercive commands and threats of abandonment formed a major part of Candace's treat-ment by AT practitioners, especially in Colorado.) It was March's opinion that Candace would not make much progress in psychotherapy without medication. As well as the Dexedrine, she was now receiving Zoloft, a medication used to treat several psychiatric conditions, including PTSD.

In June, 1999, Candace began to see a psychotherapist, Mary Sue Cherney, at the Durham Center for Child and Family Health. After another two months she also came under the care of another psychiatrist, Dr. Molly Froelich, who used a standardized child behavior checklist and two trauma checklists as guidance for her choice of medications. Froelich agreed with March on Candace's diagnoses but considered PTSD the primary problem. She tried replacing the Zoloft with Tenex, an alternative treatment for ADD that had not been approved for use in children under 12. In hopes of relieving Candace's insomnia, a switch was soon made to Effexor, a medication used for depression and for anxiety disorders.

There was also some discussion of a new possible diagnosis, bipolar disorder, a condition involving severe mood swings. Froelich now changed Candace's medication, giving her Risperdal, an antipsychotic drug that might help with apathy and lack of motivation. When given at night, Risperdal gave Candace nightmares, but with some tinkering she began to sleep better than she had.

Looking for New Treatments

Jeane Newmaker thought the Risperdal was helpful, but she was looking for other sources of treatment. She felt that in traditional psychotherapy Candace "wouldn't be pushed to deal with her issues.... Although I continued on an ex-pert's recommendations to go to anybody that they offered, suggested, or rec-ommended ... I wasn't feeling that the traditional route really served her well." At the same time, however, Candace liked the Risperdal, and when she and Jeane visited Dr. Froelich's office on Oct. 15, 1999, Candace was talkative, cheer-ful, compliant, and affectionate to Jeane.

Adoptive Disruption and Fears

In December 1999, Jeane apparently received reports from the social services agency that Candace's younger sister, Chelsea, who was in an adoptive home with her brother, Michael, had tried to choke him and that the adoption was being disrupted. Candace was told of these developments; not unnaturally, she was upset by this reminder that adoptive families are not necessarily "forever families" no matter what has been said about them. Why anyone would have mentioned such a distressing story to Candace, who was thought to be dealing with posttraumatic stress issues, is even less understandable. This event may give us one of our few real glimpses into the nature of Candace's emotional experiences, suggesting as it does a serious lack of empathy and insight in those around her.

Candace was seen by Dr. Froelich again on Feb. 4, 2000. Jeane now reported that Candace showed renewed "negativism, irritability, overall rage, and oppositionality." At this point in Candace's life, Jeane had begun to take her to Cherney less often and had begun treatment by an attachment therapist, under circumstances we will describe a little later.

Froelich saw Candace again about 6 weeks later. Nothing was reported about violent actions of any kind, whether directed against Jeane Newmaker, Candace herself, or others. Candace was described as acting infantile at this session, cuddling in Jeane's lap (presumably something Jeane had wanted), talking in a baby voice. She pushed away the blood pressure cuff and resisted at first, but later became talkative and did not want to leave. She was not aggressive. According to Froelich's notes, Candace showed affection and signs of attachment. (These signs were not specified, and it is questionable whether a child of this age has specific attachment behaviors that would be readily observable in such a setting.) She acted a bit more like a younger child, according to Froelich, and did "things you just don't usually see with kids not complying." There was concern about the reported tantrums at home and their indication of "primary attachment issue," or dysfunctional attachment.

At the March office visit, Froelich was told that Candace would be going the next month to see an attachment therapist in Colorado. The psychiatrist noted later that none of her records about Candace were ever requested by the Colorado therapists.

LIFE OUTSIDE PSYCHIATRY: SCHOOL AND FRIENDS

This extensive discussion of Candace's psychiatric experiences has made it sound as if she had no other life. But, of course, like any other child, she went to church and school and played with neighborhood friends. We know only a little about Candace's catechism class and other church experiences, but she seems to have been well-thought-of there. As for neighborhood friends, there is a strange contrast between the positive reports of adult neighbors and Jeane

Newmaker's statements in court that Candace had been sexually aggressive with other children and had threatened them as well. If this aggression did indeed happen, no one else seems to have been aware of it.

Starting School

Our most reliable information about Candace's life outside the psychiatrist's office comes from school records and reports and teachers' memories. There were no behavior problems that seemed of concern to the school. Candace could have been the school bully if she had wanted to. She was bigger than the other kids in her grade because she was almost a year older, having lost a year as a result of her foster care placement, and she had street smarts from her past experiences, while her classmates came from relatively sheltered families with well-to-do, high-achieving parents from Durham, a university town. But Candace was the opposite of a bully, taking a protective interest in smaller kids and those in wheelchairs. She was said to have started the year standoffish, but by the end was more comfortable and secure as she made friends she had a chance of keeping.

Candace was not an academic high achiever in the first grade, but neither was she a failure as Jeane Newmaker later said. In fact, Jeane's active involvement with Candace and the school was much approved by school staff, who gave Jeane the credit for helping Candace get through a difficult transition. Candace apparently seemed quite normal to everyone. That she was on medication and in an ADD study at Duke was apparently not known to the school staff.

Second grade was more difficult. Candace worked hard. She was fondly remembered later by her teacher, Janet Pinkerton. But she seemed to have trouble following in class, even though she read well enough that she later tutored a younger child in reading.

Disorders and Accommodations

After that school year, Jeane Newmaker wrote to the school asking for special accommodation to be made for Candace, who in Jeane's opinion had a learning disorder associated with the ADD she was being treated for. The school began to pay more attention to Candace's academic performance, which went on slipping in spite of attempts at intervention in the classroom. Accommodations for disabilities such as learning disorders (for example, extra time to do a test) are required under the Individuals with Disabilities Education Act, but decisions about accommodations are based on professional assessments, not the opinions of parents. The school therefore arranged an outside evaluation by Dr. Andrew Short. His report at the beginning of Candace's third-grade year did not show that she was sufficiently disabled to receive an accommodation, but he noted that she was being treated for ODD.

Candace was now on an academic watch list, with some accommodations made for her homework. She was given a classmate buddy to help her focus on oral presentations, but none of this seemed to help. She struggled through third grade, working below grade level all year long. She had particular difficulty putting words on paper, although she had a great imagination. At home, Candace and Jean fought and argued over how to do her homework, which according to Jeane was a significant source of tension.

The Individual Educational Plan

More testing during that year showed that even Candace's reading was failing to progress. She now qualified for specialized accommodation. The school staff developed an Individual Educational Plan (IEP) to try to bring about some educational progress. The IEP was based on the conclusions of a team who observed Candace in the school setting. Their diagnosis was a fairly common one: a learning disorder involving auditory processing problems, or difficulties with listening to and understanding the spoken language. The initial IEP was drawn up to allow Candace resource-room work, school activities carried on outside the regular classroom. This would have allowed many hours of intervention work a day by a teacher working with a relatively small group of children. But Jeane Newmaker was not pleased with this plan and asked for an alternative IEP. She wanted Candace mainstreamed—taught in a regular classroom—although this arrangement would permit work specialized for her learning disability only one hour each week.

At Jeane Newmaker's request, Candace entered fourth grade with an IEP that placed her in a regular classroom. Her achievement under these circumstances was adequate in most subjects. In her regular fourth-grade class, Candace stabilized as a low average student, making mostly Cs and Ds with a couple of Bs. Math and spelling were hard for her, but she did well in creative things such as art and story-telling. In spite of what Jeane Newmaker later claimed, Candace was in no danger of having to repeat the grade. Her teacher for the year described Candace as respectful and pleasant, giving no disciplinary problems whatever. Candace was very sociable at school, hugging her teacher, having lots of friends, and being a leader among the girls. She went to sleepovers at other girls' houses and had them at her house too.

FORESHADOWING A SYSTEM FAILURE: MOTHER BECOMES THE CASEWORKER

These psychiatric and educational details should not lull us into forgetting the reason for this book. Candace was dead before that fourth-grade year was over. As far as we can tell, her death was not intended by anyone, nor do the details given so far give an adequate explanation of how it came about.

If we look carefully at the story so far, however, we see the beginnings of a problem. No individual, test, or treatment failed seriously, but neither did they function together. No one knew the whole story, and no one was in charge—except possibly Jeane Newmaker.

Case management and coordination of services were the bywords of the helping professions in the 1990s. The basic idea behind these terms was that we may waste a good deal of time and money if we provide certain services without knowing what else an individual needs or has. Housing, counseling, nutrition, educational accommodations, and medical and dental services all need to be provided in an integrated way. Case managers pay attention to what a person needs rather than committing their energies to running a housing project or a counseling center where individual needs can go unnoticed. Some cities, such as Milwaukee, developed elaborate and effective wraparound programs during this period, coordinating services so everyone working with a particular child would be completely in the picture.

When we look at Candace's story so far, however, we see a serious lack of coordination. The psychiatrists and psychotherapists did not report their findings to the school, and only one asked for teachers' reports or evidence of school performance and behavior. The school had no access to psychiatric information unless Jeane Newmaker gave it to them. If Jeane wanted to withhold information about Candace's psychiatric medication, there was nothing to stop her. If she wanted to report the ADD diagnosis and ask for educational accommodations, she could do so; the only hitch was that the school needed to get an independent evaluation before giving accommodations under the Individuals with Disabilities Education Act. (One has the impression that they would have done exactly what Jeane asked if the law had not required otherwise.)

In other children's cases, a school or county social worker might become responsible for collecting and passing on information as it was needed. Somehow, though, it seems that Jeane Newmaker became her own caseworker. The professionals believed her, relied on her, and even confided in her. Perhaps it was Jeane Newmaker's status as a pediatric nurse that caused her to be treated as a professional by professionals. Perhaps it was her earnest manner and the difficult task she had apparently taken on. For whatever reason, she entered into decisions about Candace in a way that would never have been permitted to the child's birth mother. The resulting events remind us why a surgeon does not operate on her father-in-law and why a lawyer who represents himself is said to have a fool for a client. Jeane Newmaker's active presence in the professional system twisted decisions in a way that caused a serious failure, one that might well have been prevented if she had not mixed the role of mother with that of professional.

ATTACHMENT THERAPY: FIRST STEPS

Neither Candace's school nor her psychiatrists diagnosed her as having a disorder related to emotional attachment. Dr. Froelich was attentive to attachment issues, but even she was primarily concerned with PTSD as a source of problems for Candace. None of the people we have mentioned so far had suggested that there could be a special treatment to solve Candace's problems by causing her to form an emotional attachment to Jeane Newmaker. Indeed, the psychiatrist John March's statements about Candace should have been read as a warning against the very kind of treatment that eventually caused her death. It was Jeane Newmaker, in her self-chosen role as case manager, who brought AT into the treatment picture.

In December 1998, as Jeane said later, the "placing social worker in the county I was using had informed me of a workshop that was to take place in January. And we had talked occasionally, and she knew I was having difficulty with negative behaviors and wondered if I didn't want to attend." She did attend the workshop, a presentation on attachment therapy given at the Guilford Attachment Center at High Point, North Carolina, about 50 miles west of Durham.

The Reactive Attachment Disorder Diagnosis

The workshop discussed a syndrome called Reactive Attachment Disorder (RAD), a childhood disorder described in the *Diagnostic and Statistical Manual* (DSM-IV), with diagnostic criteria somewhat less precise than those given for many disorders. Some of the criteria given for RAD are possibly applicable to Candace. Others seem inappropriate, and still others apply to children younger than Candace was even at the time of adoption. One of the symptoms described for RAD is "markedly disturbed and developmentally inappropriate social relatedness in most contexts, beginning before age 5 years." This would involve either "persistent failure to initiate or respond in a developmentally appropriate fashion to most social interactions, as manifest by excessively inhibited, hypervigilant, or highly ambivalent and contradictory responses (e.g., the child may respond to caregivers with a mixture of approach, avoidance, and resistance to comforting, or may exhibit frozen watchfulness)" or "diffuse attachments as manifest by indiscriminate sociability with marked inability to exhibit appropriate selective attachments (e.g., excessive familiarity with relative strangers or lack of selectivity in choice of attachment figures)."

Again, we do not know much about Candace's behavior before she was 5. We do have information about her behavior in school at age 6, however. She does not seem to have been unable to respond to social interactions (in fact, we might guess that Jeane Newmaker would never have adopted her if she had been unresponsive). On the other hand, Candace does not seem to have been indiscriminately sociable, because she was described as standoffish with her classmates at the beginning of the year.

The RAD diagnosis is not based on the symptoms just described alone, but also depends on information about the child's early experiences. To be diagnosed with RAD, the child must have experienced at least one of these: persistent disregard of the child's basic emotional needs for comfort, stimulation, and affection by the caregiver, persistent disregard of the child's basic physical needs, or repeated changes of primary caregiver that prevent formation of stable attachments (e.g., frequent changes in foster care). Although Candace's birth family was somewhat rough-and-ready, as we will see in chapter 2, it seems doubtful that she was subjected to any persistent form of neglect or disregard. She did experience a series of foster homes, but these changes all occurred after she was 5, years after the period during which emotional attachment ordinarily occurs.

Diagnosis by Checklist

It seems unlikely that Candace should have received the RAD diagnosis, based on the diagnostic criteria presented in DSM-IV. However, the Guilford Attachment Center workshop provided a checklist and described a constellation of undesirable behaviors characteristic of RAD kids (or, as some support group members dubbed them, RADishes). The workshop also informed its participants that 95% of adopted children have RAD and thus cannot give or accept love. This was apparently just the diagnosis Jeane Newmaker had been looking for.

She did some homework about RAD and the unorthodox approach recommended by the workshop presenters. Although RAD is in DSM-IV, Dr. Lachiewicz, who had been seeing Candace, had never heard of it. Jeane Newmaker later said, "Working in the medical center I had some experts around to ask for referrals, and to tap people's brains to ask about the next step. So I felt like I was researching it well.... Not that RAD could explain every single one of her prior experiences, but it sure sounded right to a lot of people." Unfortunately, but unsurprisingly, Jeane's "experts" were not people who knew about attachment therapy. Few in the helping professions were familiar with it or with the ideas behind it, nor was there serious research to be found on the subject even if Newmaker had explored the question systematically.

Starting Holding Therapy

Jeane Newmaker signed up with the Guilford Attachment Center and began to attend group sessions with other concerned parents as well as taking Candace to a new kind of treatment with an AT practitioner, Norma Beheler. This treatment, called holding therapy, was based on the same principles as the techniques that would eventually kill Candace. In their sessions, Norma Beheler and an assistant would hold Candace across their laps, immobilize her arms, grab her face, and shout at her, instructing her to obey commands to kick her feet or to shout answers—the very coercive commands and traumatic reminders that the psychiatrist John March had felt exacerbated Candace's condition.

Violence and Resistance

In the course of these holding sessions, Candace would become activated, to use the AT term. She would head-butt, pinch, and spit as she fought with the practitioners. As Candace became more violent, Jeane Newmaker became more of a believer. By the end of 1999, she was taking Candace to High Point once a week.

Not surprisingly, Candace disliked the treatment. According to a statement made by Norma Beheler, Candace would lie to get out of holding therapy. She would say, "I can't breathe," "I want to die," "I have to go to the bathroom." She would make similar untruthful remarks outside the therapy setting, according to Jeane. But Norma Beheler and Jeane interpreted the comments as really meaning only "I want this over. I want to get out of it. I don't want to do this anymore." As we will see later, no expression of pain or discomfort is taken at face value during AT.

Meeting ATTACh

Toward the end of 1999, Jeane Newmaker seems to have decided that Candace needed still more in the way of this treatment for RAD because she was clearly not getting better as a result of what she had experienced. Jeane discovered on the Internet an organization of interest: the Association for Treatment and Training of Attachment in Children (ATTACh). ATTACh was planning a conference in Alexandria, Virginia, in early October. The big names of AT would be there. In particular, Jeane Newmaker would have a chance to meet Bill Goble, a member of the Board of Directors of the Guilford Attachment Center and one much praised by the AT practitioners.

At the ATTACh conference in Virginia, Jeane Newmaker met and talked to Bill Goble, an attachment therapist with a large following and a Ph.D. from the Union Institute, an unaccredited institution in Ohio. Goble provided Jeane Newmaker with a copy of the Randolph Attachment Disorder Questionnaire (RADQ), a form put together by Elizabeth Randolph, a Colorado AT practitioner (and discussed in detail in chapter 7). Jeane's responses to the questionnaire produced a score for Candace that indicated a severe case of RAD. This, plus some telephone discussions, prompted Goble—who had never seen Candace—to recommend intensive treatment by Connell Watkins in Colorado. Nancy Thomas, a therapeutic foster parent steeped in the AT philosophy, was also present at the ATTACh conference and also recommended Watkins.

There was also support from other mothers who were at the conference and described behaviors that seemed familiar to Jeane Newmaker. Some mentioned that AT was controversial, but Jeane was not concerned. As she said later, "I wanted help for Candace."

ATTACHMENT THERAPY: PREPARING FOR THE TRIP

Jeane Newmaker had made up her mind to take Candace to Connell Watkins in Colorado, but this could not happen instantly. The next few months were complicated ones, with applications and forms to send to Watkins, many phone calls, and a mixture of holding sessions with the High Point therapists and office visits with Dr. Froelich and Mary Sue Cherney, the psychotherapist. The parents' support group from High Point added to the excitement with advice and encouragement.

Jeane Newmaker does not seem to have concealed her plans to take Candace to Connell Watkins. She was convinced that she was doing the right thing, and she received support all around. Referring to Dr. Froelich, she later said, "She was hopeful about it. She had contact with another child who had had similar treatment. There was—she didn't say anything negative about not going, not trying it, not giving it a try." Mary Sue Cherney was also encouraging. "Nobody told me, 'you are out of your mind, Jeane, don't go.' I felt like I had lots of support to go, and people who were willing to be there when we got back." Connell Watkins had insisted that there must be some follow-up holding therapy available after Candace returned to North Carolina, and Norma Beheler was available for this.

Contradictions and Consultations

The AT practitioners and the psychiatrist noted rather different situations during these agitated months. Beheler and her assistants were telling Jeane how worried they were about her and wondering whether she could manage to go to Colorado earlier. They felt Candace was showing seriously threatening behavior toward her adoptive mother. After one session of holding therapy, Beheler even suggested that Jeane Newmaker not return to Durham that night with Candace, expressing the fear that Candace might try to kill her by grabbing the steering wheel. Jeane had to get back to work and did make the drive, without any untoward events.

At about the same time, Froelich was noting that Candace was showing no dangerous ideation whatever. Another contradictory set of statements occurred before long. Beheler felt that on March 13, 2000, Candace was making progress and talking about some of her trauma and her anger with her birth mother. Only four days later, Froelich recorded a definite setback in Candace after months of slow but steady improvement. Whether Candace's moods and behavior were erratic or whether the psychiatrist and the AT practitioner simply had different concerns is difficult to tell.

As the departure date came closer, there was increased interest and excitement in the High Point support group. Other members of the group had made the same trip, and they gave advice on matters such as where to rent a car. They even suggested the possibility of financial reimbursement from the North Carolina social services department, further legitimizing the treatment. Some advised Jeane Newmaker that she should stop Candace's Dexedrine dose (a step that should not be done without consulting a physician, and then never abruptly). One mother, Pam Molinatto, was very enthusiastic about a technique called rebirthing that she felt had been a wonderful experience; this technique was to be the one that resulted in Candace's suffocation.

THE TRIP TO EVERGREEN

In April 2000, Jeane Newmaker and Candace were on their way to a small clinic, Connell Watkins Associates, run by the unlicensed therapist Connell Watkins in her home in Evergreen, Colorado, not far from Denver. Under Colorado law, Watkins, a social worker, was permitted to work without a license but was supposed to have registered with the State, paid a fee, and attended a workshop on legal issues associated with therapy (in fact, she had not done this). For insurance purposes, Watkins presented herself as working under the supervision of a licensed social worker, Neil Feinberg, and used his license number; he was later to testify that he had not supervised her.

In the little mountain town of Evergreen, with its trees and its icy mountain streams running over rocky beds, AT was a cottage industry with many practitioners. Watkins had for some years been involved with the larger Attachment Center at Evergreen, but had left to set up her own AT operation. Working with Watkins was another unlicensed therapist, Julie Ponder, who was also originally trained in social work. Watkins and Ponder were helped by two staff members, Brita St. Clair, who had already had many telephone conversations with Jeane Newmaker, and Jack McDaniel, neither of whom had formal training in any discipline related to psychotherapy. (McDaniel, in fact, was a construction worker laid off after an injury, and his relationship with St. Clair was the main reason for his involvement.)

Brita St. Clair later recalled her initial meeting with Jeane Newmaker on April 10, 2000, as "like a picture of someone escaping from a POW camp." Jeane handed Candace over to Connell Watkins and rushed upstairs to greet her telephone friend St. Clair, "crying, just so glad to be here, desperate."

Examining Candace

Connell Watkins did not request records from Candace's North Carolina psychiatrist. On the second day after her arrival, Candace was seen for about 10 minutes by a psychiatrist long affiliated with Watkins, Dr. John Alston, who commented on the case when he later testified at the trial of Watkins and Ponder. Alston concluded that Candace very much fit the standard profile he had for children brought in by Connell Watkins: She was "superficially compliant and cooperative, literally almost all of [these children] will tell you what they think you want to hear in very much a pain-avoidant, self-protective sense." In response to his question about why she had come for treatment, Candace replied, "So I could get help." Asked what problems she had, she said, "I do not bring love into my heart, and I say no a lot." Did she want to get better? Candace replied that 80% of her did, but 20% "still wants to be the boss of myself." (These phrases do not sound like an ordinary 10-year-old's words, and in fact they are stock phrases repeated endlessly in AT.)

On the basis of his interview with Jeane Newmaker about Candace's behavior at home, Alston diagnosed Candace as having a bipolar disorder, a diagnostic category that had been considered by Dr. Froelich in North Carolina. Alston testified that this was a common problem in the 2000 children with attachment disorders he had seen over 20 years. "I had a very, very, very strong suspicion that this girl had a bipolar ... disorder of a mixed type, moderate to severe, with even transient psychotic features." Alston agreed that there were aspects of PTSD, but ruled out the ODD previously diagnosed. He disagreed entirely with ADD as a diagnosis for Candace. We should note that Alston did not review either psychiatric or school records, nor was he aware that staff at Candace's school thought she had an auditory processing disorder. The major outcome of the visit to Alston was an order to change her medication, gradually increasing the Risperdal and eliminating the other drugs.

The Treatment

In chapter 3 of this book, we will give a detailed description of the treatment Candace received from Connell Watkins and her assistants, as well as a discussion of the assumptions and reasoning behind AT. For our purposes in the present chapter, a brief description will be sufficient. The reader should keep in mind some general principles behind this treatment: that the child's anger needs to be released for emotional attachment to a parent to form; that cheerful, affectionate obedience is evidence of attachment; and that it is possible to reenact or recapitulate past developmental events such as attachment and thus cause a new, desirable outcome.

The intensive AT treatment in Evergreen was planned to take two weeks. Jeane and Candace arrived in Colorado on April 10 and Candace died on April 18, 2000. During that week, Candace did not live with her mother but stayed with Brita St. Clair and Jack McDaniel, her therapeutic foster parents. Candace saw Jeane only occasionally and for brief periods.

Candace underwent almost daily sessions of holding therapy like the treatment she had experienced in North Carolina. She was physically restrained, roughed up, and shouted at for periods of hours. She carried out more hours of strong sitting, in which she sat tailor-fashion, immobile, and silent. She had a session of compression therapy, in which Jeane Newmaker, a large, stout woman, lay on top of the child and licked her face. Candace also had sessions of art therapy with Julie Ponder and participated in psychodramas intended to make her reject her birth mother in favor of an attachment to her adoptive mother. She was frequently threatened with abandonment by her mother (and we have noted John March's description of her sensitivity to such threats).

Rebirthing

On April 18, Candace was put through a rebirthing session, a crude and inaccurate reenactment of the birth process, from which she was supposed to emerge as her adoptive mother's true daughter, emotionally attached and psychologically committed to the relationship. She was wrapped in a flannel sheet to simulate the tight fit of the womb, and Watkins and the staff, with Jeane Newmaker, placed sofa pillows on top of the child. The adults pressed rhythmically against the pillows in imitation of the contractions of labor. Candace was supposed to wiggle her way out through an opening at the top of the sheet, but as she repeatedly told the adults, she could not do so. Eventually, she could not breathe, either.

Watkins videotaped all these procedures, so there is little question about what happened. For the first 40 minutes of the 70-minute rebirthing, Candace begged, screamed, and choked. For the last half hour she was silent. When she was finally unwrapped, she was blue and had no heartbeat. Emergency medical help was summoned, but too late.

Candace Is Dead

Emergency medical technicians answered the 911 call to find that Ponder and Jeane Newmaker were attempting CPR. But Candace had no breath or pulse. Eventually, the EMTs were able to place a breathing tube and put Candace on a mechanical breathing device. Her pulse returned and the Flight for Life helicopter was brought in.

Candace arrived at Denver's Children's Hospital by helicopter after the 30-mile trip from Evergreen on April 18. By everyone's account, she was dead in all but the technical sense. She was breathing with a respirator and had a heartbeat, but her brain had died. Her pupils were fixed and dilated. She would be kept breathing mechanically for another 20 hours.

Life Support and After

Candace was kept on life support systems in the intensive care unit until Jeane Newmaker arrived later that afternoon. As a pediatric nurse, Jeane understood the prognosis—that there was no possibility of bringing Candace back. Jeane Newmaker stated some quick decisions: Candace's organs should be harvested for transplantation and the body cremated. She would take the ashes back to North Carolina.

Matters could not be this simple, however. The hospital staff were made aware that there was police interest in the case. There would be a forensic autopsy, which could well conflict with organ transplantation. More than one county would be involved, because Candace was dying in Denver County but her death was the result of events in Evergreen, a town in Jefferson County to the west. In addition, there was the fact that Children's Hospital does not have a forensic pathologist on its staff, because the hospital does not do general work and rarely needs to preserve evidence of crime. Even if all these legal hurdles could be passed, there were still many practical matters connected with organ transplants. The National Transplant Center needed to be contacted, and arrangements were needed for transplant surgeons and transportation of the organs.

Jeane Newmaker was not crying as she had been when she arrived at Evergreen. She was annoyed and frustrated by the delays and the procedural confusion. Duty-staff members later described her as storming around the hospital floor, giving orders and demanding answers. Sheriff's deputies who interviewed her at the hospital characterized her later as uncooperative, abrasive, and controlling: "a real bitch," in their words. But it is hard to know, of course, whether their memories of Jeane's behavior were colored by their knowledge of the events leading to Candace's death.

A decision was finally made by the hospital staff: Candace would remain on life support until the transplantation teams were ready. The Jefferson County District Attorney's Office agreed to the organ harvesting. At 9 o'clock the next morning, life support was turned off and organs were removed. Several were in good condition and were used in transplants. The stomach had an ulcer as a result of the prolonged use of life support. The lungs could not be used because of an active infection caused by vegetable matter that had entered the airway when Candace vomited during the rebirthing. Most of the heart was too damaged by the prolonged lack of oxygen to be usable.

Autopsy Results

The autopsy showed no trace of drugs in Candace's blood but an undissolved, fragmented tablet of Effexor in the stomach and esophagus. The brain was removed and examined and found to be considerably swollen, with the brain stem damaged by compression. There was no other evidence of disease except the lung infection. The report of the pathologist, Dr. Gail Deutsch, said, "This ten-year-old child died of cerebral edema and herniation caused by hypoxic-ischemic encephalopathy. An underlying condition leading to her cardiorespiratory arrest and subsequent hypoxic-ischemic injury was not apparent in the organs available for examination." In short, Candace was physically a normal, healthy 10-year-old girl until she was killed by a lack of oxygen.

The remains of the body were released and cremated. Jeane Newmaker was questioned by sheriff's deputies and then allowed to return to Durham. She told few people what had happened. Candace's school held a memorial service with a collage of photographs Jeane gave them. Candace's short life was over.

THE LAW GOES TO WORK

The laws of North Carolina and Colorado did not—and perhaps could not—prevent Candace's death. However, the violent death of a child does not go unnoticed. The preparation of Candace's death certificate was the beginning of a process that would eventually bring the AT practitioners to trial on a charge of reckless child abuse resulting in death.

The Death Certificate

Dr. Kurt Stenmark, an attending physician at Children's Hospital, had the task of filling out Candace's death certificate. He later testified that the coroner's office had provided a chilling videotape. It showed a perfectly normal little girl being wrapped in a sheet, and the same child being unwrapped 70 minutes later, cyanotic and without a heartbeat. Dr. Stenmark had never heard of the rebirthing treatment or of attachment disorders before. He read some of the police reports and attempted to gather the information that was needed. Whereas the other sections of the death certificate were neatly typed, he chose to fill in the cause-of-death section by hand. He noted that Candace Newmaker's brain stem had herniated on April 18 between 0944 and 1052 when it was pushed out of her skull by the rest of the brain, which was swelling because of lack of oxygen. The lack of oxygen occurred "due to or as a consequence of mechanical asphyxiation" while Candace was "restrained during [a] therapy session." This was the final word: Candace was smothered by her therapists, while her mother watched.

Dr. Stenmark's last task on the death certificate was to check whether the manner of death was natural, an accident, suicide, or homicide. Deciding that a coroner or a jury should determine whether the event was intentional, he checked "accident." He did not believe that the AT practitioners actually intended the child to die.

Charges and Arrests

The Jefferson County coroner now signed off on the death certificate and prepared a report for the Sheriff's Office. The investigator, Detective Diane Obbema, and her colleagues had been waiting for this since they had interviewed Jeane Newmaker and the others who were present when Candace was killed. There was discussion with the District Attorney's office about the criminal charges that should be filed. Second-degree murder was considered, but the question of intent would be an obvious problem for a jury if this were the charge. Other charges seemed to make successful prosecution more likely.

Arrest warrants were issued. Julie Ponder, Brita St. Clair, and Jack McDaniel were booked on May 18, 2000, each on a single count of reckless child abuse resulting in death. Conviction on this charge would carry a prison term of 16 to 48 years. Probation was not an option. Ponder, St. Clair, and McDaniel were released on bail. The Colorado Mental Health Grievance Board prohibited these three and Watkins from practicing psychotherapy until the charges against them had been resolved.

A fourth arrest warrant on the same charge was issued for Connell Watkins, but she was in Hawaii visiting her elderly parents. Watkins was informed that the charge had been filed and that she must return to Colorado immediately or she would be arrested in Hawaii and extradited. She returned voluntarily and was arrested at the Denver airport. Three other charges would later be brought against Connell Watkins: criminal impersonation, obtaining a signature by deception, and unlawful practice of psychotherapy.

A fifth warrant was issued for Jeane Newmaker, charging her with criminally negligent child abuse resulting in death. This was a lesser charge but still carried a possible 4- to 16-year prison sentence, with probation and other options available to the judge. Jeane, who had returned to North Carolina, was also told to return or be extradited. She returned to Colorado on May 24, was booked and released on bail, and went back to North Carolina, where she had been suspended from her work as a pediatric nurse and reassigned to administrative duties at Duke University Medical Center.

THE TRIAL OF THE ATTACHMENT THERAPISTS

The trial of Watkins and Ponder for child abuse resulting in death was exactly that. It was not a trial of AT or of any of the techniques or ideas associated with it. The jury saw the videotape of Candace's treatment, but they received little or no explanation of the reasoning behind the practitioners' actions. There was no Colorado law forbidding or even regulating AT. Although a bill called Candace's Law was later passed and forbade rebirthing, such legislation had not been in place in April 2000. Watkins and Ponder could not be tried for a practice that was not illegal. The District Attorney's office sought information about AT but did not attempt to make the treatment itself the focus of the trial.

This approach to the trial was similar to that used in the few known related cases. In the Minnesota case of *Martinez v. Abbott,* for example, where a change in custody was ordered because the child's caregivers used AT techniques such as lying down on top of her, the judge's decision did not condemn AT but noted that the caregivers had gone too far with it. So far, no court has dealt directly with the principles and practice of AT. The few cases have focused on harm done to children and have considered this under the traditional rubric of child abuse or similar offenses.

The Trial and the Evidence

In April 2001, Watkins and Ponder were brought to trial on the charge we stated earlier. St. Clair and Newmaker testified at Watkins and Ponder's trial in exchange for limited immunity on their own charges. Jeane Newmaker, who was to have been tried separately on her lesser charge, plea-bargained, testified at Watkins and Ponder's trial, and was not brought to trial herself.

Videotaped Evidence

The trial of Watkins and Ponder proved to be a remarkable source of information about AT, about the reasoning of the practitioners, and about the specific techniques used in their treatment of Candace. The videotape was especially revealing, showing as it did the physical rhythms of the holding therapy and the voice tones of Candace and the practitioners. It was extremely distressing to watch, for the jurors and the rest of those attending the trial. Watkins had been right when she said to a police officer, "The videotape is going to hang us." But the very existence of the videotape raised as many questions as it answered. Surely the videotaping implied that Watkins and Ponder had no intention of killing Candace, for what criminals in their right minds would create such a record? On the other hand, videotaping of psychotherapy is by no means a common practice and would generally be done only for specific research purposes. Therapists normally keep careful case notes, and this, it appeared, Watkins did not do. Jack McDaniel, a high school graduate and erstwhile construction worker, was at one point spoken of as keeping notes, but he seems a most unlikely candidate for a job that needs meticulous attention. Whatever the reason behind the videotaping, it provided an extraordinary focus for the jury as well as insights into the thinking of Watkins and Ponder.

The videotape removed all doubts about what had been done to Candace and answered a number of questions about the AT approach. It did not provide evidence that Watkins and Ponder had caused harm intentionally, and could even be argued to show the very opposite. The argument of the trial could not turn on either of these points.

The Defense's Position

The prosecution took the approach that Watkins and Ponder should have known Candace was being hurt by the rebirthing and should have released her much earlier than they did. It was noted that other "rebirthed" children were kept confined for only a few minutes. Watkins and Ponder responded that children always say they are dying and that they cannot breathe in those circumstances, and that no children before Candace had died. Thus, Watkins and Ponder argued, they could not have known that Candace was really suffering, although an observer less experienced than they might have thought she was.

(There was never any clear explanation of the prolongation of the treatment to 10 times the length other children had experienced.) According to this argument, of course, Watkins and Ponder could not be seen as either reckless or abusive.

The defense offered for Watkins and Ponder went beyond the idea that they could not have known what was happening to Candace. Their attorneys argued that Candace had died *during* treatment but not *because of* treatment. They presented the speculative defense that Candace had already had heart problems and other physical ailments, perhaps exacerbated by medication, and that these had been the real cause of her death, perhaps only coincidentally at the time when she was undergoing a strenuous treatment. The evidence for this was most tenuous. Candace had been under the care of psychiatrists for several years, and at least one of these, Dr. Froelich, had performed physical examinations, noting her blood pressure, height, and weight but no potentially fatal problems. Alston's examination when Candace arrived at Evergreen was brief and cursory, but he noted nothing that implied physical illness. The autopsy had shown only problems that appeared to have resulted from her experiences with Watkins and Ponder. (Indeed, the heart valves were in good enough condition to be used for a transplant.)

Essentially, the three-week trial was a meticulous presentation to the jury of physical evidence, testimony from people who had known Candace, character witnesses and admirers of Watkins, and the statements of expert witnesses on both sides. The sheet in which Candace had been wrapped for rebirthing was displayed so the jury could see the rip that Candace's struggles had made down one side. There was discussion of whether Candace would have been able to breathe through the flannel fabric. Jurors occasionally dozed off, although not while they were watching the 11 hours of videotape.

Conviction

One of the authors of this book (L. R.) was present when the verdict was brought in and wrote the following description: "The verdict came in after about 5 hours deliberation, during which time the jurors DID test the sheet and found it hard to breathe through. P[onder]/C[onnell]W[atkins] were sitting at their table, marble-faced as usual. They had the same demeanor after the judge read the jurors' list of counts—guilty on all. Sentencing is set for June 18th (an all day affair). Then the matter of bail bonds came up—Truman [Watkins's attorney] asked for C[onnell]W[atkins'] bond of $250,000 to stay effective until sentencing. Ponder has a $40,000 bond that hadn't been renewed. Heller [Ponder's attorney] was calling on a cell phone right there in court to get confirmation of renewal. Judge Tidball looks at the paper and says C[onnell]W[atkins] had a $40,000 bond, not $250,000, and [her] house was valued only at $201,000. They should have taken care of these matters earlier, says she, and remands them immediately into custody. C[onnell]W[atkins] and P[onder]'s faces crack—shock and terror; big sobs! They weren't prepared for this. Two sheriff's deputies waiting in the back of the court are on them lickety-split; one has passed behind his back, without looking, a pair of cuffs to Obbema [Detective Diane Obbema, who had had the job of analyzing the videotape and presenting it in court].... C[onnell]W[atkins] yells out, "Not yet" and grabs her daughter. (Overly dramatic, perhaps, considering that she's only going to be in the clink until Monday when Truman arranges for the requisite $200,000 bond.) Ponder, however, is not going to manage that sort of bond; she is shaking, taking off her earrings. Off they go, one by one through a secret door to a tiny elevator just next to their table and down to the underground tunnel to the jail across the road. It was a stunning sight—like the earth agreed with the verdict and swallowed them up."

Ponder and Watkins were later sentenced to the minimum mandatory sentence, 16 years in prison. Both have appealed the verdict.

REFERENCE

The material in this chapter is based on the official transcript of the trial of Connell Watkins and Julie Ponder in Jefferson County, Colorado, April 2000, and on observations by the authors.

Chapter 2

The Backstory: People and Systems Behind Candace's Death

It has become almost banal to talk of "the banality of evil." In Candace Newmaker's case, the fact that evil acts can be banal is plain in the videotaped evidence: pet dogs wander through the room where the child is dying, a severely disabled woman makes humming noises in the background, Connell Watkins and Julie Ponder discuss real estate prices as they lean on what must by now be Candace's dead body.

To understand the reality of Candace Newmaker's case, we need to see how a death in agony and terror grew out of a series of very ordinary mistakes rather than from depraved intentions. In part, Candace's death was an administrative failure, involving a caseworker whose semiofficial championship of AT gave the practice legitimacy. Some of the blame may be placed on the Peter Principle, as so many of the people involved took on responsibilities that were just a little more than they could deal with.

Candace did not die as a dramatic sacrifice by priestesses of a satanic cult. She died because of the ignorance and misguided meddling of her adoptive mother and the AT practitioners she had hired. Candace died because professional groups are reluctant to let legislators regulate their practices and do not know how to do this themselves. She died because human beings were more eager to jump on a bandwagon than to think through complicated and difficult issues. She died because a North Carolina therapist thought he was clever enough to cut corners and make a diagnosis with a checklist and a phone conversation. In a sense, she died because a large number of people thought their convenience and dignity were more important than the consequences of their actions.

Still, no single event, plan, or intention brought about Candace's death. Behind that tragic event were multiple factors acting in interlocking ways. Such multiple factors form systems whose actions can have unpredictable outcomes.

In the present chapter, we leave the narrow focus of the story we told in chapter 1 and try to take a *systems approach* to understanding what happened to Candace.

The Systems Concept

The use of a systems approach is one of the most important characteristics of modern psychological thought and is especially useful in the study of child development and family processes. Basically, it is the idea that every person affects others as well as being affected by them. All the individuals who mutually affect each other form a system.

Systems of social interaction are complicated things. The mutual influences of people in a system can vary without any outside factor causing them to do so, simply because variability is part of the nature of systems. Sometimes small changes in one member of a system can bring on major changes in the way other members influence each other. At other times, what appear to be major events can have only a small impact. Each system has its own rules, and we can usually know what those are only by watching the system at work.

Jeane Newmaker, Candace, Connell Watkins, and other individuals in both North Carolina and Colorado were members of systems. They affected each other and were affected in return. We do not have enough information to know exactly how these systems worked or what could have been done to prevent the fatal outcome of their mutual influences. However, we can describe some personal, group, and situational factors in the mix that caused Candace's death. In this chapter, we deal with what is known about the interlocking systems that were at work.

CANDACE AND HER BIRTH FAMILY

In chapter 1 we examined Candace's life as the adopted daughter of Jeane Newmaker, which was the second half of her life and the part we consider causally related to her death. Now it is time to look at the background of Candace's birth family, whose parental rights were legally terminated not long before Candace was "matched" with Jeane Newmaker. We might and should expect to have no information available about Candace's background before her adoption. Under North Carolina law, as in many states, even the child's adoptive mother should not have had access to such information. But confidentiality seems to have played very little role in this case, and extensive news reports have provided facts that would normally have been kept private. Our discussion in this section is drawn largely from the investigative work of Carla Crowder and Peggy Lowe of the *Rocky Mountain News,* as well as from courtroom testimony at the Watkins-Ponder trial.

Angela and Todd, Candace's Birth Parents

Candace was born Candace Tiara Elmore on November 19, 1989, in Lincoln County, North Carolina, a rural area in the southwestern portion of the state. Her mother, Angela Maria Elmore, was 18, and this 9-pound daughter was her second baby but the first she had kept to raise.

Angela spent years in intermittent foster care and had given birth to a boy when she was 16 and still herself a foster child. That child was given up for adoption. Relevant to that decision was the fact that Angela had been designated a "Willie M." child, a North Carolina category involving a diagnosis of mental illness and an order for continuation of social services beyond the usual end point of age 18. It is not clear whether the Willie M. designation was based on specific symptoms or on Angela's evident need for continuing care. Angela had two placements in group homes for emotionally disturbed children and was said to have displayed outbursts of violence.

Like many young women who give up a child, Angela was interested in "replacing" the adopted baby. When she was 17, she married Todd Evan Elmore, a 23-year-old from Winston-Salem with a record of petty criminality. Angela's pregnancy with Candace was planned, and she listened to classical music and read stories aloud to her unborn baby as she had heard would be good to do.

Two more children were later born to Angela and Todd, who got by with some help from Angela's mother, Mary, and her husband, David Davis, who was a mechanic working for the North Carolina Department of Transportation. Angela had some temporary jobs and a brief period of beauty school. The young family lived in trailer parks, apartments, and housing projects.

Domestic violence was part of the Elmores' lives, including a dropped charge of assault against Todd. As a newspaper report later described it, "Angie was scared enough to pack up her children and leave in 1992. Candace celebrated her third birthday in a battered women's shelter. Angie saved photos of their party. Candace's wavy brown hair hangs in freshly cut bangs as she blows out candles on her grocery-store cake, decorated with a wild-haired troll doll" (Crowder & Lowe, 2000).

Like many children in dysfunctional families, Candace seems to have taken on a parental role, taking care of the younger children and trying to separate her parents when they fought. In apparent approval, Candace's grandmother described her as having been "half-grown when she was born."

Attention from Social Services and the Law

Concerns that the children as well as Angela were suffering from abuse arose when one of the children had scrapes across her back. Angela's explanation was that the child had fallen out of the insecurely-latched door of their trailer, but social services workers continued their investigation of the family. Angela and Todd moved to a new county to evade the investigation, but this move naturally did more harm than good. When they were found, the three children were taken away in spite of their protests and were temporarily placed in foster care.

At this time in the 1990s, family reunification was considered a major aim of social intervention agencies. The agency's goal would have been to restore the children to their parents if at all possible and to institute services such as counseling that would improve family functioning. Angela committed to a series of counseling sessions. As if to demonstrate that family counseling requires participation of all members, however, a fight between Mary and Angela put an end to this effort. The event that precipitated a second social services action occurred on a day when Candace was at her Head Start center (and her attendance there is yet another statement of the concern of social services workers for the Elmore children). Angela and Mary quarreled so seriously that Mary took the only car and left. Angela had neither another car to use to pick up Candace nor a telephone to contact the Head Start program. Eventually social services workers called Mary, who naively or unthinkingly told them to keep Candace overnight—probably not understanding that such a decision can be interpreted as abandonment of the child, with all its legal consequences.

Those legal consequences did follow. The children were placed in foster care. When Angela went to court to ask for their return, the judge noted the foster parents' reports of Candace's fits of temper and rebelliousness. He refused to return the children to their mother, whom he saw as the cause of their problems, referring to her former status as a Willie M. child. Mary and David Davis did not ask for custody, feeling they could not take all the children and care for David's elderly mother as well and feeling, as is common, that it would not be "fair" to take one child and not the others. Termination of Angela's and Todd's parental rights was ordered, and the children became free to be adopted.

The Previous Generation, Poverty, and Social Class

Intergenerational issues were an important part of Candace's family picture. Her grandparents, especially the step-grandfather, David Davis, gave what they could in affection, money, and groceries. But dysfunction was deeply embedded in this family system. Mary, Angela's mother, was abandoned before she was old enough for school, left with her older sister on a street corner in Morgantown, West Virginia. Mary's subsequent life in 17 foster homes may have been only slightly better than the earlier period, from which she remembered eating a neighbor's garbage.

Mary married when she was 16, gave birth to Angela and to a son, and moved with them to North Carolina. There, she soon lost her job and, living on the street, gave up her daughter to foster care.

The roles of poverty and social class differences in this scenario are evident. Had Mary's parents been affluent or even had adequate resources, they would have felt less of a need to free themselves from their children—although, of course, child abandonment can occur for reasons other than poverty. Had Angela not already been classified as a Willie M. child in need of services, social workers might have been less attentive to Candace and her brother and sister. If Angela had had a car or a telephone—if Mary's education had allowed her to see the implications of having Candace kept overnight—if neither Mary nor Angela had come to see foster care as a normal part of a child's life—every reader can continue this litany.

Social Class Effects

Although it is easy to emphasize financial resources as a factor in family functioning, social class should probably be seen as equally relevant here. Class differences in the United States are rarely discussed, but are both subtle and very real. To middle-class social services staff, and to judges, too, the Elmore-Davis clan might well not seem to be "nice people." One reason for this would be their explosive fighting and outbursts of temper.

Families teach their children "display rules" that govern socially correct emotional behavior—for example, when it is suitable to cry or how loud a person can laugh in public without drawing disapproving glances. Families teaching these rules do not necessarily know they are doing so, but they like or dislike their children's actions as those actions fit family and class assumptions about behavior.

In the middle class, temper tantrums may be tolerated in the very young, but even kindergartners have learned not to fly off the handle easily. They have learned through reward, punishment, and modeling to express their annoyance in well-chosen words, gestures, and facial expressions. In American lower-class life, however, physical expression of anger is tolerated in adults and even expected from any person of spirit. Candace had learned the same display rules that allowed her mother and grandmother to have a screaming fight followed by the removal of needed transportation. In one sense, the judge was right to think that Candace's display of temper in the foster home was rooted in her mother's behavior.

JEANE NEWMAKER: A CONTRASTING LIFE

It would be a serious exaggeration to blame Jeane Newmaker's difficulties with Candace on the class differences we have just discussed. However, adoptive mother and daughter clearly had different backgrounds. Jeane Newmaker came from a "leading family" of Warren, Pennsylvania, a small town in the northwest part of that state. Her grandparents' mansion had been a town landmark. But, given the difference in the effects of affluence, Jeane Newmaker's family was little more functional than Candace's birth family. Jeane's father, John, had serious drinking problems, especially after his brother died in a sports car accident.

According to the investigative reporting of Carla Crowder and Peggy Lowe of the *Rocky Mountain News* (2000), John Newmaker was ordered by a court to seek rehabilitation treatment for his drinking after two arrests for driving under the influence of alcohol. He subsequently divorced Jeane's mother to marry a woman he had met in the state psychiatric hospital where he had gone for treatment. John Newmaker died in 1987, a year after Jeane's mother died of cancer while being cared for by her daughter. Jeane Newmaker testified at the Watkins-Ponder trial that she had sought counseling for depression after the deaths of her parents.

With a master's degree in nursing from the University of Virginia, Jeane Newmaker took a job at the Duke University Medical Center in the early 1980s. She worked as a pediatric nurse and was licensed for a time as pediatric nurse-practitioner, a position of some authority and responsibility. Nurse-practitioners have advanced training in diagnosis and management of common medical conditions, provide individualized care, and are involved in prevention and in patient education. It is not clear what curriculum Jeane Newmaker followed in her training more than 20 years ago, but current pediatric nurse-practitioner programs involve courses in experimental and nonexperimental research, psychophysiological health problems, and family responses to children's health difficulties. If Jeane Newmaker had similar training or had kept up with the field, it is hard to see why her "research" on AT amounted to a few casual questions to staff members at Duke University Medical Center. It may be, however, that her training had emphasized respect for authority more than independent investigation. It is also possible that like many students, she forgot all she had learned about research and did not relearn it because no one required her to.

Jeane Newmaker's living situation in Durham, North Carolina, was more elaborate and comfortable than her salary alone might have supported. A trust fund from her grandfather, the mansion-owner of Warren, Pennsylvania, made it possible for Jeane to buy a comfortable five-bedroom brick house near a golf course—a considerable contrast to the trailer parks of Candace's early memories or her more recent experiences with foster families.

THE THERAPISTS AT EVERGREEN

The town of Evergreen, Colorado, contains enough AT practitioners and advocates to form a complex system of their own. As is the case for most systems of any age, the members of this system have their own history individually and together. That history includes a number of brushes with the law as well as more ordinary day-to-day functioning for quite a few years. The account of AT in Evergreen that you are about to read is correct in terms of the practices of specific therapists, but remember that particular organizations in Evergreen have changed their names frequently, and practitioners have changed their affiliations, so it becomes more difficult to trace the history of a group than of a person.

Robert Zaslow

The beginning of AT in Colorado, in the early 1970s, seems to have occurred with the arrival in Denver of Robert Zaslow. A psychologist once on the staff of San Jose State University in California and later to live or travel in Germany, his present whereabouts are unknown (he may be deceased). Zaslow was an advocate of a physically rough version of holding therapy that he called Z-therapy. According to one of his papers, Zaslow practiced this technique on a number of children, including a girl at the Colorado School for the Blind, who, the paper implied, later regained her sight. Zaslow claimed that Z-therapy was a cure for autism and a wide range of other problems, including eczema and acne.

Foster Cline

A Colorado physician, Foster Cline, admired Zaslow's technique and credited Zaslow for his own use of the treatment, dedicating a book to Zaslow, whom he described as one "who with irascibility and incredible ego, showed love and dedication midst negation and attack by those of lesser genius." According to a letter to the *Rocky Mountain News* by Mark Vlosky (2000), a Colorado psychologist who saw the treatment in use, Zaslow's and Cline's approach was "brainwashing torture. It involves holding children tightly and poking them until they are reduced to quivering puddles of tears and fears." Cline appears to have started the use of this technique at the Attachment Center at Evergreen, where Connell Watkins was at one time employed.

In 1993, the Colorado State Board of Medical Examiners investigated a case involving Foster Cline; in 1996, they forbade him to practice holding therapy or to use "therapy that includes aversive physical stimulation or verbal abuse." (Cline kept his medical license and later moved to Idaho.) This action was based on the case of an 11-year-old boy who had been sent to the Attachment Center at Evergreen but managed to run away and report his experience to the police. Under Cline's guidance, the boy had been given holding therapy by Connell Watkins and by Michael Orlans, the latter a coauthor of papers in a recent book about AT (Levy & Orlans, 2000a, b). Orlans later said he had been charged with child abuse, but claimed that the boy had actually beaten himself with rocks, bruised himself, and blamed Orlans—an anecdote somewhat reminiscent of two-year-old David Polreis, who was supposed to have beaten himself to death.

Connell Watkins

Connell Watkins, the central therapist in Candace Newmaker's treatment and death, was born in California in 1946. Her family name was Cooil, and her father was a plant pathologist who later joined the faculty of the University of Hawaii. Connell graduated from Washington State University at Pullman in 1968 with a degree in psychology and a minor in sociology. In 1973, at about the same time Robert Zaslow was doing his Z-therapy at the Colorado School for the Blind, Connell, now married to "Hap" Watkins and the mother of a daughter, was finishing her Master's degree in social work at the University of Denver. The Watkins family moved to Fort Collins, where Connell was a social worker for the state of Colorado.

After a later move to Evergreen, Connell Watkins became involved in work with Foster Cline. She became known and admired by the AT community for being blunt and "tough," "very oppressive, very abrasive, very arrogant," according to a newspaper report (Crowder & Lowe, 2000). She does not seem to have looked for continuing professional education of a formal nature, nor did the state require it of her.

Colorado law did not ask for Watkins to be licensed as a therapist, and even registration of unlicensed therapists with the state was not needed until 1988, when registration with the state Mental Health Grievance Board became a requirement. Watkins registered in 1995 but had let her registration lapse by the time Candace Newmaker died. She had also left the Attachment Center at Evergreen to start her own organization, Connell Watkins Associates.

At her trial, it was noted that Watkins had used the license number of a licensed Evergreen social worker, Neil Feinberg, for insurance purposes. This would have been a legitimate action on Watkins's part, but Feinberg testified that he had never supervised her as such usage would imply. Had he done so, however, we might have expected a no less tragic outcome. Videotapes made by Feinberg at ACE, apparently for instructional purposes, show him doing a version of holding therapy that even the most restrained language would characterize as sadistic. Feinberg made Watkins's treatment of Candace look like the amateur work of a playground bully, but he testified in court that he had learned from her and admired her skill.

Terry Levy

Terry M. Levy is another important figure in the Evergreen AT group, not because of innovations in treatment but because he has published books with respectable publishers and has presented workshops for professional continuing education credit at conferences of the American Psychological Association. Levy is a psychologist whose curriculum vitae claims a doctoral dissertation in clinical psychology, but *Dissertation Abstracts* lists the thesis under the category "general psychology." Levy's résumé does not state where he did a clinical internship or other clinical training usually required if the doctoral work is not in an APA-approved clinical program. One of Levy's coauthors and coworkers is Michael Orlans, whose erstwhile patient was said to have beaten himself with rocks. Levy, Orlans, and their colleagues claim they no longer use physical restraint as part of treatment, but they have published no description of their current practices nor given any reason for the change. Levy was once associated with the Attachment Center at Evergreen, the group that employed Connell Watkins at one time.

Julie Ponder

Julie Ponder, who was tried together with Watkins in the matter of Candace Newmaker's death, was not a long-term member of the Evergreen group. Also a social worker, in her early 40s at the time of Candace's treatment, she was licensed in California but not in Colorado. Like Watkins, Ponder seems to have regarded continuing professional education as an informal matter. She was said to have come to Colorado to work with Watkins, who of course could offer no certification or degree program. Similarly, Ponder picked up the rebirthing technique through a few sessions with Douglas Gosney, a Californian who was passing through town. Ponder's version of art therapy, which appeared on Candace's treatment videotapes, appeared to involve standard interpretations. Ponder did what she had been taught to do but did not have the skill needed to make the session anything very useful for working with Candace. Ponder's California license to practice marriage and family therapy was recently revoked.

ORGANIZATIONS AND SUPPORT GROUPS

Our focus on Candace at Evergreen may make it appear that AT is primarily a North Carolina and Colorado practice. In fact, there are practitioners in too many other states to describe in this book. Some states, such as Georgia, even pay for adopted children to receive AT treatment. Examining AT-related organizations and support groups may give some idea of the spread of AT practices.

Theorists of family systems have pointed out that small systems may be embedded in larger systems, and members of small systems may be influenced by the large systems even without face-to-face contact. Jeane Newmaker's membership in a parent support group indirectly affected Candace, even though the other parents never saw the child. Organizations and support groups advocating AT are larger systems that influence family systems and groups of practitioners alike. In addition to this embeddedness of small in large systems, many individuals in the AT community play overlapping roles and move from one system to another. Parents who have identified their children as "RADishes" may later become therapeutic foster parents as Brita St. Clair did. AT advocates from a small number of treatment centers are a major source of officers of related organizations, as well as conference presenters and authors.

ATTACh

The major organization advocating AT is the Association for Treatment and Training in the Attachment of Children (ATTACh). This group aspires to be "the international leader in the education and promotion of attachment theory (sic) and services." ATTACh was the group at whose conference Jeane

Newmaker met Bill Goble and Nancy Thomas, who recommended that Candace be treated by Connell Watkins.

Members of the Evergreen AT group, including Terry Levy, Paula Pickle, and Elizabeth Randolph, have been major figures in ATTACh. Foster Cline was a founding member of the group.

ATTACh and the Credibility Problem

ATTACh has a newsletter, "Connections," available on the organization's Website. In the December 2001 issue of "Connections," the then president, Todd Nichols, made the following statements: "I am constantly surprised at the lack of acceptance [of AT] by many academicians, medical doctors, psychologists, and other professionals. Since I joined ATTACh almost four years ago, I have frequently heard concerns expressed about the way attachment therapy is perceived by many outside the field. All too often, their perception is based on inaccurate, incomplete, or outdated information. The Board is taking action to combat these misperceptions. These steps will enhance our organizational credibility and build on the foundations we've already created."

What steps was the ATTACh Board taking to enhance credibility? We might expect funding for research to demonstrate the efficacy of AT techniques, but instead it appears that style has triumphed over substance. The steps involved the hiring of AveryHartley, Inc., a Denver public relations firm who agreed to provide services not only for the ATTACh organization but for all ATTACh members on a fee-for-service basis.

According to the AveryHartley Website, the company's goal is to help clients "strengthen their competitive position through innovative marketing and communications solutions." They offer "to tap the power of television, radio, print and interactive media to [the client's] advantage" and to teach clients how to talk to reporters and "answer the toughest questions with complete confidence." AveryHartley also offers help with regulatory or public affairs issues and with crisis management. The company does note, however, that "no amount of messaging can make up for the lack of solid integrity and quality products and services." (This may not be a problem, of course, if the public is unable to evaluate the services effectively.)

ATTACh and the DSM-V Committee

The ATTACh newsletter for December 2001 contains another interesting statement about the activities of the organization. Among a list of ad hoc committees is included a DSM Committee that "will be involved in developing a description of Reactive Attachment Disorder for the DSM-V [the projected fifth edition of the *Diagnostic and Statistical Manual of the American Psychiatric Association*]." Although ATTACh may well have appointed such a committee, this curious statement is not congruent with the plans of the American

Psychiatric Association, whose staff published a revision of the manual (DSM-IV-TR) in July 2000.

The APA plans to appoint DSM-V workgroups some time in 2005 or 2006. Emphasizing that the recent editions of the manual have been based on empirical evidence rather than the more traditional "expert opinion," APA has made some recommendations for groups such as ATTACh that may want to be involved. For those who are interested in adding or revising diagnostic categories, the American Psychiatric Association's Website suggests, "you might want to start now the process of putting together a persuasive evidence-based case for your suggestions. This could consist of conducting an ongoing literature review that could be used as the basis for your proposal, or if no published literature exists, collecting data and then submitting the work to a peer-reviewed journal for publication. While of course this will not guarantee that your proposal makes it into DSM-V, the most common reason for proposals to be rejected is the paucity of data to back [them] up." As we will see in our discussion of the research literature in Chapter 7, it is most unlikely that ATTACh will be able to manage this task, with or without the help of AveryHartley, Inc.

Support Groups

Parent support groups appear to play a major role in advocacy of AT. Some of these are face-to-face groups like the one attended by Jeane Newmaker at High Point. Other groups have proliferated on the Internet and seem to play a major role in the lives of the participants.

Support and discussion groups have been a feature of American life for many years, going back to the "self-help" movement, to organizations such as Alcoholics Anonymous, and to the heyday of the National Training Labs in the 1970s. Parents of children with disabilities have been especially attracted to such groups, feeling that only people who have shared their experiences can really understand and help them—and there may be some truth to this. A surprising number of members of AT support groups appear to be dealing with large numbers of foster children, caring for physically ill children or relatives, or rearing their grandchildren, and they may be right in thinking that the average person cannot fully envision their difficulties.

Self-selected Groups

Support groups like the Attachment Disorder Support Group whose list is run by Marymount University are unusual in their degree of self-selection, in addition to having rare living situations. Like members of many support groups, these parents participate because of their beliefs about their children's symptoms and diagnoses, but their involvement is also determined by their advocacy of AT and commitment to the principles of AT-related "therapeutic parenting." Monitoring of postings by members of such groups shows their consistent support for a narrow set of ideas. Participants do not suggest alternatives to the basic AT philosophy or question the efficacy of techniques such as holding therapy. Their postings may be extended complaints that they call "venting," questions about how to get insurance or Medicaid to pay for treatment, or contemptuous references to professionals who do not know about AT. Group members also spend their time supporting each other by reassurances that they are "awesome Moms" who are doing the right thing in a world full of uncomprehending critics.

Support groups' reactions to Candace's death were remarkably sparse, with only occasional comments of a "did you hear?" type. A sampling of postings from the relevant period showed no messages implying concern or withdrawal from the group. This may have been because the news media stressed the "rebirthing" rather than the more common AT techniques used with Candace. One group, the Wisconsin Attachment Resource Network, did attempt to raise money for Watkins's defense; they also posted claims that the Jefferson County police had faked a case against Watkins to take public attention off their mistakes in dealing with the Columbine killings.

THE HELPING PROFESSIONS AND THEIR INFLUENCE

AT practitioners function as a system of their own, but their activities, like those of a family, are embedded in larger systems. One of these larger systems involves legal guidelines and law enforcement, but as we have seen, these tend to come into the picture only after harm has been done. However, the AT community is also embedded in a second larger system, one that has a subtle but pervasive influence: that of the conventional helping professions, with their ethical guidelines, standards of practice, customs, and language. AT practitioners form a group that is in some ways *in* that system, but not *of* it.

Ethical Guidelines

Clinical professionals study ethical rules during their training and are constantly reminded of them during their professional lives. So do researchers working on clinically-related material. Guidelines for both research and clinical practice stress the importance of informed consent by clients or research participants.

The Informed Consent Issue

When an individual is to receive treatment, whether for clinical or research reasons, either that person or someone responsible for his or her welfare must agree to the procedure. But this consent is not adequate unless the consenting person was actually informed about the treatment, the reasons for it, the possible negative side effects, and the potential benefits, as well as any alternative treatments that might be possible. Good informed consent documents are notoriously hard to write. They need to be at a simple enough reading level to be comprehensible even to a worried, distracted reader. There should be no jargon, and as few assumptions as possible about the reader's background knowledge. As we will note later in this book, statements of probability are quite hard for most people to process accurately, yet they are an essential part of an informed consent document's statements about potential benefit or harm.

When a child is the patient, parents or guardians are responsible for giving informed consent. Young people between 12 and 18 should be asked for their informed agreement to treatment as well; children in elementary school should be informed and agree, but it may not be possible for them to understand all the relevant facts. Younger children should receive as much information and warning as possible, but their consent should be interpreted developmentally, recognizing that some preschoolers reply "No!" even to the offer of something they like.

Ethical guidelines for children's informed consent are still undergoing development, having changed considerably over the last 30 years in the direction of more stringent requirements. Strangely, the AT view seems to have devolved over the same time period. Earlier AT practitioners such as Zaslow advised documentation of children's informed consent, but more recent proponents such as Foster Cline have apparently found the idea as ridiculous as asking a child to consent to chemotherapy for cancer. Advocates of "therapeutic foster parenting," such as Nancy Thomas, give as a general rule the idea that children should be given as little information or warning about anything happening in their lives as is practically possible. Treatments by AT practitioners are undoubtedly included in this advice.

Standards of Practice: The Issue of Touch

An extensive discussion of standards of practice in psychotherapy is neither necessary nor appropriate for this book. We will confine ourselves to the issue of physical contact between a therapist and a child client.

In conventional psychotherapy with adults, conducted by professionals whose backgrounds are in psychology or psychiatry, physical contact is very rare, and when it occurs may be a source of concern because of sexual implications. The boundaries are less clearly drawn in the treatment of children, and their application needs to be age-appropriate rather than identical for all persons under 18. Infant mental health specialists and early interventionists, who work with infants and toddlers, use touch, hugging, and picking up as freely as seems needed. Preschool children may want to be held on the lap or to lean against the therapists, but their weight alone tends to discourage therapists from picking them up. In developmental psychotherapy, a technique that stresses communication, it seems that physical proximity and contact can serve communicative functions for nonverbal children. Young children who are in psychotherapy may also be in need of speech, physical, or occupational therapy, all involving possible physical contact.

As children get older, however, conventional psychotherapists become more cautious about touch. Physical boundaries are considered especially important for children who have been physically or sexually abused. Allowing some leeway for developmental delays or physical disabilities, most therapists working with children would probably consider physical contact after age 7 to be generally unsuitable.

The Code of Ethics of the National Association of Social Workers requires clear boundaries for physical contact between social worker and client. However, in a correspondence between an AT practitioner and a NASW official, there seems to have been no clear rejection of physical contact as a part of AT. Developmental appropriateness did not seem to be a criterion in this discussion.

The ATTACh Ethical Standards

Following Candace Newmaker's death, ATTACh issued a revised philosophy and a new set of ethical standards, as well as complaint forms for use by parents or AT practitioners. Safety issues were emphasized; all persons present during therapy were warned that they "were responsible for seeing that effective steps are taken to adjust or terminate an intervention process when there is *any* indication that someone's psychological or physical safety may be being compromised." The guidelines prohibited therapeutic interventions that would cause physical pain and warned that "sexual touch is never appropriate." "Shaming, demeaning, or degrading interaction" was declared unacceptable in therapy.

An important rule in the revised ATTACh guidelines stated that "the child will never be restrained or have pressure put upon them in a manner that would interfere with their basic life functions such as breathing, circulation, temperature, etc." (Some AT practitioners appear to have stated they no longer use restraint when they do holding therapy, although holding seems by definition to involve restraint; perhaps the explanation of this apparent paradox has to do with a definition of restraint as a technique that interferes with life functions.)

The ATTACh guidelines also provided for informed consent from client and parents before treatment. They did not, however, comment on the mode of documentation of informed consent or suggest a model informed-consent document or refer to professional organizations that have such model documents. There was no discussion of developmental considerations or the tailoring of the consent process to the child's age.

Unsolved Problems and Altering Views

As we have just seen, the helping professions change over time in their views of ethical and related issues. As research evidence is gathered, the professions also swing back and forth on their assumptions about basic concepts. These changes are nowhere more evident than in work with children and families, and we can see them reflected in the connections between the AT practitioners, Jeane Newmaker and Candace.

Parents and Professionals

One of the many changing professional views relevant here is that of parent-professional relationships. In chapter 1, we noted some of the peculiarities of the relationship between North Carolina social services workers and Jeane Newmaker, and we speculated that her position as a pediatric nurse had made social workers treat her as a special case.

There have been ongoing changes—even a revolution—in the way professionals are expected to act with parents whose children are in treatment. From the older assumption that the professional is the expert and keeps a distance from the client, there has been a movement toward a cooperative stance and the belief, usually justified, that the parent is the expert on his or her child. Conventional clinicians may not yet have figured out how to establish the "optimal distance" between the professional and a given client. AT practitioners, perhaps responding to the changes in the larger professional system around them, have treated mothers as expert diagnostic consultants and have varied between declaring themselves the expert therapists (the Evergreen group, for example) and advising parents how to be experts (for instance, Martha Welch, whom we will discuss in later chapters).

Research Evidence on Development

During the past 20 years, the helping professions have also seen dramatic changes in ideas about human development and personality. At one time, some of the concerns of the AT advocates would not have seemed so far from the mainstream. It was at one time thought—by John Bowlby, for example—that early separation from a parent was in itself a major risk factor, almost of necessity producing mental disorder and maladaptive behavior. However, the analysis of research evidence about developmental risks has presented a considerably altered picture, and the view of researchers and clinicians has changed and left AT concepts behind. Sir Michael Rutter, the distinguished investigator of the later development of adopted Rumanian orphanage children, recently wrote, "it is clear that parental loss or separation carries quite mild developmental risks unless the loss leads to impaired parenting or other forms of family maladaptation" (Rutter 2002, p.8). This change in viewpoint has occurred so rapidly that undergraduate textbooks have not thoroughly caught up with it, and it is perhaps not surprising that AT advocates, with their lack of interest in formal study, have not done so.

Untested Assumptions

A third rapid change in the helping professions has involved an increased understanding of our untested basic assumptions about human beings—the beliefs about love, hatred, family, and the nature of human life that we usually believe we share with every other right-thinking person. Anthropologists have been trying to tell us for some time that there is no universal agreement on these points, but serious attention to such differences is relatively recent. Where there are cultural disagreements, it is very hard for us to see them, for the process involves stepping out of our own world view and trying to see it as one of many alternatives rather than as the one that is true while the others are absurd or frightening. A recent example of this is Leon's (2002) research on people's beliefs about adoption and the connections between the birth family and the child. Americans in general believe that there is grief and loss behind every adoption. Most of us believe that the birth family grieves, that the adoptive family may possibly grieve over the loss of fertility, and that the child when older may grieve that there are some connected people somewhere but he will never know them. (AT advocates, as we will see, believe the child grieves for the emotional attachment made to the birth mother during gestation.) Leon showed, however, that even the general American view is by no means shared by the entire world. In traditional Hawaiian culture, where adoption was common, it was believed that family feeling came about slowly as a result of shared experience and care. The birth-family connection was irrelevant unless there was later experience together. People were not expected to be distressed about "having to give up" a baby for adoption, nor were adoptive parents expected to yearn for "their own children." What was regarded as a universal opinion and motivation has been shown to be not at all universal, and it is clear that clinical work should not assume that every person shares such basic views with everyone else. But AT practitioners continue to make exactly that assumption.

Isolation of AT Advocates

How can we say that the larger professional system influences AT advocates when we have just indicated three serious ways in which professional psychotherapy has changed but AT concepts have not? The influence in this case is a matter of the isolation of AT practitioners from people who might otherwise affect them as colleagues. The more the conventional professional world changes, the more the AT world becomes an isolated group on the fringe and the less AT practitioners are likely to speak or listen to those involved in conventional psychotherapy. The advocates of AT thus move into positions where they are less and less likely to think through what they are doing in the light of modern theory and practice.

Professional Education for Psychotherapists: Problems Relevant to AT

Examining the reputation of AT, we will see that it has received little or no attention from the helping professions. Yet the AT system is in many ways embedded in the larger system, and we might well expect criticism and attempts at regulation of AT. There has been very little of this. Why?

We have just noted some rapid changes in the practice of therapy and in recent research and theory. We need to remember that conventional therapists have had the job of keeping up and adjusting to these, though they may have done the job well or poorly. To keep up with fringe practices as well was probably too much for most. Both psychologists and psychiatrists receive some basic education in research design, but they may not have had the time or inclination to apply this to fringe practices they heard of primarily through the news media. Although the president of ATTACh expressed surprise that professionals rejected AT, what is really surprising is that any of them had heard of it at all. Working clinicians have enough to keep up with without keeping track of practices outside the mainstream.

A second part of our answer to "why?" may have arisen from the educational backgrounds of psychotherapists. By no means are all trained in either psychology or psychiatry, two disciplines that have traditionally stressed research. Psychotherapists can come from many backgrounds, such as nursing and social work, that have in the past put little emphasis on research training. Some psychotherapists come out of graduate degree programs such as the Ed.D. (Doctor of Education) where empirical work and evidence-based practice are less stressed. Such practitioners may be quite effective clinically but may be less inclined than those with different training to ask what evidence supports unfamiliar practices.

A final reason for the lack of professional response to AT is an insidious and difficult one. It is the fact that even conventional professional training in clinical psychology has become less and less research oriented. As Robyn Dawes (1994) pointed out some years ago, psychologists—who used to boast of their profession's concern with research training—may now receive their professional education in programs that involve little focus on research issues. Programs offering the Psy.D. (Doctor of Psychology) degree, a doctorate that deemphasizes research competence, have increased in numbers and become a major source of doctoral-level psychotherapists. When this process was beginning, Lee Sechrest, a prominent clinical psychologist quoted by Dawes, described the situation as producing "thousands and thousands of practitioners who are peripherally acquainted with the discipline of psychology" (1994, p. 17).

The system of professional psychotherapists, within which the AT system is to some extent embedded, seems to be ill-equipped to evaluate AT or similar fringe practices. Indeed, if therapists are not well versed in the evidence for their own techniques' efficacy, they may be in no hurry to offer a critique of others' methods.

Whatever their level of research sophistication, however, many psychotherapists may never come across techniques such as AT. Such treatments are not taught in accredited academic programs (not at the doctoral level, certainly), and most of the published work about AT is in obscure journals or self-published. One editor of a professional journal, to whom an article about AT was proposed, responded that he had never heard of such a thing and was not convinced that it existed. Lack of awareness may be a major reason why the helping professions have not moved to control AT.

COMPLEMENTARY AND ALTERNATIVE TREATMENTS

Attitudes toward complementary and alternative medicine (CAM) are part of the system in which AT is embedded. CAM treatments often emerge from folk medicine and are usually validated only by anecdotes, and AT may legitimately be considered one of their number. As Everett Koop, the former Surgeon General, remarked in an editorial in *Science* in 2002, there are individuals who seek out CAM treatments simply because they are unorthodox, without regard to the issue of evidence. Many others like to explore these unconventional treatments, especially when they feel that orthodox medical or psychological approaches have not been sufficiently helpful.

Over 40% of Americans have tried CAM treatments. It is even more common for parents of children with special needs to use alternative treatments as a supplement to the techniques of conventional treatment. Physicians and psychotherapists working with these families often hesitate to advise strongly against CAM treatments for fear of alienating the family and interfering with their commitment to continuing conventional treatment.

CAM advocates, like all clinicians, are coming under increased pressure to provide evidence that their methods are effective. Unlike some other practitioners, CAM advocates expect to be able to do this easily, according to the report of the White House Conference on Complementary and Alternative Medicine in 2002. They plan to move on quickly to decisions about public education and about Medicaid and other financial resources for CAM. As we will see in later chapters, providing evidence for the effectiveness of a treatment may not be easy, especially if the outcome involves emotional or behavioral changes. However, public support for CAM treatments can be a strong influence on policy and have a greater impact than evidence does.

Media Influences

The mass media, as well as word of mouth, strongly influence Americans' beliefs about CAM and may also be strongly influenced by what the public seems to want to hear. At the time of this writing, the World Health Organization has just established an investigatory group that will document and test techniques of folk medicine and CAM—"from chiropractic care and fad diets in Manhattan to porcupine quill injections in South Africa," according to a report in the *New York Times* (McNeil, 2002). Newspaper reports on the WHO investigation were an excellent example of the ways in which the media may or may not show support for CAM. The *Times* reported the concerns of WHO about the damage that could be done by folk remedies, as well as commented on possible new sources of medication. But the report in another newspaper, the *Philadelphia Inquirer* (Rose, 2002), omitted any mention of chiropractic care, diets, or potential danger and described the United Nations agency as aiming "to bring alternative ... therapies out of the shadows ... by helping countries integrate them into their health-care services." The less "highbrow" newspaper thus encouraged belief in the value of CAM practices.

Advocacy of CAM by some media outlets serves as indirect support of AT techniques, just as individuals' positive expectations do. Even CAM supporters who have never heard of AT can spread the belief in miraculous cures by techniques based neither on evidence nor on conventional theory and can thus contribute to parents' convictions that AT could be good for their children. As CAM techniques are presented in positive ways, whether in the news or in television "docudramas," help is indirectly given to the AT community, embedded as it is in this larger system.

It is possible that acceptance of any CAM treatment makes it easier for other such treatments to seem acceptable. It is certainly noticeable that messages on AT Websites advocate a whole series of CAM treatments, including EMDR (eye movement desensitization and reprocessing), a technique suggested for post-traumatic stress disorders, and Samonas sound therapy, exposure to high-frequency sounds that is claimed to alter brain functioning.

CONCLUSION

It is tempting to cast all the blame for Candace Newmaker's death on Connell Watkins and Julie Ponder. Doing this, we could feel pleased: we have found the malefactors, they have received their punishment, and the moral balance of the universe has somehow been restored. Such a conclusion, however, would be neither correct nor of any use in preventing the practice of AT. Watkins and Ponder had help in implementing Candace's death, not just from St. Clair, McDaniel, and Jeane Newmaker but also from groups of people who were nowhere near the scene of the crime. Some of these groups had never even heard of AT in any of its forms. Stopping Watkins and Ponder does not stop the potential influences of such systems on parents or practitioners.

As we will note in later chapters, there seem to be only two ways in which the systems that facilitate AT can be altered. One is public education so that parents and others who encounter AT in its changing names and forms can recognize it for what it is. This includes improved professional education and work with the mass media. The other needed approach is legislation to control the practice of AT techniques. Education without legislation is not sufficient, because parents are more likely to interest themselves in personal anecdotes than they are in demanding intellectual exercises. Legislation without education would probably just drive AT underground; in any case, legislation is not very likely to pass until education has been attempted. Both educational and legislative approaches require us to think of AT practitioners as part of systems rather than as independent perpetrators of crime.

REFERENCES

Crowder, C., & Lowe, P. (2000, October 29). Her name was Candace. *Denver Rocky Mountain News*, pp. 1A, 1M–7M, 9M–12M.

Dawes, R. M. (1994). *House of cards: Psychology and psychotherapy built on myth.* New York: Free Press.

Leon, I. (2002). Adoption losses: Naturally occurring or socially constructed? *Child Development, 73*(2), 652–663.

Levy, T. M., & Orlans, M. (2000a). Attachment disorders as an antecedent to violence and antisocial patterns in children. In T. M. Levy (Ed.), *Handbook of attachment interventions.* San Diego, CA: Academic Press.

Levy, T. M., & Orlans, M. (2000b). Attachment disorder and the adoptive family. In T. M. Levy (Ed.) *Handbook of attachment interventions.* San Diego, CA: Academic Press.

McNeil, D. G. (2002, May 17). With folk medicine on rise, health group is monitoring. *New York Times*, p. A8.

Rose, E. (2002, May 17). Alternative care gets a boost. *Philadelphia Inquirer*, p. A24.

Rutter, M. (2002). Nature, nurture, and development: From evangelism through science toward policy and practice. *Child Development, 73*, pp. 1–21.

Vlosky, M. (2000, June 5). Putting a new name on an old form of torture [letter]. *Denver Rocky Mountain News*, p. 36A.

Chapter 3

Candace's Treatment:
What They Did and Why They Did It

INTRODUCTION

This chapter tells the story of Candace Newmaker's treatment in Colorado, the treatment that ended with her death. It also tells something of the intellectual story behind that treatment—an intellectual story that combines popular beliefs, ancient religious traditions, and a distorted, simplistic view of human nature.

The Background: What is Normal Psychotherapy?

Psychotherapy is such a common part of American life today that most readers of this book have probably had some personal counseling or other treatment. Still, people who are not themselves trained as therapists may remain unsure as to what therapy is all about, even though they have participated in it. Readers may be aware, too, that different people can have different experiences in treatment and that therapists may belong to different schools of thought.

It is certainly true that there are differences among psychotherapeutic techniques and individual differences in practice. However, the great majority of treatment approaches have more commonalities than differences. The therapy used with Candace Newmaker, on the other hand, shared few characteristics with the normal range of treatments. Not only the methods but the very basic assumptions behind the treatment were so different from ordinary therapies as to belong to a different universe of discourse.

Before this chapter begins to describe the events of Candace's treatment, it may be useful to examine some specific differences between the methods she experienced and the techniques used in 99% of psychotherapeutic interventions.

How is Attachment Therapy Different?

1. Ordinarily, psychotherapy focuses on *communication* between patient and therapist as the essential aspect of treatment. For older children and adults, of course, talking is the preferred communicative method, but even very young children can be helped to communicate through pretend play or through gesture and facial expression.

   Candace's treatment involved some talking, but its major emphasis was on *transformation* rather than communication. The therapists assumed that some physical and emotional experiences could cause Candace to change without her needing to understand her past or present situations in an intellectual way.

   Communicative therapies (the great majority of those practiced today) stress putting feelings into words and changing the way a person thinks about situations. Transformational therapies, such as the treatment Candace received, can be seen as more like medical treatment or more like a magic ritual, depending on one's attitude toward them. Whether we think in terms of surgery or exorcism, the transformational approach assumes that the patient needs only to cooperate, not to understand what is happening, to be transformed and cured.

2. The majority of psychotherapeutic techniques today involve some concerns with a patient's *early childhood experiences*, but not with his or her *prenatal life*. Without denying that an unborn baby has some sensory and even some learning abilities from a time about halfway through the mother's pregnancy, psychotherapists generally assume that babies are influenced only in a very indirect way by events that occur before birth. Instead, the period of development from about 6 months to about 2 years of age is considered the most important time for the establishment of emotional and personality characteristics.

   Candace's treatment was based on the quite different assumption that events during gestation have a profound effect on the development of the baby's emotions and that this effect begins as early as the time of implantation or even at conception. Candace's therapists belonged to a school of thought that considers an unborn baby to be fully aware of its mother's negative thoughts and feelings and to be made sad or angry by them. An associated belief is that the baby also forms an emotional connection to the mother before birth and is distressed if separated from the birth mother and adopted by someone else.

3. *Eye contact* is considered by most psychotherapists to be an important tool of communication and an indication of a patient's feelings. Psychotherapists are aware that some serious emotional disturbances, such as autism, include among their symptoms an avoidance of eye contact. Psychologists who study infant development have described the use of the gaze in communication between sighted parents and sighted babies. Unlike Candace's therapists, though, the majority of psychotherapists would reject the idea that eye contact has an almost magical social and emotional power. Instead, they would consider eye contact as one of many ways of communicating human emotion, and would point out the successful development of vision-impaired babies or of those whose parents see poorly.

4. Most psychotherapists are extremely cautious about physically *touching* a patient. When working with young children, of course, they may need to use touch as a mode of comfort and communication, but they try to make the contact as respectful to the child as possible, especially if there have been any previous experiences of physical or

sexual abuse. Most therapists would use little, if any, physical contact with a child who is 7 years old or more.

Candace's therapists, however, considered touch and *physical restraint* to be major tools for treatment. As we will see later, they held Candace firmly and moved and manipulated her head and arms in one form of treatment and immobilized her by wrapping her in a sheet in another.

5. Modern psychologists, as well as psychotherapists of other backgrounds, reject the idea of *catharsis*. This concept dates back to the classical Greek drama and holds that negative emotions build up harmfully if unexpressed and can be "drained off" by deliberate expression. The Greeks believed that accumulated sorrow, fear, and anger could be relieved by watching plays in which actors expressed those emotions. A modern version has been the idea that unexpressed anger rankles, ferments, and causes trouble. Modern psychological research, however, has shown that people who act angry subsequently feel more rather than less enraged.

The average American is not aware of the psychological research and continues to accept the idea that anger has to be expressed to be defused. Children are taught to punch pillows or to have mock fights with inflatable baseball bats to "get rid of rage." Attachment therapists, too, have clung to the ancient idea that rage can accumulate or can be dissipated by physical expression. (Logically, of course, we might think that the same reasoning could apply to other emotions, so we should be careful not to laugh and let our joy escape—but somehow the idea of catharsis is applied only to the negative emotional experiences.)

6. Most psychotherapists, whatever their academic backgrounds, are aware of two sets of statistics relevant to Candace's case. The first set has to do with the *developmental patterns of adopted children.* There is clear-cut evidence that children who are adopted at an early age have no more behavioral or emotional troubles than nonadopted children and indeed may do better in some ways (Miller et al., 2000).

The second important set of statistics has to do with *youth violence.* Most psychotherapists are aware that, in spite of a few highly dramatic incidents, the rate of violent crimes among children and teenagers has gone down in recent years and is lower than it has been for some time.

The treatment Candace received, however, involved two incorrect beliefs—or, at least, the therapists expressed these beliefs to parents of potential patients. One assumption was that all adopted children, even if adopted at an hour of age, have serious emotional disturbances. The second assumption was that rates of youth violence are increasing rapidly and that the rage and distress of adopted children makes them likely to attack and kill. Therefore, it was considered urgent that Candace be treated with whatever approaches were available because she was potentially dangerous to her adoptive mother and to others.

CANDACE'S TREATMENT

The authors of this book were not present at Candace's treatment. We never met the child and never conversed with Jeane Newmaker, Connell Watkins, or

Julie Ponder. However, we can draw on a great deal of information, videotaped and written, describing attachment therapy in general and Candace's treatment in detail.

Sources of Information

Because Connell Watkins and Julie Ponder, Candace's therapists, videotaped their treatment sessions with her and these videotapes were shown at their trial, we have some specific information about her treatment experiences. We also have an analysis of frequencies of certain events on the videotapes, meticulously performed by Det. Diane Obbema of the Jefferson County, CO, Sheriff's Department and presented in evidence at the Watkins-Ponder trial.

Of course, Candace spent days in Colorado without having all her experiences videotaped, and we cannot know everything that happened to her. However, we do have material published by former colleagues of Watkins and Ponder, and we can turn to those publications for descriptions of some experiences common to children receiving attachment therapy.

Supportive Therapies

Psychotherapy is often thought of as an intermittent event; you visit the therapist once a week, and you go about your ordinary life between visits. However, when emotional disturbances are intense or dangerous, ordinary life is not necessarily a possibility. Adults who are seriously disturbed may be confined to a psychiatric hospital, where they receive medication and may have treatments such as group therapy or art therapy as well as the usual "talking" therapy.

These adjuvant or supportive therapies are also used for children. The very seriously disturbed may be in a hospital setting, where education and play opportunities are organized to fit their special needs. Some child psychotherapists recommend intensive treatment of many types even for children who are not hospitalized, and a child may receive treatment from occupational therapists, speech and physical therapists, and special education teachers as well as receiving psychotherapy.

In Candace's treatment, a number of therapeutic tools were used, including medication, art therapy, and a form of psychodrama in which the child acted out a scene with an adult who played the role of her birth mother. However, the most unusual adjuvant therapy used with Candace was "therapeutic foster care."

Therapeutic Foster Care

Candace saw little of her adoptive mother after the two arrived in Colorado, even though they slept in the same house. Candace was placed in the care of a "therapeutic foster mother," Brita St. Clair, herself the adoptive mother of several children who were said to have attachment disorders. St. Clair had worked as Watkins's office manager for some months and had been taught the attachment therapy philosophy.

Therapeutic foster parents working with attachment therapists are responsible for the care of children who have been brought for a two-week intensive period of therapy as well as for a number of children who spend extended periods of months or more in treatment. The therapeutic foster parent has responsibility for the child at most times outside of visits to the therapist. She provides supervision and food as well as giving the child chores to do and a schedule to follow. The therapeutic foster parent gives the child whatever medication has been ordered and reports on the child's behavior to the therapist.

Philosophy of Therapeutic Foster Care

The philosophy of the therapeutic foster home is based on attachment therapy's theoretical foundations and includes a number of other ideas that have been promulgated by Nancy Thomas, the author of written material and educational videotapes on this subject. Thomas' approach begins with *demonization* of the children—perhaps not quite literally attributing to them the nature of satanic beings but coming about as close to this as reality admits. For example, in one educational videotape, Thomas says she does not allow children staying in her therapeutic foster home to say grace at meals "because you don't know who they might be praying to."

The therapeutic foster home philosophy, as Thomas has shaped it, assumes that the children in treatment are *malicious, hostile, and viciously destructive.* Without treatment, they will grow up to be people like Ted Bundy, serial killers without conscience whose great pleasure will be to hurt the innocent. Thomas claims that 80% of the children she cares for have already killed and are especially dangerous to helpless animals and infants. In Thomas' writings and videotapes, she repeatedly presents an anecdote about a 5-year-old who tore the heads off a litter of German shepherd puppies—a feat that seems beyond the strength and coordination of a child of that age, if not beyond his motivation.

Children in therapeutic foster homes are also thought to be *manipulative and exploitative* of others. Their expressions of affection, sadness, or distress and their requests for help or comfort are said invariably to be attempts to fool or manipulate the adult, who must resist them at all costs. If an adult yields to the child's ploy, the child is said to feel that he or she "wins," and such a feeling worsens the child's emotional disturbance. Elaborate scams are said to be characteristic of these children; one of Thomas' repeated anecdotes involves a boy who bloodied himself climbing out of a window, went to a neighbor's house claiming to have been in a car accident with his mother, and had rescue workers summoned, all for no reason except the love of power and manipulation.

Because the children are expected to be manipulative, Thomas advises keeping them away from other people or having them wear dark glasses in public to conceal the sad expressions they may turn on strangers. She suggests that those who see children with marks suggestive of physical abuse should show their sympathy for the adult caregivers. In one educational video, Thomas defines the evidence that someone is a good parent to a disturbed child as the fact that the child still has his head, arms, and legs attached. Many children, she says, have perished "because of what they made their moms and dads do to them."

The general approach of the therapeutic foster home, then, involves a serious and even fearful attitude toward the child, who is perceived as potentially destructive and dangerous. Restrictions and unpleasant experiences are necessary for the child's own sake, and it would be irresponsible for the therapeutic foster parent to be sympathetic or to yield to a child's apparent needs rather than maintain complete adult authority.

Training Techniques in the Foster Home

The therapeutic foster parent is in charge of two techniques intended to change the child. The first, *compliance training,* involves repeated commands that the child is to obey in a "fast and snappy" manner, cheerfully and accurately. Errors, as we will discuss later in this chapter, are attributed to the child's resistance, not to inability to comply. One of the videotapes of Candace's treatment shows her in a brief compliance training session with Brita St. Clair at Watkins's office.

In this session, Candace was sitting down when St. Clair called out, "Candace!" The child jumped to her feet, approached St. Clair, stood with her hands behind her back, and replied, "Yes, Mom Brita!" St. Clair asked her a question about how children should behave with their families. Candace answered, talking about "respect," but missed other parts of the correct answer. "Go sit," ordered St. Clair. As Candace began to sit down, St. Clair called again, "Candace!" The child came to St. Clair as before and obeyed the instruction she received to jump up and down five times. (The reasoning behind this will be discussed later in this chapter.) The earlier question was repeated and again got an incomplete answer, followed by the same sequence. St. Clair's tone seemed to express a teasing antagonism throughout the interaction.

A second tool used by the therapeutic foster parent is called *power sitting* or *strong sitting.* This is considered by some AT writers to be the essential technique for teaching children self-control. It is used in the foster home and in the therapist's office and is recommended by therapeutic foster parents such as Nancy Thomas for use in school settings.

"Strong sitting" involves sitting on the floor tailor-fashion—with the legs bent at the knees, the legs spread at the hips and entirely or partly resting on the floor, and the ankles crossed. The back is to be straight, the head up, and arms relaxed with hands in the lap or on the knees. The person doing strong sitting correctly does not speak or move and remains quiet and concentrated.

Strong sitting is supposed to be done three times a day, for a time equivalent to one minute for each year of the child's age. It should be noted, though, that timing does not begin while the child is wriggling or talking. A child may sit "incorrectly" for two hours before the timing of strong sitting begins. With three sitting sessions a day, a child might thus spend more than six hours each day in the sitting position. (In one of the videotapes of Candace, she is seen sitting for 36 minutes, although she rarely appears to deviate from the correct technique.)

Chores are assigned in the therapeutic foster home in a way that resembles the pattern of strong sitting. Children are said to be assigned about a half hour of chores such as sweeping every day, but this assignment may expand into a much greater period of time if the child resists the task or does not do the chore as well as is expected.

Discipline Techniques

Misbehavior in the therapeutic foster home may be treated by physical or other restrictions; for example, it is advised that a child who hits another child or talks disruptively in the car will have to sit with hands on top of the head or over the mouth for some minutes. If this is not done properly in the car, it is to be done for a greater period of time at home. A child who breaks or damages property is assigned extra chores until the damage is "paid for." Some responses to misbehavior seem to follow the principle that the punishment should fit the crime, and swearing or vulgar language may be punished by an assignment to manure-shoveling.

Therapeutic foster parents are taught that the children they work with need an unusual amount of *physical exercise,* and without it behave badly because too little oxygen is being circulated to their brains. Jumping-jacks or push-ups are supposed to create a better oxygen supply and improve the child's thinking and behavior.

Food and Sleep

Food is considered to play an important role in the handling of children in the therapeutic foster home. As we will see later in this chapter, attachment therapists believe that food—and sweet food above all—plays a critical part in the establishment of emotional relationships. Children are not allowed to prepare their own food or to take food from people other than the therapeutic foster parents. A child who complains about food or hesitates to eat the family meal is sent away from the table, and her food is thrown away or given to the dog. No more food is made available until the next meal. On occasions when the child is cared for by a respite worker rather than the usual therapeutic foster parent, the substitute is not to provide any sweet food for fear of interfering with emotional attachment, a process that AT practitioners believe is based on gratifications of that type.

Children in therapeutic foster homes are to go to their rooms early in the evening to give the foster parent a break. If they are attending school or being tutored, they do their homework alone in their rooms. No night lights or open doors are permitted after bedtime, even when children have unusual concerns about security and trust. An alarm set on the bedroom door sounds if the child opens the door during the night.

Schooling

Children who are in therapeutic foster homes for months do not necessarily attend school, which is presented as a privilege, not a right. They may receive tutoring, but this is not the task of the therapeutic foster parent. When the children do attend school, an arrangement sometimes made for them is a "take-a-hike" policy, in which any misbehavior whatever at school is followed by power sitting in another classroom or by being taken home to do chores.

Cuddling

The picture is not complete, however, unless we add that the ultimate goal of attachment therapy and therapeutic foster care is to create the emotional connections with others that underlie empathy and moral behavior. It is one of the tasks of the therapeutic foster parent to create emotional connections and then transfer them so that the child becomes emotionally attached to the permanent parent, biological or adoptive. The formation of the attachment is thought to result from an experience the foster child is to have each day: cuddling, rocking, and being given sweets by the foster parent. This is done at the decision of the adult, not when the child requests it. Exactly how the transfer of the attachment to the permanent parent is to take place is the concern of the attachment therapist, not the therapeutic foster parent.

Holding Therapy

When she was not at the therapeutic foster home with Brita St. Clair, Candace was taken to Watkins's office for therapy. There, she experienced several therapeutic techniques. The major form of treatment was a form of physical restraint called holding therapy, which she had already encountered in North Carolina.

Those Present During a Holding Session

In Candace's experience in Colorado, Watkins was sometimes the only person restraining the child during holding therapy. At other times, Watkins was joined by Jack McDaniel, a general helper and former construction worker who later married Brita St. Clair, Candace's therapeutic foster mother. According to courtroom testimony, it was expected that Candace would be violently resistant to treatment and that a strong man would be needed to control her physically. (The predicted spitting, biting, and head-butting never materialized, however.)

The Holding Position

To perform holding therapy, the adult or adults sat on one end of a sofa; Candace lay back, her head in Watkins's lap or her arms, her body across McDaniel's lap if he was there, and her legs extended along the sofa. Her left hand and arm were behind Watkins, and at one time the hand was sat on by McDaniel, who sat on her legs at another point. Watkins, when alone with Candace, held her right hand; when McDaniel was present, he held the right hand and moved it slowly up and down, back and forth.

This position enabled Watkins to hold Candace's face and to force eye contact. It also allowed her to bounce or shake the child's head, to grab or cover her face, and to shout into her face at close range—all of which she did.

The Events of a Holding Session

Det. Diane Obbema of the Jefferson County Sheriff's Department had the unpleasant task of watching the videotapes of Candace's holding therapy and counting the length and frequency of particular events. According to Det. Obbema's testimony, on one day Candace had two holding therapy sessions, one 49 minutes and the other 20 minutes in length. Det. Obbema noted that in these two sessions Watkins grabbed or covered Candace's face 48 times, shook or bounced the girl's head 83 times, and shouted into her face 68 times from distances of a foot or less. In another set of holding sessions lasting about two hours, Watkins grabbed or covered Candace's face 90 times, she shook, jerked, or bounced Candace's head 309 times, and the therapist yelled into Candace's face 65 times.

Although Candace was acted upon by Watkins throughout the holding therapy, it would be wrong to imagine the child as being passive and uninvolved. She was not allowed to remain that way. Candace was repeatedly told "Kick!"—to perform a repeated scissors kick that drummed her heels against the sofa—and then instructed to stop kicking. When asked a question, she was required to answer and to go on until the desired answer was given; if Candace spoke in an ordinary quiet or conversational tone, Watkins demanded that she shout.

Verbal Content

Although we have described attachment therapy as transformational rather than communicative, it should not be assumed that there is no talking involved in the process or that the content is of no importance. Talking to a child of normal intelligence can be one of the most effective ways of interesting, arousing, or enraging her—and, as we saw earlier in this chapter, one of the goals of the treatment was to "get rid" of Candace's old rage by stimulating her to express anger.

Watkins did most of the talking during holding therapy, but when McDaniel was present, he occasionally made a comment or asked a question. Generally, the talk focused on the unhappiness Candace had caused her adoptive mother and on her continuing concern with her birth mother, Angela. Her early life was spoken of as "not really your fault," but Watkins described Candace's more recent years as involving a series of deliberate decisions to be hateful and disobedient to her adoptive mother. These decisions were characterized by Watkins as "letting Angela be the boss of you."

Many of Watkins's comments to Candace were accusations. For example, Candace was told that she had wanted her adoptive mother to die and had drawn pictures of her in a graveyard, hanging, and burning. As "homework," Candace was to make a list of everything she had ever said "no" to her adoptive mother about.

Watkins made frequent threatening statements emphasizing the possibility that Jeane Newmaker, the adoptive mother, would abandon or institutionalize Candace. (In a set of holding sessions totaling about two hours, there were 49 such threats.) Candace was told that her mother might go home, but she, Candace, would definitely be staying in Colorado, no matter how hard she worked. Watkins stressed the idea that the adoptive mother did not need Candace, but Candace needed her love and care.

Insults and accusations of bad behavior formed a noticeable portion of Watkins's remarks to Candace. The girl was addressed as "a little twerp" or "jerk." Her failure to accomplish something she had said she would do was characterized as "lying," and the same term was used when Candace said she did not remember something. Watkins claimed that Candace had told her adoptive mother to "fuck off," and when the child denied using "that word," Watkins replied, "You think that."

During some parts of the holding sessions, Jeane Newmaker was present and participated by talking, although she did not take part in the physical restraint. At one point, the adoptive mother told Candace, "This is your last chance ... you can be a real jerk and stay the rest of your life. I'll go home with the dogs ... Am I serious about this? You won't come back to my house to have it be the way it was. This is your last chance, *your very last chance*. I'm having a great time. It's not hurting me."

Not all the talking was done by the adults during the holding sessions. When she could, Candace seemed to seize an opportunity for conversation with Watkins; for example, she engaged Watkins briefly in a discussion of the story of Pinocchio. Generally, however, Candace answered questions or spoke as she was instructed. She was usually compliant, but occasionally gave a spirited reply. For example:

Watkins: Do you know why you're here?
Candace: To get help.
Watkins: Why do you think you're here?
Candace: To get tortured!

Part of Watkins's technique during holding therapy involved having Candace shout repeated responses, sometimes to catch-phrases spoken in a threatening manner:

Watkins: GOT IT?
Candace: Got it!

The shouted repetitions also referred to Candace's hating her mother, wanting to hurt people, or hating Watkins for sending her adoptive mother away.

If Candace asked a question or claimed not to know something, the therapist responded with laughter, ridicule, and disbelief. Watkins inquired at one point, "Why are you always asking questions? What difference does it make?" In one sequence, Watkins referred to Jeane Newmaker's having said that "the jig is up" with regard to Candace, who evidently did not understand the expression and could not remember it exactly. Watkins and her helper Jack McDaniel made Candace try to guess the word "jig," and finally had her go through the alphabet until she got it.

Emotional Tone

Watkins's speech to Candace was not invariably harsh or directive. There were periods where she spoke quietly and even sympathetically of Candace's early life and blamed her birth mother for the problems Candace was experiencing. Even her comments that seemed intended to enrage Candace had a light quality to them, more like a schoolyard bully toying with a weaker child than like an adult carrying out a serious attack.

Candace, too, spoke in ways that were not simple responses to Watkins's instructions. However, except for the conversation about Pinocchio, most of her spontaneous speeches showed her distress with Watkins's physical restraint and handling. Candace complained of being unable to breathe on several occasions and complained that she was being hurt. Candace told Watkins "Stop it!" when her head was jerked. (At about this time, the girl apparently tried to pinch Watkins, who said, "I'll poke you very hard if you do that.") Candace complained, "Can you please quit squeezing me? . . . Please, please, you're squeezing me," and cried in pain as Watkins replied negatively, "Uh-uh."

Physical Movement

Most of the movement that occurred during the holding-therapy sessions was either performed or ordered by Watkins. In addition to the bouncing or jerking movements described earlier, Watkins manually moved Candace's face so the two maintained eye contact, and during one session squeezed Candace's face so that her mouth opened.

The reader who wants to picture the holding-therapy scene needs to recall the repeated commands to Candace to kick. The thudding of Candace's heels during the rapid scissors kick and her quickened breathing as a result of her exertions were a constant counterpoint to the other sounds and movements.

Compression Therapy

On one day of Candace's treatment, a short holding session was followed by a period of *compression therapy*. (The reader may recall from the Introduction a brief description of the death of Krystal Tibbets in Utah, which occurred during the use of this technique.) Candace was placed on the floor, wrapped in sheets so only her head could move. The parent generally lies down on top of the child, but because Jeane Newmaker weighed 195 pounds and Candace only 68, some sofa cushions were used to take part of the mother's weight. Jeane lay on Candace, demanded eye contact, and told Candace loudly what she found wrong with her. In this session, which lasted for an hour and 42 minutes, Candace did not cry or scream or join with Jeane in any emotional exchange. She complained that she was too hot and could not breathe. On Watkins's instructions, Jeane Newmaker licked Candace's face 21 times, grabbed her face 25 times, shook her head 63 times, screamed at her 16 times, and threatened abandonment 26 times. (At one point Candace said matter-of-factly, "This is stupid," but more often she appeared withdrawn and blankly unresponsive.)

Following the compression treatment, Jeane Newmaker sat in a large chair, the "mommy chair," and held Candace in her lap, feeding her a cinnamon roll and hugging and kissing her. Jeane testified at the Watkins-Ponder trial how pleasant the memory of this occasion was for her.

Rebirthing

The rebirthing session performed by Watkins and her assistants was, of course, the last step in Candace's treatment; the child lay without breath or heartbeat before the session was over. Ironically, courtroom testimony indicated that Watkins had decided to do this technique rather than another session of holding therapy because she felt everyone needed a break. Watkins apparently expected this session to be mild and easy. In previous rebirthing sessions, the children had been wrapped for 5 minutes or less. There was never any complete explanation of the reason for the extension of this session to its tragic outcome.

Candace's Introduction

Candace was introduced to the idea of rebirthing by Julie Ponder rather than by Watkins; Ponder was a therapist who was "studying with" Watkins and who had received some informal instruction about rebirthing from a visiting advocate of the practice, Douglas Gosney. Ponder explained that this process would be like being born to the right mother rather than to a mother who didn't take care of her. Candace answered "Yes" when asked, "Have you wanted to be born to this mom you have right now?," "Are you sad about that?," and "You could have been saved and not fallen out the window?" (This last question referred to a story about something Candace thought happened to her as a baby.) Ponder went on to talk about how the birth mother did not take care of Candace properly, and she explained that in the rebirthing "you'll have plenty of air to breathe. You'll have to push really hard, reach for her and pull yourself out."

Candace yawned during this explanation, and Ponder asked whether she had slept. When Candace replied that she had had nightmares about being murdered, Ponder asked whether she had been afraid she would die when she was a baby and remarked in a sympathetic tone, "Now you don't have to worry about dying." Ponder spread out a blue flannel sheet on the floor and asked Candace to lie down on it. ("Shall I take my shoes off?," Candace wanted to know.)

Positioning and Instructions

When Candace had lain down on her left side with her feet drawn up into the fetal position, Ponder began to cover her, drawing the sheet up to form a bag with the top of Candace's head near the opening. Ponder told Candace to imagine herself as "a teeny little baby" in her mother's womb, where it was warm, tight, wet, and sticky. "What did you think about in there?" "I thought I was going to die," responded Candace.

By this time, Jeane Newmaker and Connell Watkins were present, as well as Brita St. Clair, Candace's therapeutic foster mother, and Jack McDaniel, who married St. Clair not long after these events occurred. Newmaker began a speech about how she was looking forward to the birth of this baby, how nice their lives would be together, and how the baby would be safe and would have a nice life. Watkins interjected at this point that both the mother and the baby would die if the baby did not get born.

Candace was not only enveloped in the flannel sheet with sofa pillows placed on top of her, but was surrounded by the five adults, who sat on the floor, four of them leaning or pressing against her. Jean Newmaker knelt beside her head. Ponder asked Candace, "Are you ready to be born?" "Yes." "Come out head first. You have to push with your feet."

First Indications of Trouble

But now the conversation between Ponder and Candace began to indicate a problem. Candace was crying, "I can't do it . . . You're pushing on my head." She screamed, "I can't breathe, I can't do it! . . . I can't do it, somebody's on top of me! . . . Where'm I supposed to come out? Somebody's on top of me . . . No, I can't do it! I want to die now! Please! Air!" Her gasping breaths could be heard. Ponder remarked on how hard it is to be born.

"Please," said Candace. "I can't breathe. Please stop pushing on me." Sobbing, she screamed, "Please!" Ponder answered, "Sometimes it takes hours," and the adults pressed down on Candace. "Scream," Ponder told Candace, and the child obeyed.

Ponder told Candace to push harder, "You're gonna die," and Watkins agreed, "Die right now." "For real?" Candace asked. "Yes." "Please, please, I can't breathe." "You don't need to breathe when you're dead, you don't need air . . . What's it like to be dead?" said Ponder. Candace was silent.

A few minutes later, Candace could be heard to sob and moan. "Do you want to be born?" "Yes." "Let's let her go ahead and die, it's easier if you don't have the courage to live." " Please," Candace sobbed, "I gotta poop, I gotta poop." The sound of vomiting could be heard. "Do you want to be born?" Candace sobbed, "No." "Okay, stay in there with the poop and the vomit."

Ponder instructed the adults to "press more on top." Candace screamed, "I can't breathe!" Newmaker now remarked that she was "so excited to have this baby. I can't wait. I know it's hard but I'm waiting for you."

Ponder told the child, "Scream, Candace, scream for your life, go ahead, go ahead," but when there was no response but silence she pressed down harder and said to the other adults that Candace was "not willing to try." Ponder braced her feet to push against Candace as sobbing and whistling breaths could be heard.

Candace's Silence

Ponder remarked, "There's less and less air all the time." Watkins commented about how miserable people are when they're around Candace, describing her as a "walking dead little girl." There were conversations and laughter among the adults. Jack McDaniel pressed more of his weight on Candace. Ponder remarked in a light, teasing tone, "Quitter, quitter! She's a quitter!" There was silence from under the sheet.

Newmaker left the room while Ponder and McDaniel pressed on Candace's body. Ponder remarked that she had her hand right on Candace's face. "Taking a rest, huh?" There was laughter at a remark about needing a C-section. "Comfortable enough to sleep in there?"

Watkins said, "She might be ready to be born. Everybody can take a break." Ponder patted a dog that had wandered into the room. Watkins and Ponder leaned on Candace's body, talking, for some minutes. Watkins: "Let's look at this twerp and see what's going on—is there a kid in there somewhere? There you are lying in your own vomit—aren't you tired?"

Unwrapping the Child

As the child's blue face was uncovered, Ponder spoke with rising alarm, "Candace, Candace, Candace!" She started to breathe into the child's mouth. "Connell, call 911!" Newmaker, running into the room, screamed, "She's dead, she's dead! Look at her color! Call 911!" She started chest compression, shouting, "Candace! Candace!" Ponder called out, "Come on, Candace! Stay with us! Stay!"

Watkins called 911 and reported a child not breathing. She turned off the video camera. About 70 minutes had passed since Candace lay down to be wrapped in the blue flannel sheet, which now had a long tear as a result of her efforts to escape.

CANDACE'S REACTION TO STEPS IN TREATMENT

So far we have looked at Candace's treatment experiences in terms of what was done to her, and in the last section that was by far the most important issue. Looking at the entire treatment, however, we have to consider how Candace's actions guided any part of what happened. She was an active participant in the treatment situation, even when prevented from escaping from the sheet. She talked, she moved, and she could resist or comply to some extent as she chose. Her words, movements, and facial expressions cued the therapists and the foster mother to produce their own words, movements, and facial expressions. Even the tendency to ignore what Candace said was shaped by Candace's communications as the therapists interpreted them.

Resisting the Therapists

Certainly, Candace cried, complained, and resisted many aspects of the treatment. She did not want her hand or legs sat on by an adult, and she responded "Quit that!" to Watkins's squeezing of her face. At one point in a holding session Candace apparently tried to pinch Watkins. However, she did not seem either to spit or to bite, two ploys quite open to her in this face-to-face position, nor did she take advantage of the command to kick by kicking one of the adults, or even by kicking in a way that would have made the adult's sitting position uncomfortable.

Compliance

Except for her obvious increasing panic in the rebirthing situation, Candace's protests had a pro forma quality to them. She was far more compliant than resistant, although she became quite expressive of her unhappiness when a brief visit with her mother was abruptly ended.

Was There Rage?

If Watkins intended to provoke Candace to rage (see later discussion), it would appear that she did a poor job. Candace was sometimes uncomfortable and resisted physical pushes and pulls, and she complied with Watkins's directions to shout statements of hatred and anger, but she did not appear to be genuinely angry. Candace seemed indignant when Watkins accused her of having said or thought "Fuck you," but even this did not appear to be an intense or persistent feeling.

Criticism or demands for repetition from Watkins or the therapeutic foster mother did not seem to trigger Candace's anger or resentment. Her most vigorous response to one of these situations was "Oh, man!"

Candace seemed to be not only compliant but quite straightforward in her comments during the holding therapy. Asked how much she actually wanted to change, she thought and then offered "8 parts out of 10" rather than claiming an unlikely complete commitment to change. Asked about embarrassing things in her life, she told of having been "popped" with a belt in a foster home before she was adopted and volunteered that she had not even told her adoptive mother about that.

In the course of several pauses during holding therapy, Candace simply chatted with Watkins, apparently quite comfortable and without lingering negative emotion.

This analysis, of course, is based only on what was visible on the treatment videotapes shown during the Watkins-Ponder trial. The extent to which Candace was angry or resistant with her therapeutic foster mother is not clear, although she was described on the tapes as having refused to do chores at one point. Candace was "fired" from treatment and not allowed to have holding therapy one day, allegedly because she had been uncooperative at the foster home.

We must emphasize that this description of Candace's reactions does not apply to the rebirthing session. Although she began that session with an air of calm and compliance, her voice conveyed more and more feeling as she struggled without result. Still, even when Candace's voice was most expressive of her distress, she did not sound angry; what one heard was sheer terror.

THE RATIONALE: WHY DID WATKINS AND PONDER DO WHAT THEY DID?

Why did all this happen? Why did Watkins, Ponder, and the others elect to use these particular techniques? What kept them from realizing the physical danger inherent in the rebirthing method? Why did they not recognize the seriousness of Candace's pleas and respond to them?

The immediate response most of us would make to these questions might well be that Watkins and Ponder were a couple of "random nuts," and this seems to have been the media consensus following their conviction. Whatever accuracy the "nut" diagnosis may have, however, there was nothing random about Watkins's and Ponder's actions. What they did was based on a standard set of techniques, and their thinking was determined by an elaborate theoretical background, lightly supported by a few attempts at empirical studies. Those techniques and that theory contain the answers to the questions posed in the earlier paragraph. However bizarre or idiosyncratic these treatments appear—and however ineffective or harmful they may be to children—they emerge from a complex internal logic, based, unfortunately, on faulty premises.

The Goal of Treatment

To understand why Watkins and Ponder acted as they did, we need to begin by establishing what they were trying to do. The goal of all their work was to create an emotional attachment such that Candace cared for and willingly obeyed her foster mother. (Watkins and Ponder, like other attachment therapists, also referred to this attachment as a "bond" and to the process as "bonding.") This short-term goal was thought of as the foundation for longer-term consequences: good moral development, empathy and kindness for others, conscience, hard work, life success, and happiness for Candace herself.

Attachment Concepts

It may be easiest to understand what Watkins and Ponder were trying to do if we compare the concepts they used with more commonly accepted views of human functioning. As it is used in research and clinical psychology, the concept of emotional attachment refers most basically to the easily observed behavior of young children. From about the time they can crawl, babies prefer to be with familiar people, especially if they are frightened or uncomfortable. Babies at this stage may cry if a stranger approaches or if they are separated from familiar caregivers. If these babies experience a sudden, lengthy separation from familiar people, they become depressed and deeply mournful for many months and only gradually recover. Behaviors such as the ones just described make us infer that inside the baby there is an internal state we call "attachment" and that this state consists of attitudes, motivations, and emotions about relationships with other people. We could thus think of attachment as an "internal working model" that symbolizes for the baby some ideas about how people can help or harm each other.

Clinical and research work has shown that as the attached child matures, he or she acts less and less as if separation were such a great concern. But every normal older child or adult treats familiar and unfamiliar people differently, and wants to be with familiar people when sick, hurt, or frightened. The attitudes originally associated with early relationships continue to shape part of our thinking about other people.

Failure of Attachment

Can attachment fail to occur? Are there children who react in the same positive ways to everyone, and who do not grieve over serious separations? Yes, this does seem to be possible, although it is unusual. Children seem to be most ready to form an attachment somewhere between about 6 months and about 24 months of age; to become attached, they need frequent social interactions with a small number of consistent, interested, responsive people. Attachment may not occur in the usual way if the child does not have the right experiences at the right time, if she has too many changes of caregiver, or if her caregivers are aloof and uninterested in social play. The availability of food or the relief of pain are much less important to attachment than social play and pleasurable looking and talking, according to research by developmental psychologists.

What are the results of failure of attachment? It is so unusual to have attachment fail completely that this is poorly understood, but the English theorist John Bowlby (1982) concluded from one study that such children grew up without conscience or empathic concern for others. They became charming psychopaths or con artists who specialized in exploiting other people. (The term "psychopath" does not imply pleasure in harming others, but simply a sense of entitlement to what can be obtained from others.)

More often, though, problems with attachment in the early years would not produce a complete failure of empathy, but instead some lasting distortion in the internal working model of relationships. There would be a weakness in the sense of trust and security that helps us maintain long-term relationships with others in spite of disagreements. An adult coming from such a background would not be amorally charming but would have unusual problems in friendship, marriage, and parenthood.

Watkins's Beliefs About Attachment: Rage and Release

John Bowlby (1982) and other legitimate attachment theorists considered attachment to involve an internal working model of human relationships and to be a system that would continue to develop as the individual grew older and more experienced. Unfortunately for children like Candace Newmaker, however, a psychologist named Robert Zaslow (Zaslow & Menta, 1975) in the 1960s and 1970s presented Bowlby's ideas in a simplified and distorted fashion that formed the basis for attachment therapy as Watkins and Ponder later practiced it. When Watkins and Ponder spoke of establishment of attachment as a goal, they were thinking in terms of human functioning as Zaslow described it, not in terms of Bowlby's carefully researched work.

Zaslow (Zaslow & Menta, 1975) considered attachment to be something other than a set of attitudes toward other humans. He saw it as an involuntary emotional response to the face and eyes of another person, occurring when the face was presented under the proper circumstances. These circumstances involved experiences of pain, fear, and rage, following which relief was associated with the experience of eye contact. If an infant did not experience this cycle of events, Zaslow thought, he or she would not form an attachment, would not make eye contact with other people, and would show symptoms of autism rather than normal emotional and intellectual development. Children who were abandoned or abused would have felt only pain and rage, not relief, and their continued unexpressed rage would block their capacity to care for others. However, Zaslow thought, a technique of creating pain and rage and combining them with eye contact could cause attachment to occur, even if the individual was long past the period of life when attachment normally happens.

Recapitulation

What is the significance of this last idea of Zaslow's, the idea that a developmental event could be brought about even when the normal time for it had passed? Superficially, Zaslow's statement may appear to be nothing more than an assertion meant to shore up a shaky argument about human functioning. In fact, however, the idea that attachment can be forced at an abnormal time is only one example of a concept that lies behind many "alternative" medical and psychological treatments. The best name for this concept is *recapitulation,* but we should note that this term has probably never been used by any attachment-therapy writer, who would be more likely to use the idea implicitly than explicitly.

Recapitulation in speech or music means returning to the beginning and repeating or at least summarizing a statement or a melody. In the work of the possibly unreliable nineteenth-century embryologist Haeckel, "recapitulation" meant the idea that the stages of development of the human embryo paralleled and repeated evolutionary stages or steps in the development of various species from a common ancestor.

However, recapitulation in the sense that is relevant here means more than repetition or summarization of previous events. It refers to the idea that a sequence of events that has gone wrong can be forced into repetition and guided so that the right outcome is achieved.

An embryologist would not take this view, of course, because errors in prenatal development cannot be reworked. A mechanic might feel more comfortable with recapitulation, because a wrongly built engine could be dismantled and correctly reconstructed. On the whole, however, the idea of recapitulation that repairs past mistakes is a theological idea rather than a scientific one.

Religious Background of Recapitulation

The concept of repair through recapitulation appears in Jewish tradition as *teshuvah* ("return"), a process by which sins and errors can be undone and set right. Similarly, an argument in early Christian thought reasoned that Adam's disobedience to God and the subsequent troubles of mankind were corrected by Christ's obedience even to the point of suffering and death. In this view, Christ's sacrifice recapitulated the events in the Garden of Eden, undoing Adam's errors and making possible a fresh start.

Another Application of the Recapitulation Concept

Patterning is an example of a physical treatment that assumes the possibility of recapitulation. Practitioners of this fringe therapy claim that brain-injured patients can repeat their early experiences and thus force the brain to repeat its sequence of early growth and development. According to this view, if the brain-injured patients are frequently guided through the movement patterns typical of young babies, such as specific coordinated movements of head and limbs, they will regrow a healthy brain that can function as it did before injury. (There is no evidence that patterning cures brain injury or causes new brain growth, and the American Association of Pediatrics has twice issued statements to that effect, but the practice continues.)

The recapitulation concept is an essential part of attachment therapy in the same way that it is a foundation of patterning. The theory of recapitulation is the source of the idea that a child can be made to repeat a version of past experiences when the real past experience produced a bad outcome, and that having the right experiences can quickly wipe out the effects of the past and heal or cure any problems that the past produced.

Recapitulation and Rebirthing

The recapitulation assumption is also obvious in the practice of rebirthing. The past event, the one that is thought to have gone wrong, was the real birth of the child. When the birth is repeated in abbreviated, symbolic form, rebirthing practitioners assume that the outcome of the good birth to the right mother undoes and replaces the effect of the "bad" birth to the wrong mother. Curiously, however, the events of the recapitulated birth do not follow those of a real birth very closely, because an infant does not really make efforts to be born, but is passive under the forces exerted by the mother's body. (And, as we noted in a previous section, neither do the events of holding therapy reproduce accurately the social interactions that produce attachment.)

Why Reject Recapitulation?

Compared to modern thinking about child development, the recapitulation view is remarkably simplistic and unsophisticated. Current work on the development of infants, toddlers, and children is notable for its emphasis on the active involvement of the child in the world. Where attachment therapists see children as passive recipients of experience, modern developmentalists view them as acting just as much as being acted upon. Where attachment therapists see children as changing only in response to experience, modern developmentalists think of them as maturing according to their own patterns, as well as learning from the environment—and altering the environment they live in, as well. In the modern developmental view, a child would be expected to be different every day because of genetically determined maturational changes, even if he or she could magically exist without learning.

With each maturational step, the child is affected differently by any given experience. A 3-year-old learns different things from a ride on the merry-go-round than a 9-year-old does. A toddler is differently affected by the parents' divorce than a teenager is. And these facts tell us that recapitulation is impossible; however well the adults may repeat a child's early experience, the child does not respond to the events as she would have done in the past. Maturation has made her a different child than she was. We cannot step into the same river twice, and we cannot make a child have the same developmental experience over again.

Body and Mind

The centuries-old view was that body and mind are separate entities, different substances, following different rules, and temporarily connected with each other during life. By modern times, though, most educated people considered body and mind to be inseparable, and perhaps simply two manifestations or functions of the same underlying reality.

Mind over Matter

This modern idea about the connection of body and mind had a profound effect on the study of medicine. Because of our assumptions about the mind-body connection, we have the concept of psychosomatic illnesses, in which mental factors cause damage to the body, and we are concerned with issues such as the effect of stress on the immune system. We know that pain and disease can cause mental disturbances, but our great emphasis is on the way mental events affect the body. We think, for example, of psychotherapy to treat sleeping problems or eating disorders, and we advise cancer patients to keep cheerful and confident as a way of resisting their disease.

Body as a Route to Mind

The opposite assumption is true of the attachment therapists and related thinkers. Like many eighteenth- and nineteenth-century thinkers from Franz Mesmer to Benjamin Rush, they focus on stimulation of the body to alter mental processes (Rowe, 2001). They also examine physical functioning as a way of assessing mental events. These facts about the foundations of attachment therapy offer an explanation of some of the otherwise inexplicable practices of Watkins and Ponder.

Watkins and other attachment therapists used stimulation of the body in the form of holding and of tactile stimulation of the rib cage (a painful poking, from the viewpoint of the person being stimulated). Grabbing the child's face, covering the mouth with the hand, and squeezing the chin and mouth are other examples of physical stimulation intended to bring about mental change. One early practitioner of attachment therapy (Robert Zaslow, who spoke of it as Z-process therapy) suggested that informed consent should always be documented before treatment and that minor bruising was likely to occur as a result of holding. The intention of the therapist in these situations is to use physical stimulation to produce pain and fear, and thus to provoke the expression of rage, which is then "drained" or "de-activated" and can no longer block positive emotion as it was assumed to be doing.

Zaslow and other therapists also suggested that the experience of pain as a result of the physical stimulation was a symptom of the patient's resistance to emotional change rather than an indication of the intensity of poking and grabbing. If the client complained of pain, as Candace did, this was simply an indication that more pain was needed to push her past the stage of resistance into overt rage and thus to emotional healing. The therapist needed to ignore pleas and complaints to carry out the treatment that was so much needed, and this was exactly what Watkins and Ponder did.

Keith Reber (1996), a more recent writer on this topic, warned that the child who is being held will say that he is in pain, cannot breathe, is about to vomit, or is going to die. The parent (and presumably the therapist) must accept this calmly as a natural result of the treatment. The same author stressed the need for the parent to resist the temptation to feel sorry for the crying child.

Attachment therapists have also suggested that physical activity such as kicking, push-ups, and jumping jacks are needed to activate the child, send oxygen to the brain (although one might think it would be diverted to the muscles by exercise), and improve thinking ability. Chores that involve the expenditure of physical energy can be used in the same way.

Physical Symptoms of Mental Resistance

In addition to viewing physical stimulation and activity as ways to change the child's personality, attachment therapists have also considered physical actions, including speech, to be indicative of emotional status. Errors in speech or speech that is hesitant or too quiet are seen as signs of resistance to change, and efforts to overcome resistance are made by having the child shout or scream answers repeatedly. (But fluent, constant talking is also perceived as a form of resistance.) All "motor overflow" is considered to be resistance, so coughing, yawning, blinking, stretching, or wriggling would be included as indicators of the child's resistant mental state. The more the resistance, of course, the more the pressure for change should be stepped up.

According to this view, there are no accidents or mistakes. If the child forgets something, does not hear what is said, performs a task badly or slowly, says something incorrect, or breaks an object, the act is evidence of the child's resistance and need for a heightened level of physical and emotional stress. Candace's failure to escape from the flannel sheet during rebirthing would have been seen not as a "real" failure, an actual inability to find the opening in the wrap and pass through it. Instead, it would have been interpreted as evidence of resistance that needed to be countered by increased physical pressure.

Sweets and Love

A final point about the mind-body connection has to do with sweet foods. The attachment therapists have assumed that sweet foods have a powerful connection to emotional attachment and can be used to create emotional change. The reasoning here is associated with the mildly sweet taste and milk-sugar content of human milk and the readiness of the nursing infant to form an emotional connection (the latter assumed by the attachment therapists to be present from birth on). Because of this presumed relationship, children in treatment are to receive sweet foods only from the therapeutic foster parent or from the biological or adoptive parent to whom they will eventually return. To take advantage of the emotional power of sweets, the children are to have special times when cuddling, eye contact, and sweets are all combined (Thomas, 2000).

The stress on the power of sweets is not unique to attachment therapists but is also seen in the continued popular assertion that refined sugars cause hyperactivity, in spite of many well-designed studies showing no connection between the two. The idea that sugar affects both mental and physical functioning goes back to popular writings of the 1940s and 1950s, if not earlier.

Sudden Personality Change Through Emotion

Modern psychotherapy stresses understanding, remembering, and communicating as the major agents of emotional change. Even small children with little speech development are helped to communicate non-verbally in therapeutic settings. Psychotherapy that focuses on cognitive functions involves a slow process of thought and problem-solving, gradually leading to changed feelings, attitudes, and behavior.

Conversion Experiences

From the ancient human past until today, some people have assumed that real emotional change occurs rapidly and as a result of powerful physical or emotional experiences. Religious conversions, for example, are usually sudden changes in emotion and attitude, not gradual changes in belief brought about by reasoning and experience. The practice of exorcism involves the assumption that a "possessed" individual can suddenly change as a result of the rituals that distress the possessing entity and cause it to flee, restoring the real personality.

World War II and After

World War II, the great war of propaganda and attitude manipulation, was followed by a period of fascination with sudden emotional transformations. There was particular interest in the idea that an individual could change as a result of events that he or she was not even aware of—that someone else could cause a transformation in ways unknown to the victim (or patient, as the case might be).

During the 1950s and 1960s, public fascination with transformations increased, producing serious concerns about post-hypnotic suggestions and brainwashing, neither of which has been shown to have anything like the power the American public feared. The idea of subliminal perception got a similarly fearful reaction and even the attention of Congress, although there was never any good evidence that emotion, motivation, or behavior could be manipulated through stimulation too weak to be noticed.

The Sixties

During the 1960s and 1970s, popular psychotherapy movements, described in Chapter 8, took transformational approaches, especially with regard to the use of drugs and alcohol. Addictions were seen as curable through profound emotional experiences, and at the same time, the experience of drugs such as LSD and mescaline was thought to open deep, transforming insights into the self. Physical manipulations such as Rolfing, a painful deep massage, were similarly regarded as potentially transformational.

The AT practitioner's physical and emotional attempts to "release rage" come out of this same transformational approach. What appears to the rest of us to be deliberate cruelty is based on an ancient system of belief in the possibility of sudden transformation. This view raised its head frequently during the twentieth century but was repeatedly rejected by well-trained psychotherapists. Unfortunately, child patients such as Candace Newmaker are not in a position to argue about the philosophy that is causing them pain.

REFERENCES

Bowlby, J. (1982). *Attachment.* New York: Basic Books.

Miller, B., Fan, X., Christensen, M., Grotevant, H., & van Dulmen, M. (2000). Comparisons of adopted and non-adopted adolescents in a large, nationally represented sample. *Child Development, 71,* 1458–1473.

Reber, K. (1996). Children at risk for attachment disorder: Assessment, diagnosis, and treatment. *Progress: Family Systems Research and Therapy, 5,* 83–98.

Rowe, C. (2001, May 30). Modern efficiency displaces historic psychiatric hospital. *New York Times,* p. B5.

Thomas, N. (2000). Parenting children with attachment disorders. In T. M. Levy (Ed.), *Handbook of attachment interventions.* San Diego, CA: Academic Press.

Zaslow, R., & Menta, M. (1975). *The psychology of the Z-process: Attachment and activity.* San Jose, CA: San Jose State University Press.

Part II

The Facts Behind Candace's Case: Realities of Emotional Development and Childhood Mental Illness

Chapter 4

Some Facts About Normal Emotional Development (and What the Attachment Therapists Believed)

When babies are born, they already have unique personalities. They have individual reactions to hunger, pain, comfort, sounds, and sights. As they get older, those personality differences become more obvious in some ways and less obvious in others, and we who are watching begin to focus on certain kinds of characteristics as the essence of individuality. We especially emphasize the way people respond socially and emotionally. When we talk about the *personality* of an older child or of an adult, we are usually thinking about their tendencies to be sociable or solitary, pleasant or irritating to be with. We also consider the individual's reactions to others—quick hostility, patience, tolerance, fearfulness, solicitous kindness, and so on. Most of our interest in personality is directed toward the individual's experience and expression of emotion, rather than what he or she thinks intellectually about other people. This was certainly the case for Jeane Newmaker, who seems to have been much more concerned about whether Candace felt love for her than with the child's opinion of her life as an adopted daughter.

When we consider adults, we generally assume that people can be emotionally healthy in many different ways. Many possible personality patterns accompany good mental health, rather than just one good outcome of early emotional development. As individuals, we may like some personalities better than others, but we would not describe most people we dislike as being disturbed or mentally ill. In other words, we recognize that there is a wide range of healthy personalities, and we do not expect or even want everybody to be the same.

But how did those different adult personalities come about? When they were newborn babies, the adults were already different from each other, but they did not necessarily start out as exactly the same kinds of people they later became. As different kinds of babies, they had different experiences. It was the unique combination of innate characteristics and of experiences that created the unique personality of each adult. In this chapter, we look at some well documented ideas about early development and compare them to the unsupported theory behind attachment therapy and therapeutic foster parenting.

SOME BASIC IDEAS ABOUT HUMAN EMOTIONAL DEVELOPMENT

The adult personality develops gradually and as a result of many small, subtle events. This detailed process of development is difficult to observe in oneself and is far more complex than most people assume.

Most people's thoughts about their own development assume simple relationships between experiences and effects, although few events in personality development actually work that way. An example of a simple, linear effect would be the learning that might occur as a result of punishment. "My dad spanked me when I took my brother's money, so I learned to tell right from wrong." This type of explanation is rarely, if ever, adequate for the understanding of personality development. The steps of change it implies are far larger than usually occur in the real world. Many steps are probably omitted, because not stealing money is not exactly the same as knowing right from wrong. And it is unusual for a single experience to produce such a powerful change, so there were probably other events as well.

Transactions at Work

Instead of simple linear effects, *transactional processes* are more likely to be the mechanisms by which experience shapes personality. In a transactional process, each of two people has an effect on the other; each changes as a result of what the other does. After a period of time, they influence each other in a different way than they did before (Sameroff, 1983). (This interconnection is one aspect of the systems approach we discussed in chapter 2.)

If we thought of parents and children in a linear relationship, we would focus on parents teaching children, rewarding or punishing children, providing role models for children, and in other ways creating experiences that cause children to change. This is a common view of parenting and the one shared by Jeane Newmaker and the attachment therapists.

Looking at parents and children from a transactional viewpoint, however, we see that their relationships as much more complicated than the attachment therapists believed. The child influences the parent as well as the parent influencing the child. The parent chooses particular actions partly because of characteristics of the child in question, continuing or stopping what she is doing partly because of the child's response. Thus, the parents of a chronically ill, irritable baby may not smile at the baby often but may respond to the baby's distress and fussing by touching and speaking soothingly. If the baby seems happier, the parents may go on with the soothing speech or try it again another time. If the baby does not respond well—perhaps not hearing the parent's voice over its own crying—the parent may do something else or give up in discouragement. Through many incidents of this type, the parent and baby come to affect each other in new and different ways. If things go well, members of the family come to relate to each other more and more positively. Alternatively, the relationship may deteriorate as parent and child each expect the other to be sad or angry and hard to deal with; the parent sees himself or herself as a bad parent or the child as a bad child, and the child feels alone and helpless.

Transactional processes such as the ones just described may take many months or years to have an effect on personality. Each event may be so brief or small that a casual observer can hardly detect it—perhaps only fractions of a second for a change in facial expression. The people involved in transactional change are not ordinarily aware of what is happening themselves. Transactional processes are hard to see and to investigate, but they are probably the main way in which experience shapes a child's personality.

Treating Parents Too

The importance of transactional processes in development means that efforts at personality change through child psychotherapy cannot focus on the child alone. Treatment needs to work on changing the ways in which the parent and the child affect each other. Similarly, parent education programs need to be concerned with changes in the parent's attitudes and feelings as well as with techniques of dealing with the child. These are characteristic focuses of well-established therapies and programs, but, as we have seen, not of attachment therapy or therapeutic foster parenting.

Nature Cooperates with Nurture

Someone investigating the study of child development today would look in vain for the once-famous nature-nurture controversy. We no longer ask whether heredity or environment is more important. Without both, it would be impossible for an individual to develop, emotionally or otherwise. Both nature and nurture are present and influential at all times in any human being's development.

Systems

The continuous presence of nature and of nurture does not mean they work, or work together, in the same ways in all situations. No single rule allows us to predict outcomes of all combinations of heredity and environment. In fact, there is every reason to think that nature and nurture combine differently 1) at different times in life, 2) for different aspects of the person, such as intellectual functioning, physical growth, and emotional life, and 3) in different species. These different combinations follow their own rules, as we discussed in our earlier comments on systems at work.

We need to be extremely careful about generalizing from one time or aspect of development to another. The rules about cooperation of heredity and environment that are true about an infant do not necessarily apply to a 14-year-old. Rules about nature's and nurture's effects on mathematical ability do not necessarily apply to the development of control over emotions. Rules about ducks do not necessarily apply to humans. But, unfortunately, the mass media have had a tendency to jump from a study of brain development (for example) to a conclusion about "what must be true" about the emotions, or from research on nonhumans to "what must be true" about mothers and children. The same point can be made about the theorists who presented the ideas that became attachment therapy—particularly their tendency to assume that developmental events that characterize infants are possible among children at much later ages.

Early Development: Very Important or a Little Important?

Is there a special impact from experiences that occur in early life? Do they shape emotional development in ways that are difficult to duplicate or to overcome in later years? During the past 100 years or so, answers to these questions have tended to fall into two opposing extremes. One extreme was the claim that there is nothing especially powerful about early childhood experience; indeed, said the proponents of this view, because the child was too young to remember what happened, early experiences were of little or no importance. The other extreme, which had some roots in Freudian theory and others in studies of animal behavior, declared that all the important experiences occurred in the early years, setting in place for life many aspects of physical development, cognitive ability, and emotional individuality.

Why such extreme statements? The usual reason for severely opposing views on a question is that the question itself is difficult to answer, and the issue of the importance of early experience is especially difficult to deal with. We want to know whether an individual's development is more influenced by early experience or by later experience. In fantasy, we can imagine what would happen if a person had some early experiences and then lived to adulthood without any other experiences, or what would happen if someone survived early childhood without experiencing anything and only had experiences after age 7. In practice, obviously, this cannot be; anyone who is conscious is having experiences, even if they are only that "nothing's happening."

But what if we simply looked for children who had very different experiences in the early years and later on? Couldn't we answer the question of the importance of early experience that way? Good parenting in the early years could be followed by later childhood in a poorly run orphanage, or early abuse and neglect by years of loving family life. We could see which children turned out better, those with good early lives or those with good later lives. This seems like a way to answer the question, but if we look back to our earlier discussion of transactional processes, we will see why it is not. The problem is that the effect of early good or bad experiences helps determine how adults treat a child years later. Children who have been treated well act differently toward adults than those who were neglected or abused, and the adults behave differently in their turn. To put it another way, the children provide a different set of stimuli for the adults and trigger different responses from them. The adults' behavior is influenced without their even being aware of the fact. For instance, children who have been abused and neglected are often poorly trained in self-care techniques. They may not bathe often or effectively, and their use of toilet paper may not be very thorough. They do not expect to change dirty clothes, because they have often not had clean clothes regularly provided for them. As a result, they may be smelly and unattractive in comparison with children whose mothers have kept them clean and taught them carefully. The adoptive or foster parent may not feel much like approaching such children and may find it difficult to teach them cleanliness—in part because the parent did not expect to have to do this. The adults' surprise and negative emotional responses influence the way they act toward the children, so that in fact the children's early experiences play a role in determining their later experiences. The two sets of experiences do not exist independent of each other, so we cannot figure out what their separate results might be (Speltz, Greenberg, & DeKlyen, 1990).

Of course, no researcher would dream of doing a controlled experiment in which children received deliberate good or bad treatment, because the researcher's first responsibility is to avoid the possibility of harm. Even if a researcher could ethically do such an experiment, there would be practical problems; it would be very difficult to train caregivers to treat children in predetermined ways. For a multitude of reasons, then, we have no way to detect the exact influence of early experience or to decide which of the extreme views about this is the correct one.

The Difficult Middle Ground

By now it should be no surprise to the reader that neither of the extreme views of early experience is presently considered to be a correct statement about human development. However, the reality of the middle ground is not easy to put into sound bites, so it will probably never be as acceptable as the extremes to the average person having an argument with a friend. Some statements supporting the extraordinary importance of early experience have even been made by national organizations in recent years (Shonkoff & Phillips, 2000). Nevertheless, the most realistic statement about early experience is probably something like this: "Early experiences are very important—but so are many things that happen later."

AT and Early Experience

Where did Candace Newmaker's therapist stand on the importance of early experience? The ideas behind attachment therapy include a paradoxical belief both in the primacy of early experience and in the possibility of manipulating a person to return her to the vulnerability or plasticity typical of early development. This is not the same as our earlier statement about the importance of both early and later events. The claim of AT advocates would be that later experience ordinarily has little impact on the personality that was created in early life but that the attachment therapist, using specialized techniques, can recapitulate earlier events and produce a new, positive personality outcome. The attachment therapy view is different from both the extremes we discussed earlier and from the middle ground we suggested as a realistic view of development. This AT belief about the effects of early experience is really a matter of a different universe of discourse from that of most therapists, rather than simply the drawing of a different conclusion.

Stages of Development

The question we have just been discussing has further implications. The possibility that different rules apply during early as compared to later life suggests a simple form of a useful developmental concept: stages of development. If we think about development in terms of stages, we make certain assumptions. (Sometimes this is done for the sake of argument rather than because we can prove that the assumptions are correct.) For example, if thinking in terms of stages, we assume that a child's life can be divided into distinct periods of time (age periods), each of which is qualitatively different from the others. This means that during each age period the child is a somewhat different person than during other periods; she does different things, or does them in different ways than at earlier or later times. Each of the age periods has certain typical behaviors or abilities associated with it, and that is what makes it a stage rather than just an age range. Children at a particular chronological age are not necessarily just alike, but the idea of stages suggests that all children progress through a sequence or series of characteristic changes just as all other normal children do. The orderliness of development is a much more important part of the stage concept than exact ages are.

A stage is thus a period of time during development, associated with a range of ages, during which children's behavior and abilities are qualitatively different than in earlier or later periods. Stages occur in a predictable sequence, so identifying the current stage for a child lets us know what is likely to happen next, although not just when it will happen.

Do stages really exist in the child, or are they simply in our heads—useful ways for us to think about children? We are probably on firmer ground, on the whole, if we just consider stages to be helpful descriptions, and the same is true for other related ideas. However, the idea of stages has led developmentalists to ask a number of important questions about children's lives. For instance, we can ask whether certain stages are more sensitive or vulnerable, more affected by experiences, than others are. The idea of a stage that is a sensitive or even a critical period was very popular in the 1970s and forms part of the theory behind attachment therapy.

Sensitive Periods

A sensitive period is a time in a child's development when experiences affect development differently than they would either earlier or later. (Notice that this does not just say that early periods are more vulnerable; according to the idea of a sensitive period, a child could be too young to be influenced by an experience, as well as too old.) This idea is a generalization from the study of some birds and some nonhuman mammals, who seem to have brief periods in early development when they are powerfully influenced and changed for life by certain experiences. It is arguable whether we should generalize in this way from the rules for some animals' development to the rules about human development. It may be that humans have longer periods when they are especially ready to learn certain things, such as language or emotional communication. However, human changes of this kind seem to take place over many months of transactional processes, and there are probably many aspects of human development that do not work this way at all (Cicchetti & Beeghly, 1990).

Attachment therapy has a paradoxical approach to sensitive periods, just as it does to questions about early experience. It assumes both that there is a period of life that is especially important for emotional experiences and that attachment therapists have special techniques that allow reshaping of the personality after the sensitive period is over. Unlike the majority of ideas about either human or animal development, however, attachment therapists' views place part of the sensitive period for emotional development in the time before birth, a point that we will discuss later in this chapter.

STEPS IN EMOTIONAL DEVELOPMENT: AGES AND STAGES AS THEY USUALLY OCCUR IN INDUSTRIALIZED SOCIETIES

There is still much research to be done on child development. Until it is done, we probably should not claim that all human beings in all cultures follow the same emotional stages. However, we have some good descriptions of how development proceeds for healthy children growing up in families in Europe and

North America, as well as scattered studies of children in other circumstances and places. This section describes the stages of emotional development we might expect to see in a child growing up in the United States today. Please note that the children we discuss are growing up in homes with families and are being shaped by them—but, in true transactional fashion, the children are shaping the families too.

As we discuss each of these developmental stages, we will comment on the view AT advocates take and the extent to which they use relevant concepts in their work.

Prenatal Life

Do unborn babies have a complicated mental life? Do they hear and understand what people say around them? Do they even have some sort of awareness of their mothers' attitudes toward their pregnancies?

These are not easy questions to answer in systematic, empirical ways. The unborn baby's behavior is concealed from us most of the time, although modern devices such as ultrasound have let us have peeks into the protected environment of the womb. We know that in the later part of pregnancy, the fetus certainly responds to sound stimuli. Some research has reported that the unborn baby actually learns to recognize some sounds and shows this fact in behavior after birth. (We will discuss this work a little later in this section.)

However, if we reason on the basis of other information, it seems unlikely that an unborn child can have abilities that a neonate does not have. Generally, we see an increase in ability with age. If a baby a month old cannot understand spoken words, why should it have been able to do so before birth? As for understanding the mother's attitude toward pregnancy, even adults would have trouble doing this without understanding her words or seeing her facial expression or body language.

Prenatal Learning

The scientific study of early development suggests that the unborn baby may learn from some types of experiences but that it does not understand what adults say or feel nor does it develop any emotional preference or attachment for the mother before it is born. However, believers in theories that are not based on scientific studies have very different opinions. Attachment therapists, for example, assume that unborn babies are deeply aware of their mothers' acceptance or rejection of the pregnancy and that the babies grieve after birth if they felt unwanted before. There is also the assumption that a mutual emotional connection between mother and child develops during pregnancy and that separation, even immediately after birth, causes distress, mourning, and anger in the child. This view of prenatal life is shared by many unorthodox belief systems, such as Scientology, in which it is thought that a person can be guided to recall memories right back to his or her conception. Such beliefs seem to be based on the idea that memory is not a function of the nervous system, as biological research has shown, but instead is stored simultaneously in every body cell, even a fertilized ovum.

Those who claim an active, conscious mental life for the unborn have sought empirical support for this belief in various studies of prenatal learning. There are well-designed studies by De Casper and others (De Casper & Spence, 1986) that show babies reacting differently to stories their mothers read aloud before the babies were born than to other stories. But the babies paid more attention to the familiar than to the unfamiliar stimuli, which is an unusual way for newborns to behave. It is not clear what such studies mean, but it is doubtful they indicate that a fetus has an adult-like state of consciousness that it later loses.

Birth Experiences and Personality

The idea that normal birth is a traumatic experience of separation from the cozy life of the womb goes back many decades but has little evidence to support it. Imaginative writers have described the newborn as blinded by painful light and "burning" as air enters the lungs for the first time. Although the newborn baby has been in the dark and needs to adapt to bright light, which might briefly be uncomfortable, there seems little reason to think that the first breath should be painful, any more than that the first swallow of milk should hurt.

Certainly the process of vaginal birth involves a lot of pressure, even molding the skull temporarily into a different shape. But this seems to be advantageous for the baby, as it expels fluid from the lungs and prepares them for a rapid initiation of air-breathing. A baby born by Cesarean section experiences much less pressure on the head and body than a vaginally-born child, but is characteristically in need of more medical help before it functions well on its own. The normal birth process should probably be considered as energizing rather than traumatizing.

Babies who experience difficult births and sustain physical injuries are indeed slightly more likely to be violent as adults than others are. However, there is no evidence of any simple cause-and-effect relationship here. Sick or injured babies have different backgrounds and different later experiences than do healthy babies, and so do their families. There are also plenty of violent adults who had simple, easy births and plenty of good citizens who had birth injuries. (The difference may have to do with the extent to which the families were able to buffer the experience, a concept we will discuss toward the end of this chapter.)

Reenacting Birth

Would it really be possible to therapeutically reenact the important features of birth during later life, as Candace Newsmaker's therapists claimed to do? This is unlikely in many ways. Birth is a process of serious physical transitions.

The obvious one is from inside the mother's body to outside, but the baby also changes from one who gets oxygen from the umbilical cord to one who breathes air; from one whose nutrients come through the bloodstream to one who sucks, swallows, and digests; and from one who is floating but cramped to one with plenty of space and the constant effort of fighting gravity. Once these processes are complete, it is impossible to go back. It is possible to mimic the birth process through rebirthing but never to actually recapitulate it. We also note, however, that the technique used with Candace Newmaker was a rather unrealistic version of birth, because the child was asked to kick and move to cause herself to be reborn. In fact, babies are extremely quiet and passive during the process of birth and are simply moved along by the mother's involuntary or voluntary muscle contractions.

Emotional Self-regulation

Caring for or just watching a very young baby, we find it hard to see any emotional development going on. The baby seems to lack many of the emotions we see in ourselves, other adults, and older children. He or she does not seem frightened or affectionate or sad. The emotions that are apparent are also remarkably intense and unsubtle compared to those of an older person. Yet the baby of a few months is going through a dramatic emotional change that is the foundation of more mature life—the beginning of emotional *self-regulation*.

Newborn infants seem to be at the mercy of their environment. If they are distressed by pain or hunger, they continue to cry until they fall asleep with exhaustion unless an adult comes to help them. They spend a good deal of time either upset or asleep and have only rare brief periods when they are ready to learn or to play with people. Ideally, the baby slowly develops the ability to calm down when upset and to have quiet alert periods when she can pay attention to people and things.

How does the baby learn to do this? Usually, the infant's cries summon an adult, who tries to provide comfort in various ways. Some of the techniques work better than others, and a caring adult notices this and uses the effective comfort measures more frequently. Through these experiences, the infant gradually learns what is comforting and, as much as possible, tries to achieve the comforting experience. For example, a particular body position or the feeling of the thumb in the mouth may be a comforting experience that the baby can manage alone, after an adult has helped provide the experience a few times.

Comforting and the regulation of uncomfortable emotional activity thus occur for the baby in a social context in early life. Without another person, comforting is much less likely to happen. Gradually, though, the baby learns some of its own techniques for calming down—although no human being ever achieves complete control over reactions to all distressing events. By the time a well-developed baby is 3 or 4 months old, she has developed some ability to self-comfort and has the foundations of emotional self-regulation that allow for further development.

The concept of self-regulation has not been used much by attachment therapists, who seem to consider the first two years of life to operate as a single stage rather than to be divided in the way we are describing here. The AT advocate's view is that the baby's emotional attachment to the parent emerges from many experiences of the parent's power to control and comfort when the baby is in a rage of frustration at an ungratified need. These are thought to occur repeatedly over a two-year period and to be a necessary foundation for love, empathy, and compliance.

Attachment

A baby who can self-regulate a bit is ready to move on to new steps in emotional development (Greenspan & Greenspan, 1985). He or she begins to pay more and more attention to people, who are more interesting to the baby than anything else in the environment. Caregivers who are emotionally involved with the baby are captivated by the baby's attentiveness and interest, and their social play becomes increasingly pleasurable for both child and adult. Their mutual pleasure in social play seems to be the foundation of the baby's emotional attachment to familiar adults.

If the infant is cared for by a small number of consistent caregivers, and if the caregivers are emotionally involved, sensitive, and responsive, the baby will usually show a new kind of emotional reaction by about 7 or 8 months (Sroufe, 1996). The baby begins to show different attitudes toward familiar and unfamiliar people. He or she seems anxious when approached by strangers or threatened with separation from unfamiliar people. In a strange place with unfamiliar people, the baby does not try to explore its surroundings; if familiar people are present, the baby moves around and investigates the room, returning now and then to a familiar adult who seems to serve as a secure base for the baby's exploration. This may also be the time in development when an infant is likely to start wanting a familiar blanket or teddy bear for comfort. As we will see in chapter 5, however, not all babies show exactly the same attachment-related behaviors, and there are some systematic ways of describing the differences among them. The baby can behave differently with different familiar people, as we might expect from our earlier discussion of transactional processes. Attachment behaviors also show up differently in different circumstances and are more likely when the child is frightened, hurt, or sick.

Attachment is the term we apply to the baby's internal state that results in the behavior changes we've been describing. The internal state involves both feelings and thoughts or expectations about the self and other people. It is an "internal working model" or way of symbolizing social relationships. As we will see later, this internal working model changes with maturation and experience. The original attachment behaviors and experiences are an important starting point, but not the end of emotional development.

The AT View

Attachment therapists rarely mention the role of play and pleasurable social interaction in the development of attachment. As we noted earlier, they stress a cycle of need, rage, and gratification as the motivation for attachment to a familiar caregiver, considering this to have begun many months before the period we are discussing here. We may also need to point out that attachment therapists assume the process begins prenatally, so that the biological mother is the person to whom attachment is most readily made; this is thought to cause difficulties for adopted babies, no matter how early their adoption occurred. According to a research-based view of attachment, however, the process has little or nothing to do with genetic relationships or with prenatal life. The experiences that create attachment begin with social interactions after the fourth month or so and can involve any consistent, sensitive, responsive caregiver. Finally, rather than stressing a changing internal model of thoughts and feelings about others, attachment therapists think of the attachment process as an endpoint of development that does not proceed or alter in later years without special intervention techniques.

The Social Emotions in Toddlerhood

When a baby has formed an attachment to certain familiar people, he or she becomes increasingly attentive to those people's facial expressions. Especially when the baby is unsure of a new person or situation, she looks carefully at a familiar caregiver's face. If the caregiver looks relaxed and happy, the child is less anxious and may start to investigate; if the caregiver looks anxious, the baby backs off. This inspection of the adult's face is not a matter of seeing whether the caregiver is angry at the baby and will punish her for exploring, but instead involves looking for the caregiver's feelings about the unfamiliar situation. This process, called *social referencing,* allows the baby to use the caregiver's emotional reactions to learn vicariously about the world.

Social referencing is also a way for the baby to learn what the caregiver feels about things the baby does or about the baby himself. But this learning does not work very well until the baby thinks of himself as a "self," a separate and consistent individual. This does not happen until about 15 to 18 months of age, quite a few months after attachment behaviors are seen. The baby shows us his or her new ability by mirror self-recognition: looking into the mirror, the baby notices a spot of rouge that has been put on the face and touches his hand to the spot, thus showing us that he remembers what he ought to look like, can tell what is wrong, and realizes what part of the felt body is equivalent to a part of the seen mirror image. After a couple of months more, the child looks embarrassed when he catches sight of himself in the mirror, rouge or no; he turns away, hangs or turns his head, and smiles.

Between social referencing and self-recognition, the toddler can now think about himself and about other people's reactions to him. His opinions of himself begin to be shaped by others' reactions, and he responds with pleasure to positive reactions and with distress to negative ones. He begins to be capable of social emotions such as shame and guilt, whose impact we will discuss a little later. Social emotions can be very powerful motivators and help to make the child want and work for the parents' approval of his behavior. They can also cause immense frustration, fear, and loss of emotional control when the child feels threatened by others' disapproval (Lewis, 1992).

The AT View

Attachment therapists do not appear to use concepts such as social referencing in their attempts to explain children's attitudes toward others. Instead, they assume that a child's willingness to comply and to seek parental approval is entirely based on an inner change (attachment) that resulted from the parents' relieving the child's frustration in the first two years or from therapeutic techniques later on. They consider this aspect of development to result from the child's comprehension of adult power and authority—the understanding that the adult is "boss" and that the child is both limited and protected by this fact.

Social Emotions: The Preschool Years

By the time the child is about 3, the social emotions—emotions in response to other people's evaluation of the self—are well developed and are important motivators of behavior. One view of the social emotions (suggested by Michael Lewis, 1992) has divided them into two categories: 1) positive versus negative feelings about the self and 2) global evaluations, or feelings about the whole self, versus evaluations of separate specific aspects of the self or of behavior. A social emotion can be classified into one of each of these categories. For example, the term *guilt* describes a negative evaluation of a specific aspect of the self, while *shame* is a negative evaluation of the whole self, of the person's very existence. (Please note that shame and guilt do not mean at all the same thing, even though the words are sometimes used interchangeably in everyday speech.) On the positive side, *pride* means a positive evaluation of some specific aspect of the self, and the old Greek term *hubris* can be used to mean a global self-satisfaction.

Most 3-year-olds are probably capable of all these social emotions. However, for better maturation and mental health, it is a good thing if the child does more specific and less global self-evaluation. When there is pride in some ability or action, there is a positive tendency to try to repeat or maximize the source of pride. When there is guilt about an act, there is a motivation to avoid repeating the act and perhaps to apologize or to try to make up for harm done to someone. But the global self-evaluations are not about voluntary actions. The child who feels hubris has nothing he or she needs to do, because the whole self seems so wonderful; the only motivation might be to escape or attack any threat to this feeling. Similarly, a sense of shame allows for no escape or correction, because it is the individual's own existence that is felt as the problem. The only solution to shame is to destroy the self or attack the person who is seen as the source of the shameful feeling. In an older child or adult, this reaction may appear as the response to being "dissed," and the behavior that triggers it may be as minor as being looked at by someone.

The AT View

AT practices appear to make little deliberate use of these concepts. In fact, the therapist makes a point of addressing criticisms and insulting remarks to the child in treatment. Triggering shame reactions may be seen as a way to provoke the rage expected to clear the emotional blockage and prepare the child for a loving relationship. In the videotape of Candace's treatment, ridicule and laughter—common triggers of shame reactions—were frequent occurrences, as was teasing in the form of refusing information. In AT-related therapeutic foster parenting techniques, the frequent expression of disapproval of the child and the flaunting of adult power are two practices that could well provoke shame and rage, especially in children whose backgrounds had inclined them to global self-evaluations.

Internal Working Models of Relationships: The Preschool Years

Preschoolers are beginning to escape from the baby's feeling that safety and security come only from the presence of a familiar adult caregiver. They have better physical and cognitive skills and greater knowledge of the world and can do many more things for themselves. Preschool children begin to develop greater autonomy. Their parents work with them to develop self-care, confidence, and social skills.

Negotiating

At this period of life, parents and children are at the beginning of what has been called a goal-corrected partnership (in the language of John Bowlby [1982]). In such a partnership, each person alters his or her plans in recognition of the needs and goals of the other. For example, parents recognize the preschooler's need for "five more minutes" at some activity, and the preschooler becomes aware that the parent's need to stop for groceries on the way home means they had better get going.

An important theme in the developing partnership is *negotiation of separation*. Parents and preschoolers work together in planning the separations and reunions they will experience. A goal of their joint planning is to maintain the child's sense of security and trust while increasing the number and lengths of separations, whether for the parent's work needs or simply to enable the child to play longer and enjoy other activities. The child's internal working model of relationships thus begins to include the idea that the parent-child relationship continues to exist even when a separation occurs—although of course there are limits on how long a separation can be tolerated.

A parent's and child's ability to do joint planning depends in part on helping the child understand and discuss her own feelings and those of others. Parents of preschoolers also find that the child needs help in understanding the cause-and-effect relationships of emotional life. This help may involve specific explanations—"he's mad because you hit him"—as well as consistent parental responses to the child's words and deeds. The process of joint planning of separation also introduces the child to the idea that we can anticipate how we or others might feel because there are some consistent connections between events and the feelings they produce.

Empathy

The skills needed for preschool joint planning also appear in a broader context in the forms of empathy and prosocial behavior. Empathy is both a cognitive and an emotional reaction to another person's emotion, involving both recognition of and some sharing of another's feelings. Prosocial behaviors put another person's needs or feelings before one's own; they involve comforting and nurturing acts that have no direct benefit for the comforter except that an empathic child may feel better when a sad person is happier.

Although well-developed preschoolers may be kind and comforting to others, we need to remember that another person's distress is a complex kind of stimulus. It may make a preschooler respond with a mixture of empathic caregiving and anger or fear, just as adults may find themselves involuntarily laughing at a funeral. Preschoolers often try to get an adult to help someone who is unhappy rather than trying to aid the person themselves.

The baby's internal working model of relationships said, essentially, "You'll feel better if you can stay near that familiar person. Pay attention to what they think about things and you'll be safe." The preschooler's internal working model has become much more complex. The simple attachment concerns and behavior of the first years have been altered by experience and cognitive maturation. The child's working model now includes some awareness of normal, expectable separations and confidence that the adult still "belongs" to the child in spite of the absence. It includes understanding that people can change their goals to suit each other's needs, that they can understand each other's wishes and feelings, and that they can figure out how someone else will feel as a consequence of some action. (However, we should keep in mind that a sick, injured, or frightened preschooler may easily revert to some earlier attachment concerns, especially if in an unfamiliar place.)

The AT View

Attachment therapy and therapeutic foster parenting completely ignore the role of the partnership in emotional development. In fact, they appear to be particularly concerned that there should be *no* joint planning, *no* negotiation of separation, and *no* work toward a goal-corrected partnership. On the contrary, the child is to be provided with as little information as possible, and explanations or discussions are forbidden. Even preschoolers may not be told beforehand that they are going to stay in a foster home for some period of time. The entire point of the AT philosophy is the establishment of the authority and power of the adult, whose needs and wishes are paramount. This is considered to be the only way to produce a well-behaved, empathic, considerate child who is "fun to be with." The alternative developmental path leads to serial killings, according to the attachment therapist's view. There could hardly be a greater contrast in beliefs.

The School Years: Emotional Development Continues

By the time children reach school age, normal emotional development has usually made them somewhat aware of other people's feelings and able to exert some control over their own feelings and behavior. These abilities improve during the school years as a result of transactional processes during experiences with other people. The child improves his skills in getting along with other children, with parents, and with teachers, and those others also improve their skills. The other children improve partly as a result of becoming more mature, and the adults improve as a result of increased experience, intentional problem-solving, and getting to know a particular child better. For children in good circumstances, a "benign circle" of transactions is at work. The child deals effectively with a social situation and is sought out or commended by other people as a result. He is happy and feels pride in his actions, approaching the next situation with the positive emotions that make others likely to respond positively to him. His good mood enables him to use his best thinking and social abilities and to create an even better outcome than before.

Play

A good example of a transactional process occurs during schoolchildren's rough-and-tumble play. Children playing in this way are likely to get minor bumps and bruises or even have quite painful collisions with others. When such things occur, the child needs to assess her own feelings and thoughts as well as those of playmates. Did another child deliberately cause the injury? If it was intentional, what were the playmate's goals? Will it happen again? Was it painful enough to be worth complaining about? Did the person apologize, or did she threaten another attack? What will be the consequences of different responses the injured child might make? If she complains to an adult, the culprit may be (gratifyingly) punished, but the play might also be stopped. The child learns from the outcomes of different decisions and ordinarily becomes more and more skillful at maintaining lively rough-and-tumble without getting into a real fight or being bullied by others. At the same time, the internal working model of relationships with others is extended and developed, and different rules are established for peer relationships than for relationships with adults.

Children usually continue to develop positively during the school years if they have begun with positive development. Without a sense of security and predictability in relationships, and without a concept of joint planning, it is much more difficult for them to attain a positive outcome.

The Self

As the school years progress, the child's thinking ability and knowledge have ever greater influences on emotional life. Adult instruction, role modeling, and discussion of feelings and behavior play a strong role in the child's recognition of feelings and control over emotional expression. The child's beliefs about the self, sometimes described as "self-concept" or "self-esteem," are the source of many emotional experiences. For example, a child who experiences internal locus of control (the idea that he can cause some things to happen) as a belief about the self is likely to respond with positive feelings to challenges, whereas another child with external locus of control is convinced that only luck or other people's decisions can influence what happens to him. Similarly, the child may have negative emotions about the self or others as a result of learned helplessness (a belief that she cannot do certain things) or positive feelings due to learned industriousness (a belief in her own ability).

The AT View

Once again, the AT approach pays little attention to these aspects of school-age children's emotional development, even though most such treatment occurs during the elementary school years. Attachment therapists and therapeutic foster parents give exclusive emphasis to relationships between children and adults. Problems with these relationships are assumed to result from experiences much earlier in life rather than from present transactional processes, and the problems are thought to be "fixed" by dramatic emotional changes rather than through learning to think about social issues. AT practices appear aimed at fostering external locus of control, with all information and decision-making power belonging to adults. Children in the therapeutic foster home are expected to do chores and to do them effectively, which we might expect to produce a sense of learned industriousness, but work is also assigned as punishment (for example, shoveling manure as a consequence for swearing), so positive emotions about one's abilities may not be the outcome after all. AT advocates explain their stance as a matter of teaching cause-and-effect thinking that they feel the children lack. Children who are cared for by therapeutic foster parents do not necessarily attend school, where they might experience learned industriousness in academic areas; school is considered to be a privilege for them, not a right. (This stance raises certain legal issues, of course.)

The Adolescent Years: Becoming More Like an Adult

In many ways, the adolescent years involve emotional changes like those of the preschool period. This statement is not meant to evaluate teenagers as childish but simply to stress their need to increase their autonomy and develop new skills for independence, as a preschooler does when preparing for kindergarten. Like preschoolers, adolescents do their most effective emotional and social development in the course of joint planning with their parents. Ideally, their family experiences at this time help teenagers develop more effective and useful internal working models of relationships.

Family Changes

Family relationships cannot stay the same during a child's adolescence (Walder & Ogan, 1988). Puberty itself causes behavioral changes in adolescents and their parents alike, including temporary increases in emotionality and later "sullenness" in the young of both sexes. Girls whose menarche occurs during the usual age range experience a relatively brief disturbance in family relations, but girls whose first periods are unusually early may experience a persisting decrease in parental influence and in their participation in family activities (Steinberg, 1988). A boy's puberty creates long-term changes in family relations. The boy and his mother begin to interrupt each other more often than they used to and to explain themselves less often, and the boy defers to his mother's wishes less than when he was younger. As early adolescence passes, the mother interrupts her son less, treating him more in the way she treats adult men. The relationship between father and son also changes, but in the opposite way; the father becomes more assertive with the son, and the son becomes more deferential and less likely to interrupt the father. With these developmental steps, the adolescents' internal working models of relationships become more complicated. Relationships with males and with females are thought of in different ways, for example, and relationships between child and adult considered different than those between younger adult and older adult.

Peers

The adolescent's view of peer relationships also changes during this age period. Negotiation becomes a more and more important part of successful peer relations. The existence of good cognitive and emotional skills for empathy contributes to good negotiating ability and thus to an enjoyable social life rather than one in which isolation, teasing, and bullying play major roles.

The AT View

AT practitioners ignore the adolescent's need for continued joint planning, for negotiation, and for alteration of parent-child relationships. Once again, the assumption is that the promotion of emotional attachment makes the young person cheerfully compliant and devoted to the adult caregivers. If the teenager is not devoted and obedient, it is thought that attachment has failed, and it is feared that he or she will attack and harm parents, siblings, or pets. Negotiation is not expected to be a part of family life or of the relationship with a therapist. As for peer relations, adolescents in treatment are often isolated from peers. If they do not attend school or participate in sports, they may have very limited contacts with people of their own age and few chances for development of social skills with peers.

GOOD PARENTING AND GOOD DEVELOPMENT

At the beginning of this chapter, we noted that babies are born with certain personality differences already in place and that adults have their own individualities. But we also talked about the transactional processes between parents and children and the way the family environment can support good emotional development. We now need to look at parenting practices that have been linked to good emotional and personality development and to examine their relationship to the advice given by attachment therapists.

As we do this, we need to keep a point in mind: Just as there are many individual types of healthy adult personality, there may be many adequate ways of rearing children. It may even be that children who start with one kind of basic personality will benefit most from certain caregiving practices and that those practices might not work well for a different type of child. Certainly, what a parent does needs to be fine-tuned to meet the needs of the child's current stage of development. Nevertheless, in a general sort of way, we have some information about parenting approaches that seem useful.

Styles versus Skills

Our discussion of good parenting will not focus on specific events or practices—early or late toilet-training or co-sleeping with parents. Parenting is far more about relationships than it is about skills or practices. A relationship between two people involves mutual or reciprocal attitudes, expectations, and emotional responses, and these are what cause parents to choose particular practices or to develop particular skills. Parents who are similar in attitudes and expectations tend toward particular characteristic combinations of practices as well. Their attitudes and practices together form their parental style, which probably has a much greater influence on their children than does any specific childrearing technique.

Parental Awareness

Many attempts have been made to describe differences in parental style. One of the most useful was suggested by Newberger (1980), and it classifies parents according to four possible levels of parental awareness. Parental awareness involves a combination of knowledge about child development, practical intelligence, and emotional responses to children. The parent's level of parental awareness determines his or her organized system of thinking about parenting, understanding of what the child does, and developing of policies and rules about what to do. Better child development is related to higher levels of parental awareness (Pratt et al., 1993). In Chapter 8, we will discuss how each style or level might make a parent more or less likely to become involved with the AT approach.

At the lowest level of parental awareness, the parent interprets the child's needs through the parent's own needs and desires. At this *egoistic* level, parents pay more attention to what they do than to the way the child responds; for example, they may be pleased that they have spanked the child and not notice that the child's behavior got worse. Egoistic parents do not guide the child's behavior toward a long-term goal but concentrate on stopping the child from doing things that annoy the parent at that moment, even though they permit or even reward the same actions at other times.

The more complex *conventional* level of parental awareness is one at which parents know that the child's needs are different from their own but do not understand that different children need different things. Parents at the conventional level do try to teach standards that will guide behavior, and they try to show reasons for rules.

Individualistic parental awareness includes an even more complex understanding of each child's uniqueness. Parents at the individualistic level tailor rules and punishments to match the characteristics of a particular child rather than feeling they must treat all children the same way.

The highest level of parental awareness is the *analytic* level, and it requires the greatest complexity of thought and decision-making. The child is considered a complex and changing individual—and so is the parent, who is aware of his or her own growth and changing interactions with the child. The parent's actions toward the child are determined by the needs of both and by the ways they have affected each other in the past as well as those wanted for the future.

AT and Parental Awareness

At what level of awareness do attachment therapists expect parents to function? The analytic level can probably be ruled out. Attachment therapy and related parenting advice focus entirely on the child's characteristics or problems. Although a past parent or caregiver may be blamed for abuse or neglect, the present caregiver is considered to be by definition a loving, competent person. Any inappropriate behavior from the current caregiver is seen as forced or manipulated by the child. Parents are not seen as growing or changing or in any need of growth or change. They are asked to employ specific techniques but not to seek therapy or try to understand their own attitudes. The parental approach approved by attachment therapists might be described as quasi-individualistic; it is assumed that certain children, who have not formed attachments, should be treated differently than their well-attached siblings. However, the treatment is to be the same for all attachment-disordered children, no matter what their backgrounds, their language, or the cultural milieu they come from. (Support groups refer to these children as RADishes and to other children as other types of vegetables, emphasizing the importance of group membership over that of individual differences.)

It would be an exaggeration to say that attachment therapists encourage an egoistic level of awareness in parents, but there would also be some truth in the statement. The emphasis attachment therapy places on children's lies and manipulativeness implies that the truth of a situation is always what is perceived by the parent. A child who complains of pain or suffocation during treatment is to be ignored. There is no tolerance of behaviors that are simply annoying to the parent but have no long-term ill effects, such as complaining about food or chattering inconsequentially. As a deliberate policy, children are to be kept uninformed and to be surprised by separations or changes of plan, and this is considered to be psychologically beneficial to them. It is hard to see how the constant stress on adult authority can be related to anything above an egoistic level of awareness.

Beyond Awareness and Style

As children mature, there are normal changes in the ways their parents treat them, and the alteration is necessary for good development. Different children may need different care practices, too. These facts make it difficult to discuss specific practices or parental skills as all children of all ages might require them. However, we can look at some broad concepts that are probably linked to "good parenting" in some way for all children at all ages.

Parents need to be appropriately sensitive and appropriately responsive to their children's needs and communications. In the child's early life, this means paying careful attention to the baby's cues, learning to interpret them correctly, and responding to them by feeding, comfort, social interaction, or whatever else is needed. Quick and effective responses help the child stay calm and alert and aid in the development of emotional self-regulation, the important foundation for later emotional development. As a child gets older, though, parents generally wait to respond until the child tells them what is wanted, and even then they may require the child to work for results ("No, I told you I won't fill the wading pool until you put your dirty clothes in the hamper"). Teenagers may even prefer that parents not pay too careful attention to them and may feel humiliated and intruded upon if asked repeatedly what they want to eat or if they don't want a sweater.

Appropriate sensitivity and responsiveness to the child's needs are ways of modeling *empathy*. The experience of empathic adult behavior seems to be the best—possibly the only—way in which children develop their own empathic responses to others. Cognitive and emotional empathy help prevent cruelty and facilitate prosocial, altruistic behavior from an early age.

Good parents work at *buffering* the effects of experience on the child. Skinned knees cannot necessarily be prevented, but warnings to be careful or comfort after a fall help the child deal with pain and fright. When medical or dental treatment is needed, the parent's presence, explanations, and comfort effectively reduce the impact of what could be a traumatic experience. School experiences, whether pleasant or unpleasant, have a more appropriate effect when there is parent involvement. Similarly, the teenager whose friends use drugs and alcohol can think more constructively about her own choices when there have been discussions with parents about these issues. Children of all ages can benefit from parental explanation and discussion of frightening news stories or newly learned historical facts about slavery or the Holocaust.

Parents do well to minimize the use of *physical punishment* at every stage of development. Physical punishment is linked with poor control over anger and a tendency to impulsive violence. The relationship here may not involve cause and effect, and it may simply be that parents who do not use physical punishment model other desirable ways of thinking and behaving. Nonphysical punishments such as scolding or grounding have been more difficult to study, but they may be less desirable than more positive modes of guidance, simply because of the negative emotions they engender. Whether punishment or positive guidance is used, parents are more effective when they use careful monitoring of their children's behavior to stop undesirable acts before they are well started or to encourage good behavior from its beginning. Delayed punishments have very little effect on the behaviors they are supposed to prevent.

The AT View

Attachment therapists and therapeutic foster parents make contradictory use of these ideas. For example, their ideas place a great emphasis on the need of the infant for sensitive, responsive treatment, which they regard as directly responsible for the process of attachment. Children who are receiving AT treatment, on the contrary, are to be treated with as little responsiveness as possible; their complaints and requests (such as Candace Newmaker's pleas for air) are regarded as lies and attempts at manipulation, with even physical injuries regarded as deliberately self-induced. Although great concern is expressed over the children's lack of empathy and potential cruelty, no attempt is made to model empathy for them, nor do the therapists or foster parents attempt to buffer their experiences; in fact, discussion or explanation are considered unnecessary and counterproductive. Although physical punishment in the form of spanking is not part of attachment therapy, practices include restraint and grabbing the child hard enough to cause bruising, as well as the use of "takedown" techniques, by which adults bring a child to the floor and hold him or her there for some time.

REFERENCES

Bowlby, J. (1982). *Attachment.* New York: Basic Books.

Cicchetti, D., & Beeghly, M. (1990). An organizational approach to the study of Down syndrome: Contributions to an integrative theory of development. In D. Cicchetti & M. Beeghly (Eds.), *Children with Down syndrome.* New York: Cambridge University Press.

De Casper, A. J., & Spence, M. J. (1986). Prenatal maternal speech influences newborns' perception of speech sounds. *Infant Behavior and Development, 9,* 133–150.

Greenspan, S., & Greenspan, N. (1985). *First feelings.* New York: Viking.

Lewis, M. (1992). *Shame: The exposed self.* New York: Free Press.

Newberger, C. (1980). The cognitive structure of parenthood: Designing a descriptive measure. In R. Selman & R. Yando (Eds.), *New directions for child development:* Vol. 7. San Francisco: Jossey-Bass.

Pratt, M., Hunsberger, B., Pancer, S., Roth, D., & Santalupo, S. (1993). Thinking about parenting: Reasoning about developmental issues across the lifespan. *Developmental Psychology, 29,* 585–595.

Sameroff, A. (1983). Factors in predicting successful parenting. In V. Sasserath (Ed.), *Minimizing high-risk parenting.* Skillman, NJ: Johnson & Johnson.

Shonkoff, J. P., & Phillips, D. A. (2000). *From neurons to neighborhoods: The science of early childhood development.* Washington, D.C.: National Academy Press.

Speltz, M. L., Greenberg, M. T., & DeKlyen, M. (1990). Attachment in preschoolers with disruptive behavior: A comparison of clinic-referred and non-problem children. *Development and Psychopathology, 2,* 31–46.

Sroufe, L. A. (1996). *Emotional development.* New York: Cambridge University Press.

Steinberg, L. (1988). Reciprocal relationship between parent-child distance and pubertal maturation. *Developmental Psychology, 24,* 122–126.

Walder, T., & Ogan, T. (1988). The development of social referencing in the child. *Child Development, 59,* 1230–1240.

Chapter 5

When Emotional Life Goes Wrong:
Some Facts About Childhood Mental Illness
versus the Attachment Therapists' Beliefs

That children can be mentally ill is a surprising and disturbing idea for many otherwise sophisticated people. The *Philadelphia Inquirer* columnist Lucia Herndon (2001) described the idea of inpatient mental health treatment for children as unsettling and asked, "Are there really children as young as 5 who require hospitalization for mental and emotional problems?" The answer, unfortunately, is "Yes." There are, in fact, even younger children who need residential treatment.

To understand childhood mental illness, however, we need to recognize that mental illness and institutionalization do not always go hand-in-hand. Like adults, children with emotional disturbances do not necessarily need or benefit from hospital treatment (Goldberg, 2001). The 5–10% of American children who have serious problems may often get the greatest help from staying at home and receiving treatment as outpatients. They may benefit particularly from so-called wraparound services, including respite workers to give parents a break. Many problems and many treatments and services need to be considered when we think about childhood mental illness. The present chapter gives an overview of issues about childhood mental illness and examines how these facts and ideas relate to Candace Newmaker's case.

WHAT IS MENTAL ILLNESS?

The term "mental illness" covers a wide range of behavioral, emotional, and cognitive disturbances. At one end of the spectrum, we have the very serious childhood disturbances—problems that make normal life impossible, and that are often treated in hospitals or residential schools. At the other end of the range, there are relatively minor childhood problems, difficulties that preoccupy the child and annoy other people and that may cause trouble with school performance. These minor problems are not immediately critical, but they need to be taken seriously before they start a problematic developmental trajectory in which poor schoolwork leads to employment difficulties and perhaps eventually to crime.

Problems of mental health are often found in association with other types of undesirable behavior. Bullying or being bullied, delinquent or criminal acts, drug and alcohol use, or inappropriate sexual behavior may all be among these. A wide range of types and amounts of such behaviors may be associated with childhood mental illness. Mental illness in early life also has a wide range of times of onset. Some parents identify children as being different in some way practically from the time of birth. Some problems are first noticed when the child fails to begin talking during the usual age period. Other problems may not be identified until the child reaches the public school setting. Finally, we should note that schizophrenia, one of the most serious of adult mental illnesses, is usually first seen when the person is in late adolescence.

When we look at these various aspects of mental illness, we can see that serious emotional problems do not form a simple disease state like chickenpox or measles. There are many levels of mental illness, many different related problems, and many points during childhood when trouble may first appear. And, as we discuss later in this chapter, mental illness has many complex causes rather than the single cause postulated by the attachment therapists.

Classifying Mental Illness

We human beings like to simplify life and the problems it offers us. One way we can do this is by thinking about categories of events rather than the uniqueness of each individual phenomenon. Instead of considering the special characteristics of each mentally-ill child, we classify children into groups who share a *diagnosis*. Each diagnostic group is made up of children who are considered to have the same *syndrome*.

A syndrome is a set of symptoms that tend to occur in association with each other. For example, we might find a number of children at age five who have poor or no spoken language, who rarely use eye contact or other social signals for communication, who play in repetitive or stereotyped ways, and who have peculiar movement patterns. Such a set of symptoms, found in a group of children, would receive its own syndrome name and description (in this case, *autism*). When a syndrome is described and named, there are usually efforts to discover its cause, and, in fact, the cause may become one of the ways to describe the syndrome. When the cause is difficult to determine, several alternative theories may be developed and, if possible, tested for empirical support.

The idea of syndromes is a useful one because it allows us to use a shorthand description rather than all the undigested details about a given child. It also allows children to be grouped together in a way that can show what they have in common and facilitate our understanding of the cause of their problems. However, we need to be very cautious about our use of diagnostic categories. The first problem is that all children with a given syndrome do not necessarily have every one of the characteristics considered as part of that syndrome. This is true even when there is a clear-cut physical cause or physical features of the syndrome. For example, Down syndrome (trisomy-21), a disorder of physical, intellectual, and social development, has a well-known genetic cause for its specific symptoms. Nevertheless, some individuals have most of the symptoms of Down syndrome but do not have the genetic characteristics, and others with the genetic problem show few of the specific symptoms. Just as there are great individual differences among normal, well-developed children, there is variation among children with problems of mental or physical health. Human individuality does not vanish when pathology enters, and the mentally-ill child is a unique person, not just a member of a diagnostic category.

A second problem with the syndrome approach is that the diagnostic categories we use are products of human thought processes as much as of the underlying realities of mental illness. (This statement, of course, is as true of classifications in zoology as it is of psychological or psychiatric work, and biologists frequently reclassify groups of animals as they re-think the categories they are using.) Because diagnostic categories result from observation, thought, and discussion, they change over time and may be interpreted in different ways by different people.

DSM-IV Categories

The best-known and most used list of diagnostic categories is the *Diagnostic and Statistical Manual of Mental Disorders*, published by the American Psychiatric Association. The fourth and most recent edition of this manual, called DSM-IV, came out in 1994 (with a revision, DSM-TR, in 2000). It provides descriptions of diagnostic criteria used in the identification of thousands of syndromes of mental illness. Like earlier editions, this one was revised and written by a committee appointed by the American Psychiatric Association.

Because we are most concerned here with mental health in childhood, we should note that DSM-IV was not particularly intended to be used for diagnosis of infants or young children. Many of the diagnostic criteria used in DSM-IV are appropriate only for adults. Young children, for example, may show temporary disorders called developmental dysfunctions; great distress and fear about strangers could be one such problem. A child with this sort of symptom will probably lose it without treatment ("grow out of it"), but an adult with the same kind of behavioral reaction would be seriously in need of help. An alternative approach to diagnosis of young children can be found in *Diagnostic Classification: 0–3; Diagnostic classification of mental health and developmental disorders of infancy and early childhood*, published in 1994 by the National Center for Infants, Toddlers, and Families.

Reactive Attachment Disorder

When DSM-IV was published, it included for the first time diagnostic criteria for the disorder for which Candace Newmaker was being treated at the time of her death. Reactive Attachment Disorder was the name given to a syndrome that had not been clearly described in earlier years. One member of the committee revising DSM was Sir Michael Rutter, an English psychiatrist who had been much involved with research on Romanian children adopted in the West after political changes gave access to the orphanages where they had been living. The brutality these children had experienced was of great concern on humanitarian grounds but also of considerable interest as a natural experiment on the effects of early emotional deprivation. The committee decided that the syndrome resulting from the experiences of the Romanian orphans could also result from more ordinary types of early abuse and neglect and should be included in the publication under the name Reactive Attachment Disorder.

The criteria given for a diagnosis of Reactive Attachment Disorder include both a variety of behaviors and some early experiences. (As you read this description, please recall our earlier comment that not all the criteria need to be present for the diagnosis to be made.) The reader may want to review the discussion of normal attachment behavior in the previous chapter to compare this syndrome to the events of normal development.

Reactive Attachment Disorder is identified by "Markedly disturbed and developmentally inappropriate social relatedness in most contexts, beginning before age 5 years, as evidenced by" either "(1) persistent failure to initiate or respond in a developmentally appropriate fashion to most social interactions, as manifest by excessively inhibited, hypervigilant, or highly ambivalent and contradictory responses (e.g., the child may respond to caregivers with a mixture of approach, avoidance, and resistance to comforting, or may exhibit frozen watchfulness)" (referred to as Inhibited Type) or "(2) diffuse attachments as manifest by indiscriminate sociability with marked inability to exhibit appropriate selective attachments (e.g., excessive familiarity with relative strangers or lack of selectivity in choice of attachment figures)" (referred to as Disinhibited Type). A second criterion for Reactive Attachment Disorder is that the behavior just described cannot be accounted for solely by developmental delay, as might be the case for a mentally retarded child. A third criterion has to do with the child's known past experiences and involves "pathogenic care as evidenced by at least one of the following: (1) persistent disregard of the child's basic emotional needs for comfort, stimulation, and affection (2) persistent disregard of the child's basic physical needs (3) repeated changes of primary caregiver that prevent formation of stable attachments (e.g., frequent changes in foster care)." The criteria for the diagnosis of Reactive Attachment Disorder also note a presumption that the inappropriate experiences in early life are the cause of the unusual social behavior.

The appearance of Reactive Attachment Disorder in DSM-IV does not mean the discussion of this syndrome is over. There have continued to be many new suggestions about attachment problems, especially in regard to the events of the early years of life. Some workers in this area have emphasized observational tools and classifications such as those used in the Strange Situation (see chapter 9). Others have emphasized the child's general relationships with caregivers and the quality of their usual interactions, especially the emotional tone or type of feelings and the extent to which adult and child are psychologically involved in the relationship.

Diagnosing Candace

Could Candace Newmaker have been correctly diagnosed with Reactive Attachment Disorder? Based on the information we had about her in earlier chapters and the criteria for Reactive Attachment Disorder in DSM-IV, the answer is probably in the negative. Whether Candace showed "markedly disturbed and developmentally inappropriate social relatedness" at any time is questionable. She seems to have begun to talk at an average age, suggesting that she was interacting socially with others in ways that support language and communication development effectively. She was described as clinging to her mother when removed from the home, an appropriate manifestation of emotional attachment, and crying and having tantrums in foster care—again an expectable behavior for a child with normal social and emotional development experiencing an abrupt separation. There was no description of Candace as excessively inhibited or hypervigilant or as giving contradictory responses to others at any point. Nor did she seem unusually friendly to strangers. Although her early home life was a bit catch-as-catch-can and her young mother was probably preoccupied with her turbulent marriage, persistent disregard of Candace's needs, physical or emotional, is doubtful. There were several adults who cared for Candace, but no repeated changes of primary caregiver.

How Attachment Therapists Defined Attachment Disorders

The attachment therapists seem to have taken a somewhat different diagnostic approach than the description of Reactive Attachment Disorder in DSM-IV. Their views added some criteria to those described in the Manual. In addition, the writings of attachment therapists have alluded to the diagnosis of a more serious or severe syndrome they sometimes call Attachment Disorder. They describe this as increasingly frequent in the United States and as resulting in the development of serial killers or persons with other seriously distorted personality patterns, unless it is treated with AT.

AT advocates, who often refer to Reactive Attachment Disorder simply as RAD, place great stress on the child's use of social eye contact, which is not specifically mentioned by the DSM-IV criteria (and which would usually be considered more relevant to the Pervasive Developmental Disorders such as autism). Children diagnosed with RAD (called RADishes by some parent support groups) are said to make eye contact only when lying and to avoid "eye contact for closeness." Eye contact for closeness is not defined but is presumably like the sustained mutual gaze shared by parent and infant or by lovers. There is no discussion in attachment therapy writings of the developmental appropriateness of sustained eye contact at various ages, and we might question whether children over seven normally gaze into their parents' eyes. Of course, AT practitioners consider sustained eye contact to be both a cause of attachment (see chapter 3) and evidence that attachment has occurred, so it is not surprising that eye contact should be used as a diagnostic criterion.

Some other additions that attachment therapists have made to the DSM-IV criteria are these:

Child acts phony/charming to adults outside the family.

Parent feels more angry/frustrated with this child than with other children.

Child has made accusations of abuse against parent to other adults.

Child seems to know the parents' "buttons" and pushes them often.

Child feels entitled to special treatment.

Child has rigid routines and rituals and gets upset if they are interrupted.

Child has poor hygiene.

Child doesn't seem to know right from wrong.

These criteria form part of a checklist offered to parents for use in deciding whether a child might need treatment for RAD. (We discuss the sources of this checklist in chapter 7.) An interesting characteristic of these additional criteria is their inclusion of the parents' feelings; this is not a list of diagnostic criteria that focuses exclusively on the child's behaviors and experiences, although AT stresses the idea that it is the child whose personality needs to be changed.

Some other notable differences exist between the DSM-IV criteria and those that were used in Candace Newmaker's diagnosis. For instance, DSM-IV stresses the idea of developmental appropriateness—that excellent emotional functioning in a child at one stage of development can yield behavior that would be considered a symptom of poor functioning for a child at another stage, and vice versa. The attachment therapists' criteria seem intended to apply across childhood and adolescence; again, eye contact is an example, because the making or avoiding of eye contact would certainly be different for a 4-year-old and a pubescent 14-year-old. This is especially relevant because of the interaction between developmental stage and cultural differences with respect to interpersonal behaviors. A 4-year-old of European descent has probably been encouraged to look directly at an adult who is speaking, and a 4-year-old of African descent to drop his or her eyes before an adult's gaze. For 14-year-olds, the ethnic difference could also be influenced by the age and position of the speaker as well as by the adolescent's gender.

The Randolph Attachment Disorder Questionnaire

The criteria quoted in the previous section as concerns of attachment therapists come from a checklist for RAD symptoms called the Randolph Attachment Disorder Questionnaire (RADQ) and used primarily by attachment therapists. This questionnaire (discussed further in chapter 7) asks parents to assess children on a number of criteria without providing any standards of comparison or even suggesting that the child should be compared to other children of the same age (Randolph, 2000). The use of the parent's gut responses to the questions is certainly in line with the AT philosophy that the parents are good, truthful, and knowledgeable about their children as well as deserving of the therapist's complete respect and support. (Unfortunately, as we see in chapter 8, the use of checklists in this way is often associated with deliberate quackery.)

The attachment therapists note on various Websites that the checklist alone is not sufficient for diagnosis and that the child must be seen by an experienced therapist. At the Watkins-Ponder trial, however, testimony revealed that the therapist who recommended taking Candace to Evergreen did so entirely on the basis of a completed questionnaire sent to him by Jeane Newmaker. No further diagnostic work was done before Candace began treatment.

Material on AT-related Websites describes the RADQ as a screening device but also claims that the score can be used to estimate the severity of the problem and to categorize the disorder into one of three types. This is somewhat self-contradictory, because a questionnaire that could do the latter tasks is far too sensitive to be considered simply a screening device; however, there seems to be no substantial evidence either that the RADQ is a good screen or that it does discriminate among various kinds of attachment problems. (This issue is discussed in more detail in chapter 7.)

MENTAL ILLNESS? OR SOMETHING ELSE?

Some children show signs of serious emotional disturbance from an early age, but not every child whose behavior is disturbing to adults should be evaluated as mentally ill, in spite of the attachment therapists' claims. There are a number of less serious reasons for behaviors that might appear to a casual observer to be possible symptoms of deep disturbance.

Temperamental Factors

The differences in individual personality we discussed in chapter 4 can be due to differences in *temperament*. This term refers to the child's basic biological or constitutional nature and the aspects of personality it determines—aspects that are not caused by experience but are inherent in the child (Lerner et al., 1982). Personality characteristics such as shyness or high or low activity level generally result from temperamental qualities. Even though a child's temperamental characteristics are all within the normal range, parents may not realize this and may assume a behavior is pathological when it is simply different from what they want or are used to. For example, parents whose first child was very outgoing may feel seriously worried about a later-born offspring who is temperamentally shy—and of course, the opposite is also possible.

Developmental Dysfunctions

Children may also cause worry when they show the developmental dysfunctions mentioned earlier in this chapter. These dysfunctions are common but temporary results of rapid or stressful developmental change (Hetherington, Bridges, & Insabella, 1998). Some examples are the "nearly paranoid" fear of separation many children show in late infancy; an expression of rage in the form of tantrums by 2-year-olds; stammering in preschoolers; and sullen moodiness in the middle teen years. These problems are not symptoms of mental illness and will pass away if handled with even moderate parenting skill.

Status Offenses

A related issue is the existence of status offenses. Some behaviors, such as alcohol use and sexual activity, are treated as crimes and/or evidence of emotional disturbance when they are carried out by minors but not when performed by adults. Although it is possible that status offenses can be associated with mental illness, these behaviors may instead result from family or cultural characteristics.

Disabling Conditions

Finally, we should note that some social and emotional problems may result from disabilities that are quite different from mental illness. Mental retardation, for example, often produces peculiar ways of dealing with others, even among children who receive careful guidance and instruction. Poor vision can make it difficult for individuals to do social referencing (see chapter 4) and to pick up social cues from others' facial expressions. Children with impaired hearing may display frustration in tantrums when they do not know what others are saying. And, of course, problems such as fetal alcohol syndrome affect impulse control and social communication.

CHILDHOOD MENTAL ILLNESS: AGES AND SYMPTOMS

Although many forms of mental illness are seen in both children and adults, the relevant symptoms are not identical in older and in younger people. Just as a mentally healthy child behaves differently from a mentally healthy adult, mental illness is different at different developmental stages. Some of the differences are so extreme that certain disturbances, such as depression, were at one time assumed not to exist in children at all.

Childhood mental illness is a serious matter that interferes with normal learning and development. The earlier the illness begins, the more it disturbs the developmental trajectory that would ordinarily produce a healthy, well-functioning adult. Educational losses and lack of normal social skill development can both result from childhood emotional problems. Childhood mental illness is not outgrown, and our methods of treatment are far from perfect.

Regulatory Disorders

As we noted in chapter 4, experience with parental comforting normally begins to affect an infant's behavior within a few months after birth. The baby begins to show the rudiments of self-calming and mood control. He or she is more readily comforted by an adult and becomes more regular in sleep and feeding. *Regulatory disorders* are present when there is no progress toward self-regulation and the infant remains irritable or lethargic, with poor attention skills and poor emotional control. Sometimes the child develops abnormal ways to try to calm down, such as rumination—the regurgitation, re-chewing, and re-swallowing of food.

Tactile Defensiveness

Infants with regulatory disorders may show excessive reactions to being touched. This negative response, called *tactile defensiveness*, creates distress following events that are usually soothing, such as kissing or patting. In a transactional pattern, parents can be seriously affected by this sort of response from a baby and can affect the baby in turn. Caregivers may respond with depression and doubt about their abilities to nurture a baby when their attempts to comfort seem simply to distress the baby further. Not surprisingly, parents who have such experiences approach the baby less often, and the baby gets few experiences of the effective comfort from which self-regulation normally emerges.

The RADQ and Regulatory Disorders

Some of the questions posed by the RADQ seem to be more relevant to regulatory disorders than to attachment problems. Attachment therapists are concerned about children's resistance to touch, their prolonged tantrums, and their unpredictable eating, sleeping, and toileting, all of which the practitioners interpret as control issues but which could be more accurately seen as the result of regulatory problems.

Pervasive Developmental Disorders

A group of problems receives the name Pervasive Developmental Disorders because they influence many aspects of development and seem to result from some early distortion in a child's developmental pattern. Some of these problems may be noticeable from birth. Others seem to begin during the toddler or preschool period, after the child has had an apparently normal early life. Some are found primarily in boys and others primarily in girls. Some seem to have a genetic cause. Although some are relatively mild in their symptoms, others are a serious impediment to the normal experience of life.

Autism

Autism is a pervasive developmental disorder that affects social, emotional, cognitive, and even motor abilities from an early age, perhaps soon after birth. Although autistic children are often diagnosed at age 2 1/2 or 3 when it becomes evident they are not talking, many clues to the disorder exist months earlier. Unlike other babies in the early months of life, autistic children do not seem to find the human face interesting and show little of the normal gesture communication. Adults feel that the child is self-sufficient and aloof because there is little eye contact, snuggling, or other forms of emotional communication.

Autistic preschoolers and older children are characterized by a lack of interest in communication with others, to the point where the child does not seem aware that someone else is a conscious human being. Stereotyped movement patterns, such as hand-flapping or toe-walking, continue far beyond the usual early preschool age. Autistic children cannot easily tolerate change in the environment—even very small changes such as a dinner table set for guests as well as family. They resist caregivers' attempts to do things, and respond to repeated requests with severe, prolonged tantrums.

Some high-functioning autistics learn to speak and may go far educationally. One such person, Temple Grandin, the author of *Thinking in Pictures* (1995), has described herself as using picture-symbols rather than word-symbols in her thought. She also has described her emotional life as like that of an animal, with fear the most salient emotion and no subtle or mixed feelings such as jealousy or romantic love.

The RADQ and Pervasive Developmental Disorders

Again, the RADQ contains references to behaviors that might well be autistic in nature rather than relevant to attachment. Extended tantrums with long periods of screaming, resistance to change or coercion, and above all the avoidance of eye contact—these are all features of autism that are referred to by attachment therapists as evidence of resistance and the demand for control of the environment. The RADQ also refers to odd patterns of speech, repetitive movements, and repetitive behavior; a lack of make-believe or imitative play; and an unusual fascination with objects and parts of objects—all characteristics of certain pervasive developmental disorders and in no way logically related to attachment problems. Some children who are being identified as attachment disordered by the attachment therapists may thus be more accurately described as autistic.

Holding and Autism

The holding aspect of attachment therapy was initially offered as a treatment for autism and a way to break through the apparent self-containment of the autistic child. There is no evidence that the treatment was effective for autistic children, nor was it ever widely used or taught. It may be, however, that the historical connection between holding therapy and autism is the source of the concern of attachment therapists with eye contact. The avoidance of eye contact contributes to a diagnosis of autism or other pervasive developmental disorders but is not specifically related to Reactive Attachment Disorder according to the DSM-IV diagnostic criteria.

Attachment Disorders

Because most of this book deals with the idea that emotional attachment can undergo distorted development, we can be fairly brief in this section. Reasoning from research-based evidence about early development, we can note that attachment disorders would not be expected to occur until the end of the first year of life because attachment has not progressed far before that. Unusual attachment patterns may first be evident in toddlers, who can move around on their own, talk to some extent, and do things that make it clear what their concerns are. An important point about attachment disorders is that normal attachment behaviors are initially more trouble for caregivers to cope with than abnormal attachment. Toddlers' attachment behaviors can be worrisome and exasperating—for example, crying when approached by a well-meaning stranger, acting frightened when the parent moves out of sight briefly, and treating bedtime like a terrifying experience of desertion. However, these are symptoms of good, not disturbed, mental health when they occur in toddlers and young preschoolers.

Attachment disorders usually involve symptoms such as indiscriminate friendliness to strangers and reckless behaviors that can cause physical injury, although exaggerated concerns about separation may also reflect attachment difficulties. As children with poor attachment experiences get older and enter preschool and the early grades, they may show poor reality testing (telling the difference between emotion or fantasy and reality), poor impulse control, and poor resistance to temptation. They are less likely than securely attached children to comply with adults' rules or to consider teachers to have legitimate authority. They may deliberately disobey and misbehave, behave defiantly, and obey only when monitored by an adult. Children with serious attachment problems may not know how to comfort themselves except by eating and may have neither normal social skills nor the ability to play typical of their age. Their indiscriminate friendliness may already have made it easy for a sexual predator to molest them, and they may act out this experience with other children.

The AT View of Control Issues

Attachment therapists believe symptoms of attachment disorders result from the child's overweening need to take control, to con and fool the caregiver. Recklessness and physical injury are interpreted as ways to cause the caregiver to be blamed and inconvenienced. The children are described as prone to "crazy lying" in ways that are bound to be discovered, rather than as displaying poor reality testing.

Predicting Violence

A major difference between the beliefs of attachment therapists and the view of the majority of psychologists has to do with the relationship between poor attachment experiences and later violent or even sadistic behavior. Attachment therapists claim high frequencies of killing on the part of quite young children with attachment disorders, although such events are statistically very rare. This issue will be discussed later in this chapter when we examine what is known about the causes of mental illness.

Traumatic Stress Disorders

Like adults who have been exposed to overwhelming stress, preschoolers may develop *Traumatic Stress Disorder* following experiences of physical or emotional trauma. Of course, the experiences that are traumatic for a preschooler may be different from those that would affect an adult, because the child understands and interprets events differently, as well as having a realistic awareness of his or her lesser strength and skill.

The memory flashbacks and reenactments of the traumatic event, characteristic of traumatized adults, are also seen in young children. (For example, one author [James, 1994] described a preschool child who had been raped, and who, when she saw a jar of Vaseline, would fall to the floor and begin to pound her fists on her crotch.) The preschool child is also likely to show hyperactive and disruptive behavior in connection with Traumatic Stress Disorder.

Small children with Traumatic Stress Disorder are often fearful or irritable and show hypervigilance (constant alert attention to the environment). Other symptoms such as hyperactivity or regression to the behavior of earlier months may occur. It is possible that vivid memories appear in the form of physical events such as vomiting or in episodes of physical activity such as that described above.

Older children and teenagers with Traumatic Stress Disorder show behaviors that are more like those of adults. However, their preoccupation with flashbacks may appear to be lack of attention in school or deliberate disobedience to instructions or rules.

Infants and toddlers who have experienced abusive treatment by adults may have symptoms of Traumatic Stress Disorder. They may also show certain destructive behaviors that are uncommon among children of this age because of their physical and cognitive difficulty. One example is fire setting; another is serious cruelty to animals such as intentionally strangling, cutting, or burning them. Actions such as these are serious indications of emotional disturbances that are not outgrown but become more dangerous without treatment.

Are some forms of attachment disorder actually a type of Traumatic Stress Disorder? This may be an appropriate interpretation of problems resulting from abusive treatment or from forms of neglect that involved severe pain or discomfort like that of a serious diaper rash, and, indeed, some AT writers have acknowledged this possibility. The emotional disturbance may not be caused by a lack of social interaction as much as by the experience of helplessness in the face of pain. However, as we will discuss later, either abusive or neglectful caregivers are less likely to have pleasurable, playful interactions with the child than those who are conscientious nurturers. It may not be possible to divide these factors into separate components. However, in the RADQ and similar materials, the attachment therapists lay great stress on behaviors such as fire setting and cruelty to animals as evidence of attachment disorders; they imply that every child with poor attachment experiences is a potential fire-setter and killer, even if nothing has happened yet.

Internalizing Problems

One way to categorize some emotional problems is to classify them as *internalizing affective disorders* or as *externalizing affective disorders*. Internalizing disorders involve acting as if the self is to be blamed for any displeasure, and externalizing disorders involve acting as though other people are at fault and deserve punishment. Internalizing affective disorders are characterized by worry, anxiety, sadness, and concern about the self and others.

Infant Depression

Internalizing disorders are possible even during infancy. A depressed infant is withdrawn, lethargic, apathetic, and unresponsive, without any clear-cut biological or environmental reason. (A biological reason might be physical illness, or malnutrition that reduces the child's energy level; an environmental reason could be a lack of interesting events or things to look at.) There is a tendency for the depressed baby to be unusually inhibited about exploring new places or people. As time passes, the baby becomes less adept than other infants at getting friendly responses from adults, although he or she may be more socially active with some adults than with others.

Preschoolers

Depression and sadness in preschool children do not necessarily produce the behavioral signs common to infants, nor are they exactly like their counterparts in adults. Toilet accidents and reckless play can be the results of early depression. Because preschoolers often do not have the language skills to express their feelings, they do not describe their feelings of sadness to other people as an adult might.

Schoolchildren

Many school-age children experience loneliness and social withdrawal; more than 10% say they feel lonely or have no one to play with most of the time. The sources of schoolchildren's depression are complex, but children who experience stressful life events are more likely to become depressed. They feel sad and worthless, have disturbed sleep and concentration, and may think of suicide. They may also be irritable (Cicchetti & Toth, 1998).

The internalizing disorders of school-age children may also include anxiety disorders such as school phobia, an almost unendurable fear of going to school. Like depression, anxiety disorders can interfere with development by preventing the occurrence of normal experiences.

Adolescence

Teenage girls are somewhat more likely to experience depression than boys are. By this stage of life, much of the concern about depression has to do with problems associated with it, not with the existence of the emotional disorder alone. Poor health habits such as drug use are associated with depression, as are eating disorders. It can be difficult to tell whether depression causes or is caused by the associated problems. For example, severe dieting can produce "crash diet depression," and negative mood can result from low carbohydrate intake.

A major concern about depression, of course, is the role it plays in producing suicidal behavior. Suicidal acts do not usually occur as a result of a sudden impulse but instead are preceded by a period of suicidal ideation (thinking and planning about suicide). Suicidal ideation most often occurs during depressed moods. However, suicidal acts rarely occur when the individual is in the depths of depression; a slight improvement in mood seems to be needed before the energy can be mustered for a suicidal action rather than just a thought.

School phobia, which we mentioned earlier as sometimes occurring in middle childhood, is most likely to be evident during the high school years. This condition involves severe emotional distress and is not a simple matter of skipping school because homework was not done.

The RADQ and Internalizing Disorders

Looking back at the RADQ and related materials, we can see that the attachment therapists may treat signs of internalizing disorders as if they indicated attachment problems. For example, a depressed child may struggle with poor social skills and appear to be phony in his approaches to adults, especially strangers. Depression interferes with both the experience and the expression of positive feelings toward other people. Depressed adults tend to make little eye contact, and this may also be characteristic of depressed children. The RADQ includes questions about preoccupation with suicide and death as well as about suicide attempts—all obviously associated with internalizing problems. The diagnosis of attachment disorders by attachment therapists may thus include many false positives as children who are depressed are treated as if they have attachment disturbances.

Externalizing Problems

As we noted earlier, externalizing affective disorders involve an unusual tendency to blame and want to punish others for one's experiences of displeasure. Like other aspects of emotional disturbance, externalizing behavior should be considered from a developmental viewpoint. Hitting a person when frustrated is not a sign of emotional disturbance in a toddler, although it could well be in an older child. We also have to consider externalizing behaviors situationally. There is a difference between a deliberate kick in the shin and the accidental collision typical of rough-and-tumble play. An intentional cross-check on the hockey rink may draw a penalty but was probably a rational decision and not a symptom of mental illness. Even in adulthood, physical violence may be a matter of choice, used in play, as a way of dealing with other adults, or as a child-rearing technique.

Adults often feel more concern with children's externalizing problems than they do with depression or anxiety. They are worried about what will happen if the children still hit, kick, and rage when they are bigger. Adults recognize the real dangers of uncontrolled physical violence and their own responsibility for teaching self-control to children. Highly publicized events of youth violence in recent years, despite their statistical infrequency, have triggered zero-tolerance policies in schools, which punish children for a pointed "bang-bang"-ing finger or for a nail file in the backpack. One of the appeals of attachment therapy to parents has probably been its focus on the need to prevent violent behavior.

Beginnings of Conduct Disorders

Most well-functioning parents do not interpret infant rages and tantrums as evidence of externalizing problems (nor should they). As a child enters the toddler stage and develops language and other skills, however, we would expect fewer situations to be met with all-out rage and for tantrum behavior to decrease gradually.

Preschool behavior problems may show us the first signs of a developing conduct disorder, an externalizing disorder in which anger and frustration are turned into attacks on other people (Constantino, 1992). A preschooler's unusual aggressiveness, cruelty to animals or younger children, or fire setting may be the first symptoms of conduct disorder. Later delinquent and criminal behavior is much more common among individuals who had such behavior problems in preschool than among those who did not.

Conduct disorders are more likely to be noticed and diagnosed after about age 6; they are estimated to occur in about 4–10% of schoolchildren, and four times as often in boys as in girls. When children's externalizing behavior becomes frequent or severe, it is classed as delinquent behavior. It has not become more frequent in recent years, despite frightening newspaper stories. Children under 10 do sometimes commit violent crimes such as homicide and forcible rape, but these events are rare. More often, schoolchildren are involved in property crimes such as arson and in nuisance crimes such as stealing and vandalism.

Delinquent Behavior

When an adolescent with an externalizing disorder does some kind of serious damage to people or property, this behavior is generally considered a type of juvenile crime or delinquency. More moderate externalizing behaviors may simply annoy parents and teachers, never coming to the attention of the law, and may or may not be so severe as to indicate serious mental illness. Externalizing behavior among teenagers can include reluctance to obey and escalation of aggressive verbal interchanges with adults.

Adults are easily frightened by adolescent externalizing behavior because the teenager is big and strong and actually capable of doing serious harm if he or she wants to. The mass media have made great dramas of the rare events where adolescents have killed in cold blood rather than in a fight or a car crash. AT Websites have encouraged such fears and refer frequently to events such as those at Columbine High School, claiming that these are increasing dramatically and that AT treatment is the only hope for prevention. (Of course, for the Evergreen attachment therapists, the geographical proximity of the Columbine killings was a great attention-getter.)

Two pervasive public concerns about adolescent externalizing behaviors involve the reported increase in deliberate killings and the involvement of girls in infanticide and in organized violence. We would do well to strive for a genuine understanding of these issues rather than to allow our emotions to be manipulated by media presentation of single cases and of numbers. As discussed in chapter 7, it is easy for people to be swayed by detailed descriptions of single events and to conclude that there are many such happenings. It is also easy for people to be convinced that a large percentage increase means a large increase in real numbers, but the actual numbers giving a certain percentage depend on the comparison being made. If only one girl commits a violent crime one year and two do the next year, there has been an increase of 100%, but this does not have the same significance as going from 10,000 crimes to 20,000 in one year.

In fact, there does not appear to have been an increase in the number of killings by teenagers. Although record-keeping methods have changed and it is difficult to make comparisons between the present and many decades in the past, it is clear that cold-blooded killings by adolescents occurred (though rarely) throughout the twentieth century. Infanticides by girls go back throughout the history of humanity and have probably not increased in frequency.

The RADQ and Externalizing Problems

Not surprisingly, the RADQ has a number of questions alluding to threats or actual violence. Such behaviors are interpreted as resulting from attachment issues rather than as part of an externalizing disorder.

Schizophrenia

The mental illnesses we have discussed so far have covered a range from the very mild to the dangerous. The most serious form of mental illness, psychosis, involves symptoms so severe that the psychotic individual is dangerous to himself or to others. It is quite rare for teenagers to show these severe disturbances, which do not ordinarily become full-blown until later in life. However, the major emotional disturbance called *schizophrenia* can begin with episodes in late adolescence or even earlier. Schizophrenia, we should note, is not the neurotic disorder sometimes called split or multiple personality, so beloved of the mass media. Schizophrenia is a psychosis that involves a lack of connection between the person's thoughts and emotions. In its most common forms, schizophrenia is shown in flattened or inappropriate emotional reactions. The schizophrenic individual may seem withdrawn and uninterested and be difficult to tell apart from a retarded person. In other forms, schizophrenia may involve auditory hallucinations or paranoid fears. A paranoid concern with imagined threats may trigger violent actions against people who are perceived as enemies, but this is by no means usual with schizophrenic adolescents.

In a case that received much attention in the late 1990s because of the family's prominence, Malcolm Shabazz, a grandson of Malcolm X, was diagnosed as schizophrenic at the age of 12. The boy had set a fire that caused the death of his grandmother, Dr. Betty Shabazz. Evidence brought in Family Court showed that Malcolm had, as a 2-year-old, attacked his mother and engaged in fights that left them both bleeding and as a 3-year-old had set his sneakers on fire during the night, had experienced hallucinations, and had an imaginary friend called Sinister Torch. He was bland and unemotional when talking to a psychiatrist after the fatal fire (Gross, 1997).

Schizophrenia and AT

We should note once again that this level of disturbance in early adolescence is extremely unusual. We should also note that Malcolm Shabazz had a number of characteristics that the attachment therapists would attribute to an attachment disorder and attempt to treat with attachment therapy. Such treatment could not be expected to be any more effective with a severely psychotic child than it appears to have been with less disturbed children.

WHAT CAUSES CHILDHOOD MENTAL ILLNESS?

If the authors of this book could explain where mental illness comes from, they would be extremely famous, if not necessarily rich. There are many unanswered questions about the causes of mental illness, but we are slowly developing a useful knowledge base that is helping us understand the nature of emotional disturbance. In this section, we discuss a number of the factors that contribute to difficulties in social and emotional development. It will be noted that we do not include among these some of the factors posited by attachment therapists, such as the unborn baby's assumed awareness of its mother's rejection.

The one principle the reader should keep in mind here is that the causes of mental illness are almost invariably *complex*. Two or more factors—sometimes many more—work together to produce the outcome for an individual. In addition, these factors function in the *transactional* way we mentioned earlier. The outcome results from a series of slow steps in which the child influences and is influenced by others. Even when there is a powerful genetic factor in emotional disturbance, transactional processes occur when the child's unusual characteristics cause unusual responses in adults, and those unusual responses in turn shape the child's development in ways that go farther and farther from a normal developmental trajectory. For example, adolescents with mild Tourette syndrome, a neurological disorder, have unusual tendencies to blink, purse their lips, sniff, hum, and clear their throats. Although these are minor behavior problems, the Tourette teenagers are also unusually likely to have conduct disorders, hyperactivity, or depression—perhaps as a result of the reactions they frequently get from other people (Mason et al., 1998).

Genetic Factors

The very serious emotional disturbances of childhood, such as autism and early-onset schizophrenia, probably have strong genetic or other biological components. This is also true of the various disturbances involving serious depression.

Beyond these specific genetic factors, however, there may also be biological characteristics that cause individuals to be more or less easily influenced by harmful experiences. Some children do remarkably well in environments where others have serious trouble. Biological factors are probably responsible for the *resilience* or *vulnerability* with which a child responds to a poor social environment. A child's physical health can also make a difference in her ability to thrive in less than ideal situations.

Trauma and Violence as Causes of Emotional Disturbance

Either specific traumas or the experience of persistent stress can cause disturbed feelings and behavior. Children living in impoverished inner city areas are especially likely to suffer repeated exposure to violence, injury, and death and to become hyperactive and hypervigilant as a result. Such experiences can have traumatic effects at any age, but younger children are even more likely to have serious effects on their development than older ones.

Domestic violence is unfortunately a major cause of emotional trauma in all social classes in the United States. Serious battles between parents are terrifying at both the emotional and physical level. It may be that to see one parent kill the other is the most traumatic experience a child can have.

Physical Abuse

Physical abuse of the child is also a source of emotional trauma, as the parent, normally the source of all safety and security, becomes simultaneously the cause of real pain and fear. There is much disagreement in the United States about the use of corporal punishment and the appropriateness of considering it to be a form of physical abuse. Because such large proportions of young children receive some form of corporal punishment, it is difficult to know whether practices such as spanking result in any level of emotional disturbance. However, it is clear that severe forms of physical punishment, such as beating with the buckle end of a belt or burning with cigarettes, are associated with later disturbed and violent behavior; this is also the case for physical punishment of adolescents.

Emotional Trauma

Emotional traumas such as sudden, long-term separation from familiar people may have a considerable impact on emotional development. Whether their effect is severe enough to be considered a mild form of mental illness depends on additional factors, such as the age of the child at the time of the separation and his or her later living circumstances. It is doubtful that such separation alone causes later violent behavior or other serious symptoms (Sharma, McGue, & Benson, 1998).

Can long-term emotional maltreatment be sufficient to cause trauma and create problems of emotional development? There is reason to think that this can be the case. Although one job of parents is to let their children know when they disapprove of behavior, a constantly negative emotional atmosphere can amount to psychological maltreatment. This can be defined as "a concerted attack by an adult on a child's development of self and social competence" (Garbarino, 1998, p. 3). It involves a pattern of behavior rather than an occasional negative response. Included in this pattern are some specific motives, communications, and actions.

The psychologically maltreating parent *rejects* the child by refusing to confirm the child's worth or to accept that the child's needs are legitimate ones. When a school-age child is frightened of a bully, for example, the psychologically maltreating parent may threaten punishment and force a confrontation with the feared person rather than offering comfort, protection, or help. Vicious teasing followed by criticism of the child's tears or rage ("ah, you big baby!") may be part of this pattern.

The psychologically maltreating parent *isolates* the child from normal social experiences and prevents the child from forming friendships. The child may be forbidden to speak to or play with particular other children without explanation or negotiation. The parent may model social isolation by not speaking to particular neighbors. Even brothers and sisters may become isolated from each other while living in the same household.

The psychologically maltreating parent may *ignore* the child and remain emotionally unavailable although physically present. This may not be simply a matter of evading conversations that the child tries to initiate but may also include refusing to speak to or look at the child.

The psychologically maltreating parent may *terrorize* the child, threatening and bullying with gestures such as a hand raised for a blow. The child may spend time hiding or planning how to escape if the threats turn into a physical attack. The atmosphere of constant anxiety may convince the child that everyone is as hostile as the parent and that there can never be any escape to a kind and nurturing social world.

Attachment Therapy as a Source of Emotional Trauma

Looking at AT practices, we see that many of the children in treatment have had physically and emotionally traumatic experiences in the past. What is more significant is that in the course of the treatment they continue to have them, because both attachment therapy and the associated therapeutic foster parenting include features of physical and emotional violence and pain. We would expect such treatment to re-traumatize children rather than to ameliorate the effects of earlier traumas.

Transactional and Relationship Factors in Childhood Mental Illness

From an early age, children are influenced by the past and present lives of their caregivers. The adult's mental health plays an important role here. Depression limits a parent's capacity for adequate nurturing (and, of course, schizophrenia and other psychoses make appropriate caregiving impossible). Infants are especially vulnerable to the lack of sensitivity and responsiveness characteristic of emotionally disturbed parents (Campbell, Cohn, & Myers, 1995; Zahn-Waxler et al., 1984).

Parents who are depressed or who habitually use drugs and alcohol are especially likely to be inconsistent, insensitive, and unresponsive in their dealings with their children. Caregivers who themselves experienced early loss of a parent or who were physically or sexually abused may respond to their infants in ways that are associated with unusual attachment-related behaviors in the Strange Situation (see chapter 9).

Maternal Depression

Although many young mothers experience depression, sadness, and irritability as they adapt to the first months of parenthood, the real impact of adult depression on children occurs when the mood is more serious and goes on for more than four months. It is a still more serious situation when depression in the caregiver is only one part of a bipolar emotional disorder, with swings from depressed mood to a manic, excited condition; toddlers with such mothers are more aggressive and cope less successfully with frustration.

Parents who are depressed or otherwise emotionally incapacitated may find it difficult to buffer the effects of life stresses on their child. They do not have the energy or motivation to help the child work out problems with friends or to explain and give comfort to a child faced with loss from death or divorce. It is not so much what these parents do as what they fail to do that is the problem for their children's development. The child psychologist David Elkind (1981) has pointed out the many sources of stress in children's lives and the physical and emotional impact when too many accumulate in a short time. Elkind also noted the modern problem of the "hurried child," who becomes a partner or confidante to a divorced parent, contributes to adult decision-making, and then at puberty is suddenly subjected to strict rules when the parent becomes aware that he is too independent. Neither the early independence nor the sudden surveillance offer the child the buffering needed for excellent development.

Family Circumstances

Single parenthood and adoption are often thought of as producing relationship problems that disturb the child's emotional development, but there is little reason to think that these are common causes of problems. Teenagers in single-parent families are actually less likely to use tobacco, alcohol, or drugs than those in two-parent families who have poor relationships with their fathers. Children who are adopted as infants have more problems than non-adoptees in areas such as school adjustment but actually show more mature prosocial behavior, have fewer social problems, and are less often socially withdrawn than non-adoptees—quite contrary to the predictions that would be made by proponents of attachment therapy. Children adopted after infancy are more likely to have emotional problems than infant adoptees, especially if they have been in many foster homes or have experienced neglect or abuse.

We do not have enough space in this book to go through all the possible ways in which relationships and transactional processes can influence children's emotional responses to the world. However, the examples in this section show the effect of children's experiences with their parents over periods of years, with the possibility of gradual distortion of emotional development. We may also note that in AT practice, treatment of the child exclusively, without child–parent therapy, is not likely to change a pattern of transactions that is strongly influenced by parental emotional characteristics, especially if the child is to continue living with that parent as primary caregiver. We can also repeat that the RADQ actually asks questions about the parents' feelings, thus making children of depressed or disturbed parents more likely to be evaluated as having attachment disorders. If these parents are not treated, their children will continue to be influenced by parental problems.

Cultural Factors

Living among the highly diverse subcultures of the United States, it is important for us to note that cultural differences can cause behaviors that might erroneously be interpreted as symptoms of emotional disturbance. For example, many African Americans do not make eye contact when listening but do so when speaking, and European Americans do the opposite; an African American child would thus be diagnosed by attachment therapists as lacking in the "appropriate" eye contact the therapists consider to indicate attachment. Similarly, many Spanish-speaking children, as well as young African Americans, have learned to regard direct eye contact as a challenge to authority that should be avoided when speaking to an adult. An African American child who is accused of doing something wrong will probably remain silent to convey that he is not guilty, while European American children say they did not "do it," considering silence to be an admission of guilt. The African American child would be told in

AT treatment not only to say he did wrong, but to shout it out. Failure to do so would be interpreted as resistance (Smiley & Goldstein, 1998).

In considering cultural factors behind symptoms that could mean mental illness, we need to note that parents of one group may actually teach children to do things that other groups disapprove of strongly. The level of aggressiveness considered desirable in a child varies greatly from one group to another, as does the degree of babyishness or dependency. Some groups would encourage toddlers and preschoolers to continue breastfeeding; others are horrified at the idea of an older child nursing. There have been many cases of immigrant parents being arrested for practices interpreted in the United States as sexual molestation, particularly the kissing or patting of a little boy's penis.

As a final idea about cultural differences, we can note that certain subcultures in the United States approve of criminal actions rather than disapprove. Parents from such groups are sometimes regarded as psychologically maltreating and corrupting their children; they train the child to pursue socially negative values and behaviors, to be destructive rather than constructive. The child becomes more and more skilled in undesirable behavior and is comfortable only with other "bad kids." He or she has little chance for change to a normal developmental trajectory, but the source of the problem is not mental illness in anything like the usual sense.

WHEN DO CHILDHOOD MENTAL ILLNESSES CAUSE SERIOUS ADULT PROBLEMS?

Unfortunately, many children who show symptoms of serious mental illness will grow to be adults with more or less serious emotional or behavioral problems. There are not nearly enough resources available to treat all the children in need, although some apparently effective treatments are available (see chapter 6). Most children will not grow out of it when "it" is a severe disturbance. (This is not, of course, at all the same as saying that every child with a sad life or a single traumatic experience grows into a severely disturbed adult.)

Are AT Advocates Right About How Serial Killers Are Created?

When AT advocates talk about how serial killers begin in childhood with disordered attachment, hatred, and cruelty, their ideas catch our attention and activate our fears. We know there are only a very few actual serial killers, but we read about or even meet adults who are hostile and aggressive, apparently longing for an excuse to hurt or kill.

We refer to these sometimes dangerous people as antisocial or having borderline personalities. When we look back at their childhood experiences, however, we do not see a single pattern of experiences that pushed the button to make them what they are. More usually, many risk factors worked together to create the outcome, and these may have included physical or sexual abuse. Efrain Bleiberg has suggested that these children, who do not necessarily share the same patterns of experience, do share something: a paradoxical, incongruous combination of "exquisite sensitivity and brutal lack of concern for others" (2002, p. 1). Bleiberg's description sounds much like the ways AT practitioners describe the children they diagnose: "One moment they can be engaging and appealing[;] the next moment, however, their capacity to manipulate others and their rage, demandingness, and self-destructiveness become overwhelming" (2002, p. 1). (We should note, of course, that no one described Candace Newmaker in this way, nor is Bleiberg's description congruent with the DSM standards for Reactive Attachment Disorder.) Bleiberg has speculated that such children have actually learned to inhibit an exceptional ability for empathy with others, an early talent that brought them discomfort in their particular living circumstances. He noted the extreme difficulty of working with such children, but described some treatment techniques—diametrically opposed to those of AT—that appeared helpful.

Are There Good Outcomes for Children with Serious Mental Disorders?

Occasionally a case gives us real hope when a child whose behavior was profoundly disturbed recovers and makes a life. One such case of resilience involved an English girl who at the age of 11 murdered a preschooler and two months later strangled another small child (Sereny, 1999).

In 1968, Mary Bell, who was living in poverty with her prostitute mother, killed a 4-year-old neighbor boy. She subsequently went to his family's house and asked to see him in his coffin. After her second killing, she was apprehended and sent to a reform school and later went to a maximum-security prison.

Mary was sexually molested while at the reform school. This was not her first experience of sexual abuse; her mother, whose specialty as a prostitute was the use of whips as part of sex acts, had used Mary as part of her services when the child was between 4 and 8 years old. She also tried to poison Mary and to give her away. After the murders, the mother took sexually suggestive photographs of Mary and sold information about her to the newspapers.

What could have happened to such a person? Surely this dreadful life, with its early, irrational violence, indicates a developmental trajectory that is hopelessly out of control. But, in fact, Mary Bell, now in her 40s, has been released from prison under an English law that protects the identity of criminals who might be attacked by the public. She has a teenage daughter and has made a life. When her identity was discovered by neighbors and she knew that her daughter would have to know about her, she agreed to work with an interviewer to create a book about her life. Mary Bell told the interviewer that she knows her guilt is permanent and that nothing can ever justify the killings or allay her sadness about them.

How did she turn from a vicious child killer, the very stuff of attachment therapists' stories, to a remorseful and responsible adult? Was it her punishment that caused the transformation? Or was it that even imprisonment and molestation gave her a more secure environment than her mother had done, and she took the opportunity for development that was offered to her? Did she learn new values when she was separated from her corrupting social environment? She does not know this herself, of course, and we do not know what transactional processes guided her personality to this outcome. But her story does give us hope for the resilience in even the most angry of children. It also makes us wonder what might have been the outcome for Candace Newmaker, who, when she was only a little younger than the murdering Mary Bell, died at the hands of people who were afraid she would kill.

CONCLUSION

Childhood mental illness occurs in different forms and requires different treatments than do adult emotional disturbances. The reasons for mental illness in people of all ages are complicated and not yet fully understood, but it is clear that childhood mental illness is understandable only in the context of normal developmental change. Individual personality traits and experiences such as maltreatment have powerful effects on a child's feelings and symptoms of emotional disturbance. Some mentally ill children do not recover in spite of extensive treatment, but others do change significantly as they move into adulthood.

The attachment therapy view of childhood mental illness is a remarkable oversimplification of the complexities of human emotional disturbance. This belief system dramatizes mental illness by exaggerating the frequency of cruel, violent behavior by the young. AT thinking implies that diagnosis is easily accomplished through the use of checklists, and that preventive treatment is needed in the absence of any clear symptoms. The attachment therapy viewpoint is seriously out of line with our understanding of childhood mental illness as systematic research has shown it to be.

REFERENCES

Bleiberg, E. (2002). How to help children at risk of developing a borderline or narcissistic personality disorder. *Brown University Child and Adolescent Behavior Letter, 18*(6), 1, 3–4.

Campbell, S., Cohn, J., & Myers, T. (1995). Depression in first-time mothers: Mother-infant interaction and depression chronicity. *Developmental Psychology, 31,* 349–357.

Cicchetti, D., & Toth, S. (1998). The development of depression in children and adolescents. *American Psychologist, 53*, 221–241.

Constantino, J. (1992). On the prevention of conduct disorder: A rationale for initiating preventive efforts in infancy. *Infants and Young Children, 5*(2), 29–41.

Diagnostic and Statistical Manual of Mental Disorders (4th ed.). (1994). Washington, DC: American Psychiatric Association.

Diagnostic Classification Task Force, Zero to Three/National Center for Clinical Infant Programs. (1994). *Diagnostic classification: 0–3*. Arlington, VA: National Center for Clinical Infant Programs.

Elkind, D. (1981). *The hurried child*. Reading, MA: Addison-Wesley.

Garbarino, J. (1998). Psychological maltreatment is not an ancillary issue. *Brown University Child and Adolescent Behavior Letter, 14* (8), 2–4.

Goldberg, C. (2001, July 9). Children trapped by mental illness. *New York Times*, pp. A1, A11.

Grandin, T. (1995) *Thinking in pictures*. New York: Doubleday.

Gross, J. (1997, July 30). Experts testify Shabazz boy is psychotic. *New York Times*, pp. B1, B6.

Herndon, L. (2001, July 4). Children served by mental hospital. *Philadelphia Inquirer*, p. D3.

Hetherington, E., Bridges, M., & Insabella, G. (1998). What matters? What does not? Five perspectives on the association between marital transitions and children's adjustment. *American Psychologist, 53*, 167–184.

James, B. (1994). *Handbook for treatment of attachment-trauma problems in children*. New York: Lexington.

Lerner, R., Palermo, M., Spiro, A., & Nesselroade, J. (1982). Assessing the dimensions of temperamental individuality across the life span. *Child Development, 53*, 149–159.

Mason, A., Banerjee, S., Eapen, V., Zeitlin, H., & Robertson, M. (1998). The prevalence of Tourette syndrome in a mainstream school population. *Developmental Medicine and Child Neurology, 40*, 292–296.

Randolph, E. (2000). *Randolph Attachment Disorder Questionnaire*. Evergreen, CO: The Attachment Center Press.

Sereny, G. (1999). *Cries unheard*. New York: Metropolitan/Holt.

Sharma, A., McGue, M., & Benson, P. (1998). The psychological adjustment of United States adoptive adolescents and their non-adopted siblings. *Child Development, 69*, 791–802.

Smiley, L., & Goldstein, P. (1998). *Language delays and disorders*. San Diego: Singular.

Zahn-Waxler, C., Cummings, E., Ianotti, R., & Radke-Yarrow, M. (1984). Young children of depressed parents. *Zero to Three, 4*(4), 7–12.

Chapter 6

Better Treatment for Candace: How Trained Psychotherapists Would Have Approached This Case

Gerard Costa

As with childhood mental illness, people are often surprised by the idea of child psychotherapy. Historically, clinical psychology had its start in child guidance clinics, but somehow this fact has been forgotten and replaced by images of reclining patients on couches, recounting their dreams to bearded therapists—not an accurate picture of modern treatment for either adults or children.

Perhaps the best approach to a discussion of child psychotherapy is a description of modern therapy as it applies to people of any age. Psychotherapy is a process in which a practitioner tries to guide a client to understand, think, and feel differently so the client will be able to live a more stable, emotionally comfortable, and constructive life. If the client seems to lack self-control or to make decisions that lead to trouble, these issues will be a major focus. If the client is unrealistically frightened or angry, the therapist will attempt to reduce these uncomfortable feelings or to make them seem less important. The process involves talking and the other communications we all use. This description of psychotherapy is most accurate for strongly cognitive therapies; more psychodynamic treatments spend more time in careful exploration of unconscious motivation and the emotions persisting from the client's past history. Generally, psychotherapy for children and adults attempts both to reduce the source of a person's conflicts and to enhance their strengths. In this way, the person's adaptation to life is improved.

Psychotherapy usually deals with mild or moderately severe disturbances of thinking and feeling. These may be long-term problems or may have been triggered by some recent events in the individual's life. Even problems with a biological component, such as ADHD, that are usually treated by medication are helped more when the medical treatment is supported by counseling. Severe mental illness (psychosis) generally calls for medication and possibly for residential treatment, but some psychotherapy may be a helpful supplement.

When psychotherapists work with mild problems or the "normal problems" common in everyday life, the goal is not to make the client's life somehow perfect but to prevent the development of later, more serious troubles. Expectable problems, such as mourning over the death of a family member, have the potential for causing further difficulty by interfering with necessary tasks or steps in development.

Psychotherapy often focuses on problems that have their roots in social relationships. Such an emphasis may be especially helpful when the difficulty has to do with the client's life situation, such as Jeane Newmaker's awareness that she had reached middle age without marrying and had to make some decisions if she wanted to become a mother.

Psychotherapy today tends to emphasize *communicative* more than *transformational* functions. Therapist and client discuss the issues at hand, consider possible solutions, and practice new ways of thinking about the world. They explore the reasons for the emotions the person is feeling and gradually connect past experiences with present affect. It is not generally expected that a sudden insight or recall of a memory will transform a person's life without further effort.

Cognitive and behavioral factors are the major focus of most psychotherapeutic techniques, particularly those that follow a cognitive-behavioral model of treatment. Therapists following this approach help clients learn more adaptive ways to think and behave. Although the experiencing and understanding of emotion are considered important, cognitive therapists assume that emotional distress is best relieved by changing the client's thoughts. Emotional change is expected to follow an alteration in thinking. For example, a person who is suffering from unrealistic jealousy may be helped to stop the constant repetition of thoughts about a spouse's hypothetical infidelity and will experience less painful emotions as a result. Similarly, a person who is helped to change behavior may get more happy reactions and fewer angry reactions from others and therefore will have a more pleasurable social life.

Psychodynamically oriented models take a different approach by examining the events in a person's life that contribute to his or her problems or symptoms. In this approach, difficulties in development or functioning are viewed as resulting in the formation of coping strategies or defenses that may be only partially adaptive. Affect, thoughts, and actions are understood as being influenced by unconscious motivation. For example, a child might have experienced intense parental rage and have begun to learn how to please Mommy so she is not as angry or dangerous. As this child develops, he or she may develop fear of authority and approach relationships with the expectation of fear and rejection and the wish to take care of others. This could be part of a person's character and not be consciously recognized as a problem. We refer to these as *syntonic* symptoms—those that we are so accustomed to and that are so much a part of our lives that we do not see them as problems.

CHILD PSYCHOTHERAPY

Modern child psychotherapy shares the characteristics just described, but of course there are some special features of treatment when the client is a child. Children are not just small adults. Their family lives are exceptionally important, because only under extreme circumstances can they "divorce" their families. Children also bring unique challenges to the cognitive and communicative aspects of therapy, because their ways of thinking are qualitatively different from those of adults. However, skilled clinicians can do valuable work even with quite young children.

Issues in Child Psychotherapy

We will shortly consider the ways in which psychotherapy with children is quite different from therapy with adults. Before we examine the distinctions, we review three issues central to clinical formulation and practice in child psychotherapy: *family systems*, the understanding of a child in the context of his close interpersonal relationships; *following the child's lead*, a feature of child treatment that is particularly essential for children under seven; and *developmentally appropriate practice*, therapeutic language and techniques that reflect the cognitive and affective development expectable of children at different ages.

Family Systems

In chapter 2 we brought up the idea of a *dynamic system* in which each member has an influence on each other member. We have also discussed the idea of a *transactional process*, in which people's mutual influences change gradually over time. Psychotherapists today stress both of these concepts, especially in work with children. The concern is not just with the ways parents affect children but also with the ways any child—even (or perhaps especially) a baby—influences parents. Because of this view, child psychotherapists often prefer to work with all family members rather than with the child alone.

Child psychotherapists often think of the child's role as a *transference object* (Fraiberg, Adelson, & Shapiro, 1980) for the parent—a being who can activate memories and feelings from both conscious and unconscious experiences in the parent's past. How a given child functions in this role is best seen by a therapist who observes real interactions among family members rather than relying on family reports. It is especially the case that any problems associated with attachment need to be approached by observing and dealing with child *and* parent. The parent-child relationship is viewed as the focus of child psychotherapy.

A second and more complex family-systems issue has to do with children's maturation and changing needs. Children are always changing, whether or not they are receiving psychotherapy. They do not simply stop developing and wait until a problem is solved. As children mature, they need their parents to change too. Normally, parents do respond to their children's development and begin to treat them differently, but some parents seem to get stuck with feelings and behavior that worked excellently in the past but are not constructive in the present. For example, noncustodial divorced parents often have trouble moving along with the child's maturation, and adoption of an older child could lead to similar difficulties. However, the changes in the child—and those needed in the parent—may be so subtle that a therapist will miss them unless he or she sees parent and child together.

Following the Child's Lead

Psychotherapy with adults may be quite directive, with the therapist clearly in charge, or may follow a nondirective approach shaped by the client's concerns. Child psychotherapy is generally quite nondirective. "Following the child's lead" is the byword of the foremost practitioners in this area, such as Stanley Greenspan (1990, 1992). Because many children, especially younger ones, have difficulty putting their difficulties into words, the therapist may follow their leads in play therapy by using dolls and accessories or in "floor time," where exchanges as small as a brief period of eye contact can be built on by letting the child control the type and extent of communication. Like language in adults, play in child treatment is viewed as the principal means of communication, and pretend play is often examined for themes and conflicts that reveal symbolically what a child cannot put into words.

Cognition and Developmentally Appropriate Practice

Even people who are very inexperienced with children would realize that communication in child psychotherapy cannot involve big words that a child does not know or references to knowledge that a child is not likely to have. However, we also need to remember that children have different ways of thinking than adults, as well as different knowledge and possibly different emotions. A therapist who takes these matters into account is using *developmentally appropriate practice* and is more likely to work successfully with children than one who does not.

Differences between Child and Adult Cognition

To understand the way child psychotherapy can work toward changes in a child's thinking, we need to consider how children's thinking is different from that of adults. A great deal of research has been done on children's developing cognitive abilities, but in this case we need to focus on the thinking patterns of children the age Candace Newmaker was during her adoptive life. We can probably assume that Candace's cognitive ability was in the normal range (her school performance shows us this). But we may also consider that she may have been a little delayed as compared to many children, both because of the emotional pressures of her life situation and because her birth family had not provided an ideal environment for gestural and later verbal language learning, important factors in cognition.

Concepts and Cause-and-Effect

At age 5 or 6, the point at which Candace was adopted by Jeane Newmaker, children are developing some new ways of thinking but have not thoroughly mastered them. When they use *concepts*—categories into which they can fit new information—children often forget or change the rules they use. Such a child might know she is supposed to avoid strangers but sometimes think strangers are just a certain kind of person and there may be unfamiliar people who are not classified as strangers. Having seen a man with a ponytail who was described as a stranger, for example, a child may for some time regard all men without ponytails as "not strangers." On another occasion, hearing an elderly woman called a stranger, the same child may think for a while that middle-aged men do not fit the "stranger" category. At this age, children begin to think about things that can fit into two categories at the same time (like a red circle or a blue square—an object can have both color and shape). However, children can still be confused by subcategories such as a birth mother, an adoptive mother, and a foster mother, who belong in part to the same category (mother) and in part to different categories (biological versus psychological parent).

A special cognitive problem for these kindergartners, first-graders, and second-graders is their tendency to engage in *transductive* reasoning, a peculiar form of logic in which children (and sometimes adults) link events and objects that are really not related. Transductive reasoning leads to difficulty understanding cause-and-effect relationships. For example, a child at this age may think that trees waving cause the wind to blow or, in Candace's case, that her own behavior had caused her to be taken from her birth family's home. This magical thought pattern, one that skips adult cause-and-effect concepts, may cause a child this age to be frightened by her own powerful emotions, which (to her mind) could cause the occurrence of events that exist only in fantasy.

Better Understanding of Others

By age 7 or 8, children get better at understanding categories, and they improve their ability to take the *perspective* of another person. They begin to improve their theory of mind—their idea of what another person might think or feel—and to realize that what people want can influence what they believe (Flavell, Miller, & Miller, 1993). They also begin to realize that private thoughts do not cause bad things to happen to others. These advances can be a great help to the child's progress in psychotherapy. For example, Candace's developing theory of mind could have helped her understand her birth mother's motives and actions if a skilled child psychotherapist had worked with her on this issue.

There are some limitations on the thinking abilities even of a 10-year-old, of course. Children in the school years can solve many problems and may know many facts, but they are not good at checking their own homework—or the logic of their thoughts. It is still very hard for them to think about what *might* be true or even about the hypothetical possibility that they could be wrong in their beliefs. Candace told an elaborate but not very likely story about having fallen from a high window as a baby; she was not yet cognitively mature enough to check her memory against what might really have happened. Such a memory, though it seemed real to Candace, might be symbolic in nature, representing a sense of being unprotected rather than a historical event.

PRINCIPLES AND PRACTICES OF CHILD PSYCHOTHERAPY

We have discussed some differences between adult and child psychotherapy, but there is one major idea that we need to emphasize. Important concepts of child psychotherapy today emerge from the intensive study of *infant* development more than from our ideas of adult functioning. Both historically and in the clinical treatment of children, our approach is based on the principles that govern infants' developing connections with their families. We can summarize some of these principles and then show how they apply to the emotional functioning of older children.

Principles of Infant-Parent Relationships and Treatment

Knowledge derived from work with infants and their families can inform clinical work with older children and adults. We describe six guiding principles regarding infant mental health and the nature of the parent-child relationship. Along with these principles, we describe a set of corollary principles that further inform psychotherapeutic thinking and practice with patients of all ages.

Guiding Principle 1

Infants are born with a remarkable capacity for human relatedness and are prepared from birth to develop relationships with others. A newborn's vision, hearing, smell, touch, taste, and movement are all exquisitely capable of reacting to and offering feedback to caregivers regarding the baby's physical and emotional states.

Guiding Principle 2

Most of what infants learn about human relatedness occurs in the first three years, a time of unusual biological readiness. Brain development in the first three years proceeds at an unparalleled rate, and connections made in the brain depend on the nature of the infant's experiences, particularly interpersonal relationships.

Guiding Principle 3

Pregnancy, birth, and the early years of a child's life are times of emotional change for the parent, in which his or her past and present experiences shape the relationship with a particular child. This relationship, rather than learned parenting skills, determines the parent's attitudes and actions.

Guiding Principle 4

Clinical work entails establishing helping relationships with families in need. Psychotherapists have their own emotional histories that influence work with families—especially those families whose infants and children are hurt or are not adequately cared for. The relationships of clinical work need to be supported by ongoing regular supervision and case review.

Guiding Principle 5

The family home is the setting in which we can best understand how parents and children relate to each other. Home visits offer clinicians remarkable opportunities to understand and help families in need.

Guiding Principle 6

The infant-parent relationship emerges within a unique set of cultural and economic factors that provide a historical and practical context to the family and the intervention. Parental care, expressions of emotion, use of health care, and therapeutic relationships are profoundly influenced by the culture and the economic resources of the family.

Six Corollary Principles in Child Mental Health

Throughout childhood and later development, our emotional and behavioral health can be understood according to principles similar to those just summarized. In addition to the core principles derived from the field of infant mental health, we now describe six corollary principles that inform our clinical understanding and treatment of children of all ages. The previous six principles provided general insights regarding early development and therapeutic support;

the next principles deal with aspects of the child's present development and psychological functioning that the treating therapist must consider. The following set of principles is not exhaustive, but it includes many of the factors that organize our psychological and social functioning and determine the therapist's approach to treatment.

Principle 1: Preoccupation

A child who is preoccupied with his or her internal life is less available to invest the external world with interest and attention. Children who lack consistent, caring, loving, attuned, available, responsive attachment figures often become preoccupied with basic feelings of mistrust and insecurity.

Principle 2: Communication and Language

Communication and language are not just intellectual but emerge from emotional relationships, especially from the parent-child relationship. Early disruptions in relatedness are often manifested by delays in language, play, and other symbolic expressions. All adults who form relationships with children help influence their development. When early attachment disruptions occur, the gestural and preverbal origins of language may be compromised (for example, reading of facial expressions for social situations or difficulty in reciprocal emotion or communication). The use of language to express internal emotional issues can be adversely affected.

Principle 3: Expression of Feeling versus Acting Out

When the child is able to express thoughts, emotions, problems, or conflicts in symbolic ways such as play, gestures, and language, there is less acting out in the form of undesirable behavior. Children need opportunities to have caring adults who can "feel with" them (Furman, 1992), respond to their inner conflicts, and help them express difficulties through language and play.

Principle 4: Parents Have to Develop Too

As children develop through infancy, the preschool years, and middle and later childhood, they require "different kinds" of parents to interact with. Thus therapists always need to work with parents to explore their understanding of their child's changing needs and to support their capacity to change to meet those needs.

Principle 5: Many Effects of Early Disruptions

Early disruptions in attachments, early family instability, trauma, and deprivation have effects that often continue to manifest themselves as problems throughout life. The later symptoms may take the form of a wide variety of childhood problems, such as emotional, activity, and arousal regulation difficulties; oppositionality; and internalizing and externalizing disorders.

Principle 6: All Development Is Affected by Early Relationship Problems

When early relationships are unhealthy, all areas of development can be affected and children may show delays in developmental progress. This may be seen in learning and memory problems, information processing and retrieval difficulties, and other skill deficiencies.

Candace's Case: How Could These Principles Have Been Applied?

Considering these principles, we can now discuss ways in which the social service, child protective service, and mental health systems might have done things differently with Candace and both her birth and her adoptive families. The aphorism that hindsight is always 20–20 is appropriate here, and we are in a better position than people who worked with the families to judiciously evaluate the best practices for Candace and the large number of children like her. It is not our intention to vilify her therapists, her adoptive mother, or the systems in North Carolina and Colorado that were responsible for Candace's care. We must, however, recognize that events have now come to light that occurred in private, closed settings but that reveal both professional practice and systemic failures that can teach valuable lessons. Knowing the tragic outcome of that case, we can review the unfolding events, as the people involved could not, and envision different decisions and a different culmination.

Ways of Helping

In considering the kinds of help needed by families in trouble, we can discuss a wide range of helping strategies. We will prepare for our discussion of alternative approaches to Candace's case by reviewing five major categories of help. These categories are derived from work on infant mental health (such as ideas discussed by Fraiberg, 1980; Weatherston & Tableman, 1989; Lieberman & Pawl, 1993), but they are strategies for mental health interventions along the whole developmental spectrum through childhood and adolescence.

Building an alliance is the process of engaging a family's involvement in treatment through consistent, reliable, predictable, genuine care. This may include home visits, telephone contact, reflective listening, nonjudgmental acceptance, emotional support, and other services.

Concrete services address the everyday needs of the family (food, child care, shelter, clothing, health care, transportation). Part of this is accomplished through systems advocacy: working with collateral agencies that provide services such as housing to educate them about the needs of children and to advocate that those needs be adequately addressed.

Developmental/parental guidance is a helping strategy that provides information in a nondidactic way, sharing information and ideas about children's developmental changes, needs, and behavior. This may involve use of anticipatory guidance, observation, and reflection, modeling, and providing materials such as toys.

Supportive counseling involves observing and empathically sharing what happens in the family, identifying and supporting feelings, and providing support and encouragement. The supportive counselor also models problem-solving strategies, provides honest and empathic impressions, and helps with links to other support services.

Dyadic (parent-child) psychotherapy is an approach that comes out of work with infants and their parents, but it can also be applied with older children. This is a specialized intervention with the primary purpose of helping the parent develop insight and a deeper understanding of experiences and emotions. There is a focus on past experiences that may be interfering with the formation of a healthy relationship with the child. In this strategy the relationship between child and parent is seen as the client, and a psychotherapist attempting this approach must understand fundamental notions of psychological development, including unconscious motivation, transference, defenses, and coping strategies.

Child Mental Health Issues in Candace's Situation

We have examined principles that can inform our understanding and treatment of child psychotherapy cases and have described some helping strategies. In the next section, we review Candace's treatment and identify specific factors that led the course of treatment awry. These factors, including beliefs and systemic forces, resulted in the failure of the treating clinician to attend to essential aspects of Candace's difficulties and culminated in tragic commissions and omissions.

Saving the Child

Candace's case seems to have included a feature that is very common when children are placed in foster care. As often happens, the child protective system reacted principally to child welfare and child safety concerns, with a priority on saving the child that did not necessarily look at the needs of the parent or of the parent-child relationship. Contact with the birth mother was sporadic, and there was probably little contact with the grandparents. Such disruptions in contacts with familiar attachment figures are experienced by children as painful and erosive of trust and security. As we noted earlier, children soon become preoccupied with uncertainty about the reliability of others in their world when these circumstances occur.

Pressure of Permanency Planning

Careful administration of concrete services and dyadic psychotherapy did not occur in Candace's case, not because of decisions of mental health professionals but because of systemic considerations. One of the unfortunate consequences of well-intended *permanency planning* laws, which usually establish a one-year limit for children in foster care placement, is that child protective agencies make decisions against the background of a ticking clock. Time pressure may not allow the use of supportive strategies even if they are available. Protective services move quickly toward permanent out-of-home placement when psychotherapy is not quickly available, if support services such as transportation are lacking, or if families are not easily engaged (and we can suppose that Angela Elmore, Candace's birth mother, did not fit the profile of an easily engaged client). Although it is true that children cannot wait for parents to get better, the system needed to balance the pain of separation against the benefits of placement and to allow for more individualized decision-making that could have allowed Candace's family to be reunified.

Parent-Child Factors

We discussed earlier that the relationship between parent and child is the client in dyadic psychotherapy. Even when dyadic psychotherapy does not occur, we would expect at the very least that every family member would be considered part of the problem when a family seems to function poorly. Yet, in Candace's case, there seem to have been no questions raised about the mental health of her adoptive mother, Jeane Newmaker.

It must be emphasized that parenthood through adoption is as powerful as birth parenthood in activating psychological material within the mother. For every parent, the child can serve as a significant *transference object,* and in every case we must wonder who *this* baby is and what he or she means in the mind of *this* mother. Jeane Newmaker wished to be a parent, and what that wish meant to her was based on her own history, as was her emotional reaction when she began to parent Candace.

From accounts of Candace's behavior before and after her adoption, and given her early history, we can understand that she may have been difficult to parent at times. Her experience of inadequate care and disruptions, with consequent emotional and behavioral difficulties, was likely to have made her sometimes oppositional, distractible, "hyperactive," and so on. Disordered relationships such as Candace experienced can produce regulatory disorders too, so that she may have had difficulties in handling her own levels of emotional excitement, arousal, and attention and may have had problems with self-calming. There seems to be little evidence that Jeane Newmaker was provided with information about these possible problems or guidance on how to deal with them.

Planning Treatment

Ideally, Candace should have received multidisciplinary evaluations that would have helped her adoptive mother work with her and would also have assisted in planning for psychotherapy and other appropriate treatments. The fact that these steps were omitted represents a serious breach of professional conduct and ethics. What appears to have occurred, instead, was a premature closure of diagnostic reasoning. The therapists involved sought to confirm the belief that Candace had a psychologically based attachment disorder, that she alone owned the problem, and that medication and the AT ritual would repair what was wrong.

WHAT DID JEANE NEWMAKER BRING TO THE RELATIONSHIP?

Every family member has a unique combination of strengths and weaknesses, and Jeane Newmaker, of course, was no exception. We need to examine what we know of her, as well as what we know of Candace, to understand the parent-child factors we mentioned earlier. The tragic nature of this story means we will look more closely at Jeane Newmaker's weaknesses than at her strengths, but we do not mean to imply that she was without positive qualities. As is the case for many of us, some of her characteristics were both strengths and weaknesses—her persistence in her professional advancement and the work she went through to adopt Candace were also reflected in her commitment to the AT treatment that killed her child.

We will discuss three issues that Jeane Newmaker seems to have brought to her relationship with Candace. Two of these involve common problems of adjustment. The third indicates a degree of pathology and would have made the first two problems much more difficult to work with.

An Adult Child of an Alcoholic Family

Jeane Newmaker's father's alcoholism was described in chapter 2. We know that Jeane sought treatment for depression following her parents' deaths, but we have little more specific information about her relationships with them. Like all families, alcoholic or otherwise, the Newmakers were unique, and Jeane's reaction to the parents' influences was also unique. Nevertheless, we can look at some of the growing body of information on adults who were children of alcoholics and see some characteristics Jeane shared with that group.

One of Jeane's characteristics that was consistent with those of adult children of alcoholics was the tendency to love people who can be pitied and rescued, such as abandoned children. This was accompanied by an overdeveloped sense of responsibility. Like other individuals whose parents were alcoholics, Jeane tended to be most concerned about other people and their faults and to have a diminished ability to examine faults in herself.

Several studies of adult children of alcoholics report higher levels of depression, anxiety, generalized stress, and low self-esteem, stemming from the absence of a calm, empathic parental relationship in earlier life. We can imagine that Jeane may have thought she could heal herself through her child, creating in her relationship with Candace much of what was missing in her own life. She behaved as if she wished to rescue Candace from abandonment and to create the perfect emotional attachment, but Jeane's own need for this achievement emerges as the critical feature of her history with Candace, even more than Candace's developmentally appropriate need for a family.

Depression: Vanishing Chances of Parenthood

For Jeane Newmaker, as for most women, success in life was partly dependent on the creation of a family of her own. Her professional success alone could not counterbalance the sense of loss associated with her continuing single, childless life. To be a mother may have seemed to her like the final step in achieving solid adulthood. As a child of a dysfunctional family, she may have fantasized a perfect family that she would create to make herself happy and wipe out the childhood memories of anger and alcoholism.

Physical infertility can cause sadness and depression that last for years. Even after a child is adopted or conceived through assisted reproductive technology, the sadness and sense of loss may persist (Shapiro, Shapiro, & Paret, 2001). In Jeane Newmaker's case, we may need to draw a parallel between physical infertility and "social infertility"—the failure to establish a social relationship in which pregnancy and motherhood are possible. We do not know what love relationships Jeane had in her past, but she was by her late 30s clearly looking for alternatives to parenthood via marriage. Giving up the idea of a timely marriage would involve a sense of loss, of a door closing; anticipating menopause and the real end of fertility would give a similar feeling. Even beyond these specifics, the sense that some part of her life would remain unlived would possibly trigger thoughts of barrenness, waste, and even death. Our parallel between physical and social infertility suggests that these feelings would persist even after the adoption, creating sadness and depression that would interfere in Jeane's establishment of a genuine relationship with Candace. We may suggest that a serious problem for the Newmaker household was that Jeane could not overcome her depression to love Candace, whether or not Candace was able to love her adoptive mother.

The Possibility of Narcissism

The two emotional problems we have discussed, an alcoholic family background and fertility issues, are common enough. Most individuals manage to deal with such problems with or without therapy and to adjust to a considerable extent. However, it seems possible that Jeane Newmaker's adjustment was much complicated by a *narcissistic* personality structure.

In referring to the possibility of narcissism, we are considering an element of more serious character pathology. According to the *Diagnostic and Statistical Manual* of the American Psychiatric Association (DSM-IV), Narcissistic Personality Disorder (NPD) involves a pervasive pattern of grandiosity, a need for admiration, and a lack of empathy. Narcissistic persons presume they are superior and behave in self-aggrandizing ways (Beck & Freeman, 1990). They are easily offended and withdraw when they feel slighted. They need to be admired, and their purpose in relationships is to provide themselves with confirmation of their special qualities; a partner, adult or child, who does not do this is a target of rage and contempt. Their stress is on appearances rather than the emotional reality of relationships. Of course, such an adult character is likely to have emerged from early failures to have her own empathic needs met.

As Jeane's explanations for her behavior and the events that led to Candace's death are examined, what seems to emerge is a profoundly narcissistic character. Jeane appears to have lacked a capacity for empathy for Candace. She was preoccupied instead with her own neediness as a mother and her own wish to have the child regard her as a mother (reflected in the unusual change of Candace's middle name to Jeane's own). This preoccupation caused her failure to recognize the deadly crisis the child was facing. We also know that Jeane followed rather blindly and compliantly the recommendations of the AT practitioners, accepting readily their conclusion that Candace, not Jeane, was at fault. This perspective would have been gratifying to her narcissism.

Another point supporting the idea of narcissism was Jeane's behavior with respect to Candace's brother's and sister's adoption disruption following a serious physical attack of one on the other. Jeane, amazingly, shared this information with Candace in apparent complete disregard for the emotional impact it was bound to have. Her motivation in this situation is not clear, although it may have been to communicate to Candace the possibility of abandonment and to do this in a way that would appear innocent to Jeane herself. Although it is disturbing that such information was shared with Jeane (an action that was actually contrary to North Carolina law), the truly disturbing thing is that she passed it on to an 8-year-old. Again, in line with the possibility of narcissism, we saw that Jeane took Candace traveling for the summer as soon as the child came to her; this presented an appearance of a happy family but was completely without empathy for Candace's need to adjust to her new life and have it become familiar and routine, especially before starting school.

A narcissistic personality structure, with its unrealistically high expectations and easy vulnerability to rejection, would have magnified enormously Jeane Newmaker's perception of Candace's "faults." A distressed 6-year-old's temper tantrums could easily be read as rejection of the adoptive mother. Even the most affectionate school-age child is not likely to act admiring or to make a great point of caring for a parent, as Jeane may have expected and needed her to do. No doubt Candace did sometimes tell Jeane she hated her—many quite normal children do make this announcement in moments of conflict. Emotionally healthy parents can tolerate this flash of hostility, but a narcissist could react with extreme distress. In one of the Colorado sessions, Candace was asked why she was there and replied that it was because she said "no" to her mother. Such an ordinary event of family life might have clashed unbearably with narcissistic fantasies and expectations. And, of course, if Candace had expressed longing for her birth family or had not seemed to hate her birth mother sufficiently, this would have been interpreted by a narcissist as complete and unbearable rejection.

WHAT WERE CANDACE'S PROBLEMS?

We should now have a look at the other side of the parent-child factors involved in this case. Looking at school reports about Candace Newmaker, we seem to see that she had normal problems, mainly connected with paying attention in school and being willing to do her homework. At home, she seems to have had some sleep disturbances, some nightmares, and some tantrums and resistance to doing what she was told, problems that can be understood as related to preoccupying thoughts and feelings and to difficulties in self-regulation. We do not know what she was really thinking or feeling about any of this, but perhaps we could understand a bit more by considering other children who have experienced losses.

Certainly, it would be useful to our speculation about Candace's view of her life if we could know more about other children who were adopted after infancy. But most of the research in this area is focused on outcome measures—how the children do in later life, how many serious problems develop, and so on. An alternative for us may be to look at a much-researched topic that is comparable in some ways: the experiences of children following divorce.

Is Adoption Like Divorce?

Divorce is now so common that it seems normal, if still undesirable, and it may seem odd to compare it to the much rarer experience of adoption. For the older child, however, the two experiences may have something in common. Both are often preceded by months or years of family dysfunction, even by domestic violence. Both occur without reference to the child's wishes. They involve separation from one or more familiar people, and divorce as well as adoption may lead to a change of home, school, neighborhood, friends, resources, and habits. The distress and depression of a custodial divorced parent may make her (usually) behave in unaccustomed ways toward the child. In both divorce and adoption, the child's and parent's recoveries are gradual processes, and the steps the child can take are linked to his or her developmental stage. The parallels between adoption and divorce seem clear enough for us to use information about adjustment to divorce and see how it applies to Candace's experience of adjustment to adoption.

According to one way of thinking about divorce (Wallerstein, 1983), school-age children can go through several steps of recovery from the crisis but are not mature enough to complete the process until they are adolescents. If we are right in making the parallel between divorce and adoption, this would suggest that Candace could not have finished adjusting to adoption before she died. However, we can examine some steps she may have taken, basing our speculation on the description Wallerstein has given of events following divorce.

Accepting the Reality

The first task of adjustment to divorce that children have to perform is simply accepting the fact that the event is real. This may be especially difficult if there have been earlier trial separations or if one parent insists that there will be a reconciliation. Candace, too, had the task of accepting the reality of termination of her parents' rights and her adoptive placement with Jeane Newmaker. This may have been more difficult for her because she had been in foster care on several occasions and because her birth mother had apparently assured Candace that they would be reunited.

Resolving the Loss

A second task for the child of divorce is resolution of the loss, giving up the wish for the lost family and looking toward the future rather than longing for the past. Candace, like other late-adopted children, needed to do this too. In Candace's case, this process would have been slowed by the fact that Jeane Newmaker, at least once, told her of her brother's and sister's troubles in their adoptive family. The threats of abandonment that were part of AT would also have interfered with this task.

Giving Up Anger

Finally, the child of divorce needs to give up anger and self-blame and to accept the fact that he or she did not cause the divorce and has no control over what has happened. The late-adopted child may have a similar task to do, which might have made Candace especially vulnerable to the aspersions and criticisms heaped on her during AT sessions (for example, that everyone was miserable when they were around her).

Realistic Hope

Not until adolescence do children of divorce seem to be able to come to some realistic hope that in the future they will enjoy stable, gratifying relationships with others. It seems doubtful that Candace could have achieved such hope for a trustworthy family by the time she died, both because of her experiences and because of the maturational changes that seem necessary for this step.

The Role of Psychotherapy

The tasks and problems faced by children of divorce are normal problems compounded by the children's cognitive immaturity. Work with a psychotherapist can help the child make advances in some of these tasks; an example would be helping the child feel less self-blame. In the same way, appropriate treatment could have helped Candace—and her adoptive mother too—resolve their very predictable concerns and confusion about her adoption.

RECOMMENDED THERAPEUTIC INTERVENTIONS

In considering various approaches to *infant-parent psychotherapy*, Stern (1995) discussed the notion of a port of entry into clinical work with families. By "port of entry," Stern meant the clinical focus, or the approach with which the clinician enters the system. We think the port-of-entry idea is also useful in looking at older children, and we will consider three examples of approaches a therapist can take.

Ports of Entry for Child Psychotherapy

Some approaches to child-parent psychotherapy address directly the parent's inner life and representations of the child, including beliefs about the child, distortions of who the child is, and projections of the parent's own feelings onto the child. The infant mental health model developed by Fraiberg and her colleagues (Fraiberg, Adelson, & Shapiro, 1980; Lieberman & Pawl, 1993) is an example of this approach that involves home-based work, with the presence of the infant considered essential. The goal of the work is to free the parent's view of the infant or child from these distortions by helping the parent develop insight into the background of the parent's own beliefs. This approach seeks to exorcise the "ghosts in the nursery" from the parent's past; these are emotional memories that prevent the parent from seeing the child as he or she really is.

A second approach attends to the behavior of the child as the port of entry. An example of this approach is the work of T. Berry Brazelton and his colleagues (Brazelton, 1992), in which observation, assessment, and anticipatory guidance help parents better understand and interpret their child's behavior. Their implicit (and often unidentified) assumptions and beliefs about the child are challenged and altered through this technique.

A third approach, exemplified by the interaction guidance process of Susan McDonough (1995), chooses as a port of entry the parent-child interaction, particularly the parent's behavior. In this technique, videotapes are made of parent-child interactions and are reviewed with the parents, with the purpose of building on positive moments through discussion and elaboration.

We can understand that regardless of the port of entry—the parent's thinking, the child's behavior, or the parent's behavior—work of this type changes the entire system. When only behavior is discussed, shifts nevertheless occur in parental thinking about the child and about the parent's self.

Looking at Candace's Case: Treatment Ideas

Two points about intervention for Candace clearly emerge from our discussion. First, we suggest that early *infant-parent psychotherapy* with Candace and her birth family could have strengthened their growing attachment despite the evidence we have of parental and familial inadequacy. The resulting improvement would have reduced risk factors for Candace and the other children and would perhaps have prevented the tragic course of events.

Second, it is clear that both Candace's birth and adoptive *mothers* should have been incorporated into the treatment at the initial stages and throughout the work. Regardless of the differing ports of entry, all the approaches we have discussed involve direct therapy, developmental/parental guidance, and supportive counseling, and all involve the promotion of healthier *relationships* as a goal, not the remediation of the child's problems alone.

We can now consider specific therapeutic interventions that are appropriate for children with disorders of attachment and for their families. These can be used in combination with each other to produce a best-fit plan for a given child and family.

Home-based Services

Increasingly, models of home-based support such as those suggested by Olds and his colleagues (Olds et. al, 1997) are being developed, with services delivered by a range of professional and paraprofessional staff, including public health nurses, child protective agency staff, and educators. We do not know whether those who worked with Candace's birth or adoptive family were able to identify such resources in their area (although this seems unlikely, because North Carolina social services agencies are claiming their shortage of funds is so severe they cannot comply with the recent Federal Register guidelines on restraint and seclusion of children in psychiatric facilities). The account we have of Candace's life suggests that the focus of her treatment involved out-of-home services, including placement in foster care, adoption, and ultimately the intensive AT treatment program that required an extended stay in Colorado. Home-based services would have been beneficial for Candace, either in the context of her birth family or with Jeane Newmaker.

Birth Mother-Foster-Adoptive Mother Inclusion

North Carolina law recommends that even in adoption cases, efforts should be made to maintain contact between the child and the birth family. By all accounts, Candace mourned the loss of her mother and probably of her brother, sister, and grandparents, but there is no indication that efforts were made to promote contact with them. (Tragically, Angela Elmore was not even informed of Candace's death until five months after it occurred.) Therapeutic work must consider all such important relationships in a child's life. Unless it is contraindicated by circumstances (a parent in prison, a parent with severe mental illness, a dangerous parent, or an active drug abuser), efforts to provide contact, communication, and visitation between a birth and a foster/adoptive family are much needed. The experiences the child has in visiting help minimize the feelings of rejection and abandonment that would otherwise preoccupy the child, especially if parental guidance and psychotherapy incorporate the experiences into their work. When clinical intervention systems ignore or actively exclude contact between birth and foster or adoptive families, children may not fully understand the nature of the loss or their own fantasies about blame and responsibility.

The author of this chapter treated a mother and her children for three years, during which time both children were placed in a foster home 15 miles from the birth mother's residence. For nearly two years, the foster mother brought both children for weekly family sessions that included time with and time without the foster mother's presence. Through very difficult and painful sessions, both birth and foster mothers developed a relationship with one another, and when the children were reunited with their birth mother, a transition plan was developed that eased the painful separation the children had in leaving the foster family. Subsequently, the birth mother allowed visits and overnight stays with the foster mother and even expressed the wish that if she should become ill (the birth mother was HIV positive) the now-former foster mother would assume custody of the children. It is clear that such approaches require effort on the part of everyone, birth parent, foster parent, children, and therapist alike. But the alternative is that when treatment approaches attend principally to the notion that children need to be placed and cared for and that their relationships do not need care, children with disruptions in attachment will continue to have unresolved issues, especially if their treatments take an inappropriate approach to the importance of their original attachments.

The need for children to maintain contact with the birth mother is intuitively obvious to most of us, but less obvious is the need for a foster or adoptive child to have regular contact with siblings. Although most child protective systems recommend such contact on paper and also recommend that siblings be placed together, such instances have been extremely rare in my clinical work. On the contrary, most foster and adoptive children continue to wonder about and mourn the loss of their siblings. It is clear that transportation and logistical arrangements to promote contact and visits among siblings are demanding, but we should not ask children to bear the burden of such logistical difficulties, especially the continued preoccupation with their unresolved concerns.

Family Psychotherapy

In family psychotherapy, the family is the patient and treatment involves all members, even when only one has served as the identified patient who is the reason for the therapeutic involvement. Whereas there are a number of theoretical frameworks that guide family therapists, most consider the family a system of individuals in dynamic interaction. Their work involves helping family members reduce conflicts by identifying ways to enhance communication, confirm each member's value, and satisfy the needs of each. Parent-child psychotherapy is one variant of family psychotherapy. The goals are similar: the developmental needs of the child are interpreted and conflicts are examined so parents can better provide appropriate direction, limit-setting, and freedom. Chazan (1995) has described a version of parent-child treatment known as simultaneous parent-child psychotherapy in which the same therapist might treat both parent and child individually as well as together. Such work requires strict attention to the formation of clinical confidence in each member, as well as awareness of the ways in which there may be a competition between the parent-therapist alliance and the child-therapist alliance.

Child/Play Psychotherapy

Perhaps the best-known approach to children's behavioral and emotional problems is child/play psychotherapy. In this technique, although language is used as suits the developmental and emotional capacities of the child, the principal medium of communication is play, using dolls, art materials, drama, and pretend activities. The play therapist often observes and monitors themes of the child's play. The therapist offers ways to help the child verbalize these themes and their associated feelings, fears, and conflicts and offers guidance to family members accordingly.

Brodzinsky (1993) proposed a Stress and Coping Model of Children's Adoption Adjustment and noted that when children view adoption as "stigmatizing, threatening, or as involving loss, a pattern of negative emotions associated with stress—for example confusion, anxiety, sadness, embarrassment, anger—is likely to be experienced" (p. 160). Such issues would likely be explored both in child/play psychotherapy and in conjoint sessions with the adoptive family.

It is important to note that in Candace's case, with lack of contact with her birth family and with the AT treatment regimen including harsh, painful treatment and pathologizing diagnostics, she probably experienced her adoption as negative. What ensued were precisely the kinds of symptoms we described earlier—negative feelings, regarded by Jeane Newmaker as evidence of lack of attachment.

Additionally, much of the work of the AT practitioners was directed at promoting Candace's anger and hatred for her birth mother as a means of creating love for her adoptive mother. This view assumed that love for one person leaves less love for another—a horrific zero-sum concept of attachment that defies reason and is contrary to the ideas of every legitimate attachment theorist. In the circumstances shaped by AT, adoption must have felt extremely painful to Candace, yet the AT approach disallowed any empathy for her pain, instead defining her difficult behavior as resistant and manipulative. Whatever was going on with Candace, we could expect AT treatment only to make it worse and for her to develop iatrogenic problems—difficulties caused rather than cured by the treatment she received.

Individual Psychotherapy for the Adoptive Mother

If we are correct in considering Jeane Newmaker as a narcissistic personality, providing therapy for her might have been quite difficult. Such individuals tend to avoid entering therapy because they feel it defines them as inferior, an unacceptable experience for them. She had gone into therapy previously because of depression after the deaths of family members, and this is one of the situations that seems to make psychotherapy possible for the narcissist (Beck & Freeman, 1990). Otherwise, they are likely to enter treatment only after a crisis that unavoidably demonstrates the differences between narcissistic expectations of the world and reality. (We do not know whether she entered treatment following Candace's death, but a crisis of that kind would be needed for her to do so.) A therapist must be patient, tactful, clear, and firm with narcissistic clients and must model for them what it means to accept one's own human imperfections. Much work in this area would have been necessary before other issues, such as her alcoholic family background, could be addressed.

Treatment of Severe Childhood Problems

What if Candace had symptoms we do not know about? We have discussed some problems that Candace is likely to have had, as well as some treatment approaches and services that would have helped her. We have assumed, on the basis of the information we have, that her problems were moderate and treatable. But what if, unknown to us, she actually did have the vicious hostility and

homicidal rage that AT practitioners claim to result from disruptions of attachment? Could psychotherapy have been of any benefit to her?

The basic therapeutic approaches for profoundly disturbed children are basically the same as the ones we have discussed. The involvement of their parents
in the treatment is, if anything, even more important than when the disturbances are mild ones. Bleiberg (2002) has provided some useful ideas for approaching certain severe emotional problems of children and adolescents. He
pointed out that we can consider the developmental trajectory by which a child
becomes an adult with a dramatic antisocial personality disorder, and we can
consider how to intervene to change that pathway of development to one with
a more positive outcome.

Children start down a negative pathway of development for a variety of reasons, but in Bleiberg's opinion they "share a striking incongruity—an uncanny
sensitivity and reactivity." They react dramatically to other people's mental
states, and this reactiveness "paradoxically [coexists] with remarkable self-
centeredness and utter disregard for other people's feelings" (2002, p. 1). Bleiberg described such children as combining "exquisite sensitivity and brutal
disregard for others" (2002, p. 1).

The group of children under consideration may have had no worse experiences in early life than many other children who function much better. But
somehow these children have stopped using their capacity for *mentalization*—
the term Bleiberg applies to "the capacity to interpret and respond to human behavior ... in human, meaningful terms ... to 'read other people's minds' and
grasp the mental states underlying human behavior" (p. 3). Mentalization, or
theory of mind as we have called it elsewhere in this book, is a capacity that develops a great deal in the first five or six years of life. When this ability is used,
it enables a person to achieve a number of important interpersonal skills, such as
a sense of being in charge of one's own behavior, a capacity for empathy, the ability to tolerate frustration, and the ability to use symbols as we do in language.
Bleiberg did not suggest that mentalization fails to develop in antisocial children, but that they develop a strategy of inhibiting it—deliberately not using
it—because they are people who are especially responsive to other's feelings.
They are easily distressed by what they perceive of others' mental states and
have caregivers who respond to their distress in terrifying or terrified ways. The
strategy the children use to deal with these frightening situations is to stop
using mentalization. Instead, they begin to behave in ways that cause others to
give stereotyped, expectable responses, often potentially abusive. Examples of
the children's behaviors could be physical attacks, verbal assaults and insults, or
the kinds of sex-related behavior (such as mimicking intercourse) that make
adults highly uncomfortable. As Bleiberg described this, children, parents,
teachers, and therapists can "become entrapped in coercive cycles of interaction
that greatly increase the odds of maltreatment and leave everyone feeling out of
control" (2002, p. 3). (This outcome might be especially likely if a narcissistic
mother responded to every action as if it were profoundly rejecting.)

The treatment suggestions made by Bleiberg stressed many of the points we made earlier about child psychotherapy. A collaborative relationship between parents and therapists is essential to altering negative cycles of interaction. Bleiberg recommended that the therapist not confront the child's vulnerabilities, not try to link past and present emotions until the child gives the lead on this, and not try to approach important internal states (such as the conflicted feelings Candace had for her birth mother). Verbalization of moods and emotions should be encouraged. Children should be helped to gain a sense of control and effectiveness rather than allowed to feel demeaned. Mentalization needs to be encouraged by such means as pointing out the circumstances that tend to lead to certain feelings and behaviors. Bleiberg considered that such children can be seen to have made a major step toward recovery when they ask the therapist for help in solving everyday problems. It is hard to imagine a set of treatment recommendations that could be more different than these from the principles used by AT practitioners in working with children they believe to be antisocial.

CONCLUSION

As a conclusion to this chapter we will state a position about the AT view of child psychotherapy. We will also summarize the ways in which Candace was treated by AT practitioners and compare them to more appropriate treatment through conventional parent-child psychotherapy.

We want to make it clear, first, that we realize that practitioners of holding and related therapies are not identical in their views and treatments. We describe elsewhere in this book some differences between therapists who restrain children themselves and those who instruct parents how to do this. There are also practitioners who use holding but do not appear to have the same intentions or make the same assumptions as Candace's therapists. For example, Daniel Hughes (1997), in discussing holding therapy, advocated holding as something to be done to children, even against their protests. However, the model of holding Hughes recommended was to be guided by the "model of the mother holding her infant" (p. 107), and this technique required therapist and parent to be "highly attuned to the child's experience of the moment-to-moment therapeutic engagement" (pp. 107–108) for there to be any benefit to the child. Hughes also noted that if the child was not displaying a positive engagement to the holding, or if the parent reported that the child was fearful of the session, he would not hold the child but would instead "adopt a more traditional therapeutic stance" (p. 107). Hughes described empathic and mirroring verbalizations during holding, even speaking on behalf of the child's inner life, rather than the shaming, ridiculing, sometimes demeaning, and ultimately unresponsive language Candace's therapists used toward her.

The Hughes variant of holding brings a more traditional conceptual framework to treatment of attachment-disordered children. Similarly, since Candace Newmaker's death, a number of AT practitioners have stated that they no longer consider rage stimulation an appropriate part of their work. However, we still consider this model of treatment, involving the restraint of children, to be inappropriate, especially for children past the early childhood years. Holding approaches, at best, carry the message that the child is being coerced to attach, a distinctly different concept from our view of a gradually unfolding relationship. For children for whom touch may have been associated with injury or abuse, holding may reactivate traumatic memories, producing iatrogenic problems. At worst, practitioners who are not adequately supervised or are not emotionally grounded may carry holding to the extreme—and perhaps to another tragic outcome. For those practitioners, belief in the power of holding (like belief in a potion or elixir) leads them to surrender judgment or discretion. Their belief in the theory overrides care of the patient. This is fundamentally dangerous because the patient is real and the theory is an abstraction meant to guide the intervention.

As we can see by comparing material in this chapter with chapter 3's description of AT as Candace experienced it, conventional child psychotherapy is almost diametrically opposed to AT. Specifically, conventional treatment is based on multidisciplinary assessments; AT is not but depends on checklists and mothers' reports. Conventional treatment considers that early events in the child's life should shape the therapeutic process; AT uses the same treatment for all. Conventional psychotherapy rejects the ideas of recapitulation and of coercive approaches; AT has these assumptions at its core. Conventional treatment has a minimal risk of iatrogenic effects; AT runs a strong risk. Conventional psychotherapy for children focuses on the why and how of behavior, but AT is concerned with the what, especially with the child's obedience.

In addition, conventional child psychotherapists use calm, respectful language; consider eye contact as a means of communication, not of transformation; treat the child's communications as genuine; and include all family members in the treatment process, not just the child. In each case, AT has taken the opposite approach.

REFERENCES

Beck, A. T., & Freeman, A. (1990). *Cognitive therapy of personality disorders.* New York: Guilford.
Bleiberg, E. (2002). How to help children at risk of developing a borderline or narcissistic personality disorder. *Brown University Child and Adolescent Behavior Letter, 18*(6), 1, 3–4.
Brazelton, T. B. (1992). *Touchpoints: The essential reference.* Reading, MA: Addison-Wesley/Lawrence.

Brodzinsky, D. M. (1993). Long-term outcomes in adoption. *The Future of Children: Adoption, 3*(1), 153–166.

Chazan, S. (1995). *The simultaneous treatment of parent and child.* New York: Basic Books.

Flavell, J., Miller, P., & Miller, S. (1993). *Cognitive development.* Englewood Cliffs, NJ: Prentice-Hall.

Fraiberg, S. (1980). *Clinical studies in infant mental health: The first year of life.* New York: Basic Books.

Fraiberg, S., Adelson, E., & Shapiro, V. (1980). Ghosts in the nursery: A psychoanalytic approach to the problems of impaired infant-mother relationships. In S. Fraiberg (Ed.), *Clinical studies in infant mental health: The first year of life.* New York: Basic Books.

Furman, E. (1992). On feeling and being felt with. *The Psychoanalytic Study of the Child, 47,* 67–84.

Greenspan, S. I. (1990). Comprehensive clinical approaches to infants and their families: Psychodynamic and developmental perspectives. In S. Meisels & J. Shonkoff (Eds.), *Handbook of early childhood intervention.* New York: Cambridge University Press.

Greenspan, S. I. (1992). *Infancy and early childhood: The practice of clinical assessment and intervention with emotional and developmental challenges.* Madison, CT: International Universities Press.

Hughes, D. (1997). *Facilitating developmental attachment: The road to emotional recovery and behavioral change in foster and adoptive children.* Northvale, NJ: Jason Aronson.

Lieberman, A., & Pawl, J. (1993). Infant-parent psychotherapy. In C. H. Zeanah (Ed.), *Handbook of infant mental health.* New York: Guilford.

McDonough, S. (1995). Promoting positive early parent-infant relationships through interaction guidance. *Child and Adolescent Psychiatric Clinics of North America, 4*(3), 661–667.

Olds, D., Eckenrode, J., Henderson, C., Kitzman, H., Powers, J., Cole, R., Sidora, K., Morris, P., Pettit, L., & Luckey, D. (1997). Long-term effects of home visitation on maternal life course and child abuse and neglect: Fifteen year follow-up of a randomized trial. *Journal of the American Medical Association, 278,* 637–643.

Shapiro, V. B., Shapiro, J. R., & Paret, I. H. (2001). *Complex adoption and assisted reproductive technology.* New York: Guilford.

Stern, D. (1995). *The motherhood constellation.* New York: Basic Books.

Wallerstein, J. (1983). Children of divorce: The psychological tasks of the child. *American Journal of Orthopsychiatry, 53,* 230–243.

Weatherston, D., & Tableman, B. (1989). *Infant mental health services: Supporting competencies/reducing risks.* Lansing, MI: Michigan Department of Mental Health.

Part III

Preventing More Cases Like Candace's: Problems and Some Possible Solutions

Chapter 7

Science and Psychotherapy: Is There Evidence That Attachment Therapy Is a Valid Treatment?

Testimony at the Watkins-Ponder trial, as well as publications and documents on the Internet, all make one thing clear: the attachment therapists assert that their treatment works. Not only does attachment therapy work, they claim, but other treatments for attachment disorders are at best irrelevant, and at worst cause greater damage to the child.

What would practitioners of attachment therapy have to do to substantiate this claim? How can we apply scientific method to psychotherapy of any kind? If a researcher has claimed to offer evidence that a treatment is valid, how can the rest of us decide whether to trust that claim? These questions need to be answered by many consumers of research but especially by parents with the responsibility of choosing treatment for their children.

In a letter to the *New York Times*, the director of a Midwestern treatment center for teenagers advised parents to search for references before sending a child to a program. But how do people do this? Are references to be found on the Internet, through friends' anecdotes, or through support groups? How do we assess the quality of information? These questions really deal with the same issues we addressed earlier, although they appear to have easier answers.

EMPIRICAL VALIDATION: PROBLEMS AND SOLUTIONS

As a number of professional organizations have stressed in recent years, consumers, researchers, and therapists alike need to consider the effectiveness of all forms of psychotherapy. Unfortunately, this task is so complex that researchers sometimes seem to forget their goal as they become embroiled in questions about how to ask the question. Fortunately, we do have approaches to guide us through the maze of empirical *validation*—the finding of systematic evidence, scientifically amassed, to confirm or deny the effectiveness of a mental health intervention (Flyvbjerg, 2001).

Our present chapter is devoted first to discussing how evidence for psychotherapeutic success or failure is gathered, and second to a review of evidence specifically relevant to attachment therapy. We begin by looking at some recent changes in people's attitudes about the need for evidence.

Recent History: False Memory

Although the idea of psychiatric help is embedded even in American comic strips, events in recent years have caused some serious questioning of its efficacy. One of the most important triggers for discussion of psychotherapy was the "false memory" scandal of the 1990s, in which thousands of people were convinced by over-enthusiastic, under-trained, or fraudulent therapists that they had been victims of secret child abuse. Their "repressed memories" were thought to be the cause of any emotional problems or discomfort in their adult lives, and they were to overcome these by accepting the reality of the abuse and confronting the family members they thought responsible. After some years of personal turmoil, some of the "victims" came forward with evidence that the "remembered" abuse simply could not have happened, and others recanted for other reasons. Lawsuits produced restitution for a very small number of those who had been involved. The positive outcome of the false-memory epidemic was the development of a new, serious concern with quackery on the part of psychologists and psychiatrists. The American Psychological Association instituted a task force to set criteria under which a mental health intervention could legitimately be described as based on empirical evidence, systematically acquired through the use of scientific method (Chambless & Hollon, 1998).

Recent History: Managed Care

Other factors, inside and outside the helping professions, also contributed to the demand for empirical validation of therapies. The rise of managed health care led to an institutionalized preference for the quickest, cheapest, and most effective treatments and thus to a demand for evidence about what actually was quick or cheap or effective. Although mental health interventions have not achieved insurance parity with physical treatments, they quickly achieved parity in terms of demands for demonstrations of their effectiveness. Physicians and mental health practitioners alike have been encouraged to use evidence-based care, making treatment decisions based on several levels of information discussed later in this chapter.

Recent History: Expert Opinion

Thinking about evidence for psychotherapy has also been connected with a more general concern about expert testimony in the courtroom, whether about mental health issues or otherwise. The traditional criteria for evidence of this kind were based on a witness's experience and his or her standing in the professional community. The Daubert decision in 1993 set up new guidelines that focus on the empirical foundations of the evidence rather than simply the fame or reputation of the expert witness. The impact of this change is discussed further in chapter 9.

Disagreements About Empirical Validation of Therapies

Not all psychologists or psychiatrists agree that there should be scientific evidence, Daubert-style, for therapies. Post-modern thought in many fields has questioned whether human beings can collect evidence that truly reveals the nature of the world. This constructionist view suggests that even the most rigorous science reveals only what we *think* about the universe, not what the universe really is. A less stringent view holds that the social sciences have special problems and that it is a mistake to try to model them on the more objective physical sciences.

Even social scientists who rely on the use of scientific method can fear the impact of the human element on empirical testing of psychotherapies. They point to situations where peer review of an article submitted to a professional journal has been influenced by the politics or prejudices of the reviewers, or where concern has been shown, not with the solidity of the evidence, but with the implications for practical politics. Professionals in mental health and the social sciences have not always been innocent even of personal attacks on those who are perceived as disagreeing with them.

Problems Inherent in Empirical Validation

Distressingly real difficulties are inherent in the collection of evidence for psychotherapy, over and above disagreements with the ideal of scientific validation. Such problems can manifest themselves at several levels, with possible contamination of the evidence at every level.

Steps in Evaluation

To evaluate a treatment, we need to go through a number of steps. A problem that needs treatment must first become evident in some way, usually because the potential patient is unhappy, because the family is worried, or because the police or the school system become concerned with the person's conduct. The family or the individual then chooses to seek treatment, or it is sought as an alternative to prison, or the person is legally ordered into treatment. The selected treatment continues for some time; the patient may leave treatment for a variety of reasons. At this point information is collected about the patient's improvement (or lack thereof) in mood and in conduct; data collection may be repeated or delayed until a later date. Because our techniques for understanding these events are statistical in nature, this set of events must be repeated for many other patients as well.

Factors Influencing Evaluation

Each of the events just described is affected by many unpredictable factors of time and place. First, the identification of the problem may be influenced by the diagnostic categories in use by mental health professionals at a given time. They may or may not apply meaningfully to the person in question. (The famous example of this issue is homosexual behavior as a diagnostic category; not very many years ago, it was categorized as a type of pathology, but this is not the case today.) A related concern has to do with the skill of the person making the diagnosis and the accuracy of the information available to him or her. An inaccurate or irrelevant diagnosis focuses attention on the wrong emotional or behavioral issues and confuses evaluation of the therapy.

A second issue involves the patient's reasons for entering treatment. The involvement of an individual in the therapeutic process may well be less if participation is under duress.

A third concern is the reason a particular form of treatment was chosen. Is it simply all that is available in the area where the patient lives? Was this person deliberately assigned to one treatment or another for research purposes? Is the treatment one that is newly fashionable, one that a famous rock star has used, or one that was recommended by the family physician or clergyman? These factors can all affect attitudes and the willingness to do the hard work of therapy.

The success of a treatment can also be influenced by the way in which it is applied. Therapists working with different individuals cannot and do not behave identically in every session with every patient. Practitioners differ in training and skill as well as in how much they like or are interested in a given patient. In addition, like the relations between parent and child we discussed in chapter 4, therapist and patient work together in a transactional process they both influence. Finally, the length of time for which the patient continues in treatment is usually not fixed but depends on factors such as health insurance, job responsibilities, family requirements, spontaneous improvement or worsening of the problem, and even matters such as falling in love with someone who objects to psychotherapy.

Outcome Issues

After an individual's therapy is completed, we return to the problem of diagnosis but in a more complex way. What outcome criteria should we choose to decide whether the person is doing better? Who decides what doing better is: the patient, the therapist, or someone else? The classic complaint about people undergoing psychoanalysis was that they were just as unpleasant as ever but were no longer unhappy about it; would we accept such a change as evidence that the therapy was effective? And, can we expect a therapist who has been working hard with a patient to be quite objective about what has been accomplished? Our answers and choices can make a great deal of difference to the evidence for or against the validity of a treatment.

Statistics

This list of difficulties makes it sound as if the systematic study of psychotherapy is impossible. But they are simply things to be taken into account during an essential process. The most important trick researchers have for dealing with these issues is to look at large numbers of cases rather than one or two anecdotes. The assumption is that many of the differences among people average out or cancel each other out when enough people are involved; if a therapist has one patient she dislikes, she probably has another one she likes. (This statistical approach has no effect on our concerns about outcome criteria or initial diagnosis, of course, and we see later in this chapter that those considerations are of great concern when we look at attempts to validate attachment theory.)

DOING THE RESEARCH: CONCEPTS AND CRITERIA IN EVALUATION OF PSYCHOTHERAPY

Variability

When the previous section listed the various factors that could confuse research on psychotherapy, the basic issue was one of the essential characteristics of human beings: variability. The concept of variation is essential to the understanding of human development, personality, psychopathology, and everyday behavior as well as to most characteristics of all living beings. Human beings of every age change from moment to moment. This variation may be caused by the environment (by psychotherapy, for instance), but it also occurs spontaneously. Such spontaneous changes usually stay within a predictable range of variation, but that is about all that is predictable—except for that fact that change does and will occur.

The reality of constant change means that whatever we can measure about a person is not likely to be just the same when we measure it again a little later, even though "nothing happened" to make the person change. Neither is one person likely to be just like another, or one group identical to a second. One size does not fit all and often does not even fit the same person twice in a row, even when nothing has occurred to make this the case. We have to be very careful about assuming that any changes in people have been brought about by psychotherapy, because we cannot assume that they would have remained unchanged in the absence of treatment.

Statistics

Because of these changes and differences, we need to look at groups of people in research rather than at anecdotes about individuals. We also need to describe what we measure in statistical terms. Averages and the less familiar measures of variation give us our best possible descriptions of people and the ways they change, even though they do not give a recognizable description of any individual.

Maturation

Because our basic concern in this book is with the effects of AT on children, we need to deal with one especially important issue about variability: the rather predictable variations in children's lives as they grow up. Not only are children individually different, but they change in a predictable fashion through maturation. Genetic and other factors cause them to grow and change physically and mentally as they get older. Research on the effectiveness of child psychotherapy is badly flawed unless it takes into account several kinds of variation: the everyday changes caused by experience and by spontaneous change, the changes that come from maturation, and any changes that may result from treatment. The last two are all too easily confused with each other.

Hypotheses and Falsifiability

Before we go on with our discussion of research on psychotherapy, we need to clarify an essential concept used in all research. Scientific investigation tests hypotheses. Rather than collecting all kinds of information in a dragnet approach, systematic empirical work looks for information that is relevant to the predictions we call hypotheses.

How do we decide what information is relevant? This point is much less well understood even by the educated public than the basic idea of a hypothesis. Ask any college sophomore studying experimental psychology the purpose of a piece of research the class is doing. Chances are the answer will begin, "Oh, we're trying to prove that ... [their prediction is correct]." On the contrary, however, scientists are supposed to try to prove that their hypothesis is wrong and should be rejected. Hypothesis-testing means doing your best to find any information that fails to support your prediction, and it does not mean searching for supportive information while avoiding all other data. We might think of a hypothesis as like a boat that will float or sink. If it is likely to sink, we want to know that as quickly as possible while we are still near land. We may even overload the boat or take it into rough waters just to test its safety. Scientific investigation similarly sets up the most difficult possible circumstances so poor hypotheses can be summarily rejected before they cause wasted time—or worse—and, as Candace Newmaker's case shows, the outcome of poor hypothesis-testing about psychotherapy can be very bad indeed.

Some readers may be thinking, "Oh, nonsense, scientists are human too. They want their pet hypotheses to be supported." Of course, this is true, but, as we will see later, many safeguards are in place to protect the integrity of the research process, and professional disgrace is the fate of researchers who try to evade them. These safeguards are especially powerful with respect to research on human subjects and, above all, on children.

The idea that scientific investigation tries to reject hypotheses brings us to the concept of *falsifiability*. To falsify a hypothesis is not to fudge data (which it sounds like) but to collect data that demonstrate that a theory cannot be true. Good theories can be falsified when they are wrong; poor theories yield hypotheses that are so vague or ambiguous that all data can be interpreted as confirming them. (For example, in a lecture, one attachment therapist suggested that certain emotional problems could be caused in infancy either by abuse and neglect or by excessive indulgence of the child's wishes.) Scientists working with poor theories find they cannot develop clear-cut predictions or decide whether data support a prediction. The adequacy of empirical research on psychotherapy thus depends to some extent on the theory behind the therapy. If it is not falsifiable, good research becomes impossible.

Preliminary Steps in Research

Whether research is on psychotherapy or another topic, it begins with some preliminary steps and not with the high-powered techniques that are researchers' ideals. A qualitative or narrative approach often has to precede carefully designed experimental work. (Indeed, some post-modernist thinkers consider these descriptive steps to be the only research techniques that make sense at all, but few psychologists agree with this stance.)

Description

In chapter 5 we discussed the description of different syndromes of emotional disturbance and the use of those descriptions in the development of manuals such as the DSM-IV. Such use of descriptions has become an institution in the United States since the basis for payment by private or government health insurance has become linked to the use of "official" diagnostic categories.

In connection with these issues, we need to note that descriptive criteria for diagnoses such as Reactive Attachment Disorder are not necessarily permanent. This point is discussed further in a later section of this chapter.

Screening

The basic descriptive work and the organization of diagnostic categories are sometimes extended to the development of screening instruments: questionnaires and checklists intended to identify people who have specific problems. A practitioner can then examine those who have scores indicating the possibility of difficulties and can try to pick out people who actually have a serious condition such as depression. A questionnaire or checklist is a rough-and-ready measure that may show many *false positives* (for example, people identified as being seriously depressed when they are not) as well as *false negatives* (in this case, people whose answers to the questionnaire do not reveal their serious depression).

Effective screening instruments are not developed in a day or as a result of scribbling some questions that seem to be right. They start with some descriptive material such as might be derived from interviews or from existing diagnostic criteria. The process continues with testing of the questions on very large numbers of people, followed by careful statistical analysis. Often researchers look for correlations (a type of mathematical relationship) between certain answers or scores on a questionnaire and the diagnosis given by a clinical psychologist or psychiatrist. They may also look for evidence that the questionnaire discriminates between groups, with people who have one diagnosis scoring differently from those independently diagnosed with a different problem.

What is the relevance of screening or other forms of diagnosis to testing psychotherapy? There are several related issues. One has to do with evidence that people in treatment actually do have certain symptoms. Without this evidence to begin with, we could hardly claim that a mental health intervention has helped those who received it. A related point is the need for standards to help researchers remain consistent and objective in their judgments. Established criteria, whether from a diagnostic description or from a questionnaire score, can be applied repeatedly by a well-trained observer. This avoids the problems that might occur if an inexperienced researcher judges symptoms in different ways before and after a group of people are treated.

Later Steps in Research

After descriptions and diagnostic categories are in place, researchers begin to move on to the sometimes daunting task of testing the outcome of a treatment. Therapies are usually designed for the treatment of certain groups of problems, and they are tested for their impact on those kinds of problems, not as general cure-alls.

Classes of Evidence

The concept of evidence-based care mentioned earlier in this chapter has given rise to the idea of three classes of evidence, each derived from certain kinds of research and having implications for the making of certain decisions (Patrick, Mozzoni, & Patrick, 2000). Class III evidence is only a step above the qualitative approach described earlier. It involves systematic descriptions such as case reports. Class III evidence may be considered more relevant to safety than to effectiveness and provides practitioners with some treatment options but gives no information about the best thing to do.

Class II evidence is a step beyond Class III, because it provides ways to make systematic comparisons, for example, between people who have received a certain treatment and those who have received a different therapy or those who have remained untreated. Class II evidence can also involve evaluations of people's symptoms before and after a course of treatment. Psychologists usually refer to the Class II level as quasi-experimental. Comparisons in a quasi-experiment are based on "natural experiments"—situations in which the researcher has no control over which people decide to have which form of treatment or over other experiences they may have. Class II or quasi-experimental research has the distinct drawback that it does not tell us what causes any differences we find between groups. People who choose to participate in one kind of treatment may be different in unknown ways from those who choose another kind, and it may well be those unknown differences rather than the treatment that causes the eventual differences between the groups. (We will see later in this chapter that the best of the studies of AT's efficacy are at this quasi-experimental level.) Nevertheless, some useful information can come from Class II studies, and it has been suggested that Class II evidence can imply guidelines for practitioners to consider in their decision-making. It should not be used to support claims about the best treatment practices.

Experiments and Evidence

The highest level, the gold standard for testing the efficacy of psychotherapy, is Class I evidence, based on experimental work. To understand how Class I is different from Class II, the reader needs to be clear about the nature of experimentation. Although everyday language uses the terms "experiment," "research," and "study" synonymously, an experiment is only one of many types of research and has characteristics of its own. An experiment is an investigation in which a researcher can cause certain events to happen in a controlled way rather than having to wait for them to happen naturally. For example, under certain circumstances, a researcher could decide which people would receive a certain treatment rather than having to wait until they themselves decide what to do. The great advantage of the experimental approach is that it allows researchers to set up an excellent standard of comparison against which to judge any effects of therapy.

In the quasi-experimental (Class II) approach described earlier, the researcher cannot be sure whether differences between groups are a result of treatment rather than of some unidentified factor such as maturation or in-

dividual differences. In Class I research, however, the experimenter can come
as close as is humanly possible to knowing that the therapy has caused any
effects that are seen. How can anyone be so sure? The certainty is accomplished through a technique called *random assignment to groups,* or randomized trials. In this approach, the researcher chooses people to receive one
treatment or another at random from an available population of potential
participants. "At random" means that every person has an equal chance of
being placed in one group or the other. Any individual characteristics that
could affect the outcome are thus equally likely to go into either group and
be statistically averaged out when the groups are compared. Any systematic
differences between the two groups' outcomes can then legitimately be attributed to the therapies themselves rather than to accidental factors. (Random assignment to groups is not the same thing as random sampling, a
procedure for choosing research subjects from a large natural population,
and random sampling is rarely, if ever, used in the empirical evaluation of
psychotherapies.)

Class I evidence provides acceptable reasons for deciding that a treatment is
best practice—an effective and otherwise desirable mental health intervention.
The lower evidence levels do not provide such reasons. As we will see later in
this chapter, none of the studies set forth by attachment therapists have provided Class I evidence.

The American Psychological Association Task Force

When the American Psychological Association established a task force to
study the empirical support for mental health interventions, the psychologists
set very stringent criteria for claims that therapies are effective. Not surprisingly, they went with the gold standard: Class I evidence or experimental comparisons where people have been assigned randomly to treatment groups. This
technique allows people participating in a treatment to be compared to people
in another group (comparison or control) that is treated differently.

But the APA task force did not stop there. They added some other criteria for
studies that would be accepted as giving empirical support for mental health interventions. One requirement had to do with the measurements used to assess
the outcome of a treatment, the measurements that would be interpreted as
meaning the therapy had or had not been effective. These measurements were
required to be both *reliable and valid.*

The reliability of a measurement refers to evidence that it yields similar
scores when used by different practitioners or that a person tested several
times will get similar scores on different occasions. (The characteristic variability of human behavior makes it unlikely that exactly the same score will
occur.) The validity of a measurement means it gives the "right answer" about
a person, or at least the same answer as another well-respected measurement.
For instance, a measure of a child's conduct disorder might be considered to

have evidence for validity if it matches a classroom teacher's report of the child's behavior.

Finally, the APA task force set the requirement that claims for a treatment's effectiveness must be supported by independent replication in at least two studies. "Independence" in this case means the studies cannot simply involve some additional measurements taken by the same researchers from the same research participants.

It would be a mistake to think that the APA task force solved all the problems of empirical validation of psychotherapy. Although few practitioners reject the importance of randomized trials, many have concerns about the manualization of therapy inherent in the task force guidelines. These critics suggest that the APA guidelines require therapists to follow a manual that dictates exactly what they will do or say. Psychotherapists usually say they cannot do this, and they certainly do not want to do it. Psychotherapists have complained that the APA task force criteria do not produce findings that can be generalized to the real world of treatment. For example, there is usually no fixed number of treatment sessions planned from the beginning of therapy unless health insurance considerations drive such a decision.

The question of empirical validation of mental health interventions is ongoing. Few practitioners would say the goal is either impossible or worthless. The need for credibility is recognized—as we see from the attempts of the attachment therapists to demonstrate their own—but there are serious disagreements about the best way to achieve it (Beutler & Harwood, 2001; Gottfried & Wolfe, 1998). One potentially valuable approach is a statistical technique called meta-analysis, in which data from many small studies can be put together to yield a more meaningful conclusion than can come from the individual investigations (Weisz et al., 1995).

Some Problems Specific to Child Psychotherapy

Gathering empirical evidence for mental health interventions is a slow, awkward, complicated process even when the people in treatment are all adults. Evaluating child psychotherapy has all those problems and several difficulties of its own.

Blind Studies and Family Influences

When adults are undergoing mental health treatment, it is possible that no one around them knows about it; therapy can be a secret even from a spouse. When children receive treatment, however, their caregivers know about it. The adults have usually chosen the treatment or given permission for it, they accompany the child to appointments, and they may ask the child what happens during therapy sessions. Parents may seek counseling for themselves, ask for advice about how to treat the child, or even try to use therapeutic techniques at home.

In the adult therapy situation, friends and relatives may be "blind" to the therapy; this term means they are unaware that treatment is occurring. Unless the person in treatment begins to behave differently toward them, they will have no reason to change their attitudes or behavior. When children are in treatment, however, their parents can hardly ignore the fact. The parents thus have reasons to change their ways of treating the child even when the child has not altered. The parents may be more relaxed because they are optimistic about the outcome of the therapy or tense and punitive because they find it embarrassing to be seen at the therapist's office. They may follow instructions given by the therapist, seek advice from Websites, or look for support groups; Internet support groups are available even when the diagnosis or treatment is unusual in the geographical area.

Children in therapy thus have at last two factors influencing them: the treatment itself and whatever family changes have resulted from new expectations or knowledge. When randomized trials are used, this second factor is assumed to average out across groups of people so any differences in outcome can properly be attributed only to the treatment itself. Good research design can thus be even more important than usual in the evaluation of child psychotherapy.

Maturational Factors

As we discussed earlier, children are constantly changing for maturational reasons. (See also chapter 4). The rate of change is greater at some times, such as during puberty, but change is always present. This is another good reason for demanding Class I randomized trial evidence about child psychotherapy.

Let us look at the sources of confusion that arise if we take a quasi-experimental (Class II) approach to child psychotherapy. Suppose we were to compare a group of children before and after they received a year of treatment. The goal of the treatment would be to help the children act less like babies and more like adults—to be less impulsive, more self-controlled, more appropriately emotionally expressive, more empathic, and so on. These are all changes in the direction that would be produced by maturation alone, although of course the intention of treatment is to speed up the changes. In a simple before-and-after study, then, we can have no idea how much of the outcome was caused by the treatment and how much by the effects of getting older.

Even when the design is more elaborate than a before-and-after study, other types of Class II approaches also have their problems. We might try to solve the difficulty described in the previous paragraph by finding a comparison group of children who did not receive treatment. We would evaluate the original group of children before and after a year of treatment and examine the change over that time, and we would do the same for the comparison group, using the same time interval even though the comparison children had no treatment during that period. We would thus be able to look for the difference between the size of the change in the treatment group and the size of the change in the comparison group. We would expect the two groups to mature by the same amount, so any other difference between them we could chalk up to the effects of the therapy.

This looks at first glance like an excellent solution to our problem, but unfortunately it is not. What we have described is a quasi-experiment, so we are looking at children whose parents chose for them to enter treatment or not to do so. Factors in the two groups of families caused the parents to make different choices. Even if we can match the groups of children so that both groups are equally troubled at the beginning of the study, it is extremely difficult to match the parents or even to know what factors determined their choice. In fact, there is by definition one major difference between the groups of families—the decision to seek therapy for the child—and this may both result from and cause many other differences that can influence the outcome.

Only a randomized trial study can deal effectively with factors such as maturation and family differences, because only when children are randomly assigned to treatment conditions can factors of this kind be assumed to average out rather than to influence the outcome. Unfortunately, assigning people randomly to groups is not always practical or simple. Human beings do not like to feel like guinea pigs, and they are usually eager to defend their children from researchers who might experiment on them.

Informed Consent

Participants in research today are required to give their informed consent to procedures, especially for experimental work. This generally involves reading or hearing information about the purpose and possible effects of an experimental treatment and signing of a document to show agreement to participate and understanding of the information. Professional journals may not publish material from sources that have not complied with informed consent guidelines or other ethical considerations.

Informed consent guidelines are different for children than for adults. Adults, unless they are incarcerated, elderly, or suffering from serious mental illness or retardation, are generally considered able to understand and agree to a procedure. Children under the age of 18 are not considered legally competent to give informed consent; their parents or guardians must do it for them. When research participants are in their teens, however, it is appropriate for the adolescents as well as their parents to give their informed consent. Depending on the circumstances, even school-age children may be asked to give their agreement after receiving a simple explanation. Informed consent for investigations of child psychotherapy is thus a more complicated matter than informed consent by adult participants.

ATTACHMENT THERAPY: PROBLEMS FOR EMPIRICAL VALIDATION

Now that we have established some guidelines for appropriate ways of testing the effectiveness of psychotherapy, let us look at the evidence for attachment therapy. Attachment therapists' publications and Websites proclaim their belief that "attachment therapy works." Indeed, in written material and in testimony at the Watkins-Ponder trial, they have gone so far as to say that no other form of treatment is effective for the problems they work with. A common statement by attachment therapists and parent support groups is that no one can possibly understand what they are talking about unless he or she has lived with an attachment-disordered child. This presents a very real conceptual problem with respect to evaluation of attachment therapy.

Public Verifiability

The attachment therapists' belief that only certain people can know about attachment disorders is on the face of it a rejection of the idea that AT practices can be studied scientifically. One of the most basic ideas of modern scientific method is that science involves communication and public access to knowledge. The social sciences have been particularly concerned with *operationalism,* the process of defining concepts in terms of the measurements used to decide whether an event has occurred or not. An operationalist approach is considered essential because it allows researchers to convey information to each other with minimal distortion by subjective interpretation. When attachment therapists claim that only they can understand attachment disorders and their treatment, they seem to reject the possibility of operationalizing or of the public verifiability of information that is at the heart of modern science.

Outcome Measures

A second serious problem for attempts to validate attachment therapy has to do with the outcome measures that attachment therapists favor. The APA task force standards require these to be demonstrably reliable and valid. However, the basic measures used both before and after AT are the reports of parents.

It is not unusual for parent or teacher reports to be outcome measures for evaluations of child psychotherapy. Normally, though, these reports can be validated by comparing them to some independent measurement of the child's behavior. The parent may say the child is less argumentative; if an independent observer and the child's teacher say the same, or if the school reports a decreased number of detentions for fighting, we have corroboration that the reports are correct. In the case of attachment therapy, this approach is impossible almost by definition. Children evaluated by attachment therapists are diagnosed almost entirely on the basis of parental reporting. (Indeed, Candace

Newmaker's initial diagnosis appears to have been made by someone who never saw her but depended on her adoptive mother's answers to a questionnaire.)

In fact, the crux of the attachment therapists' diagnosis is the report that the child is hostile, malicious, and almost demonic with the mother but wonderfully good, charming, cooperative, and well-behaved with outsiders. The bad behavior with the mother cannot be measured independently because it does not occur when other adults are present. This is considered the signature of the disorder, and the child is cured only when it is no longer present. Indeed, by these standards, if it were possible to get an independent evaluation, the child could presumably not be diagnosed with an attachment disorder.

Informed Consent

A third conceptual barrier to empirical validation of attachment therapy has to do with certain assumptions about the rights and appropriate treatment of the child. Although the usual practice would require the informed consent of adolescents to research participation, the view of attachment therapists is that children "do not have the right to stay sick." These practitioners have argued that AT can be compared to painful cancer treatments that must be carried out for the child's own good. Although Robert Zaslow (Zaslow & Menta, 1975) advocated informed consent for children undergoing his rough physical techniques, more recent AT writers have considered it unnecessary (Cline, 1992).

The withholding of information is an important tool in attachment therapy. Even preschoolers may be taken to a therapeutic foster home without warning, explanation, or information about when they will see their parents. Because attachment therapists assume that children's treatment is facilitated by keeping them anxious and wondering, they do not want to provide even the information that is usually given to children too young to consent to treatment.

As we will see in the rest of this chapter, it is questionable whether even parental consent to AT is fully informed. Parents seeking information about AT are told that the treatment works; various Websites show documents that purport to provide empirical validation for the therapy. As we will see, however, the evidence presented for these claims is unacceptably weak.

ATTEMPTS AT EMPIRICAL VALIDATION OF ATTACHMENT THERAPY

In spite of the problems offered by their own belief system, the attachment therapists have some excellent motives for attempting to present empirical evidence to support their treatment techniques. Although private insurance and state agencies have paid for attachment therapy, the pressures of managed care make these arrangements vulnerable to demands for empirical validation. In spite of their rejection of orthodox techniques, attachment therapists would reap many benefits if they could achieve affiliation with established institutions, which is unlikely as long as their treatments are unvalidated. Whatever the reasons, attachment therapists have, in recent years, begun research projects that attempt the empirical validation of their practices.

Diagnosis and Frequency Estimation

As we noted earlier, a preliminary step in the evaluation of a mental health intervention involves the establishment of diagnostic categories. Initially, for a period of some years, attachment therapists focused on the DSM-IV diagnosis of Reactive Attachment Disorder. This was the diagnosis claimed for Candace Newmaker, although, as we saw in chapter 1, the available evidence about Candace does not seem to justify this diagnostic decision. (We note at this point that RAD has been described as "not ... a particularly clear or coherent diagnostic entity" [Hanson & Spratt, 2000, p. 142]).

Checklist

The Website of the Attachment Center at Evergreen offers parents an Attachment Disorder Checklist, some of which was discussed in chapter 5. An interesting point about this list involves the overlap of items (interest in fire, failure to make eye contact, etc.) with a similar list that was at one time suggested for the detection of child sexual abuse and another that was used many decades ago to detect symptoms of masturbation (see Dawes, 1994; Unterwager & Wakefield, 1990). The checklist is presented as an appropriate screening device for initial detection of attachment disorders such as RAD.

An unusual feature of the checklist is that it includes statements about parental feelings. These include "Parent feels 'used' and is wary of the child's motives if affection is expressed;" "Parents feel more angry and frustrated with this child than with other children," "Parent (especially 'MOM' [sic]) feels intensely rejected by this child," and "Parent feels that no matter what he/she does for the child it is never enough." This novel inclusion of items about the parent in a checklist about the child's symptoms is a reflection of the attachment therapists' consistent assumption that the parents' beliefs, actions, and perceptions are all correct and it is the child who must change.

New Diagnosis

In the past several years, attachment therapists at the Attachment Center at Evergreen (Colorado) have described what they consider to be a form of attachment disorder (AD) that is more severe and dangerous than RAD. They have described this disorder as not yet in DSM. To receive this diagnosis, a child must meet the criteria for both RAD and for either Oppositional Defiant Disorder or Conduct Disorder (both in DSM-IV) or some other psychiatric disorders.

The RADQ

For purposes of screening and classification of attachment disorders, attachment therapists such as Elizabeth Randolph use a questionnaire called the Randolph Attachment Disorder Questionnaire (RADQ). Randolph (2000, 2001) has stated that the RADQ distinguishes children with AD from those with Conduct Disorder or other psychiatric disorders, although this claim seems inconsistent with the idea that AD includes both RAD and Conduct Disorder criteria.

Thinking about the RADQ seems to have undergone some changes over the past several years, because the information offered on the Attachment Center at Evergreen Website is contradicted by the RADQ test manual in its 2000 form. The test manual offers information about the development of the RADQ and its foundation on questions from the Attachment Disorder Checklist. Studies of reliability are said to have shown correlations of better than .8, indicating a high probability that similar answers would be given to the test if it were taken again. However, there seems to be only one form of the 30-item test, so parents who were retested might well remember their previous responses. (We also note that the figures .8 or 80% appear with strange frequency in the AT literature; statisticians become suspicious when the same number pops up again and again.)

The question of validity is pursued in the test manual, but, once again, there is no means of independent validation of an assessment. An unusual issue is brought up by the manual with respect to parents' difficulties in giving accurate responses. It is considered necessary for the tester to go over the test and ask the parent to reconsider answers, a procedure that obviously stands in the way of determining the parent's own opinion. Where validity is claimed on the basis of correlations with other tests, there are few significant correlations.

A curious feature of the RADQ is its use of rather dramatically phrased statements. For example, the parent is asked to respond to the items "My child acts *amazingly* innocent ..." and "my child has a *tremendous* need ..." (words underlined in test statements).

Subtypes

The RADQ manual gives an extensive discussion of the use of the test for assigning children to attachment disorder subtypes. Randolph has proposed that children with AD (diagnosed primarily with the RADQ) can be divided into four groups on the basis of their scores on RADQ subscales. In one publication, Randolph (2000) has given these groups the names used for four behavior categories to classify toddlers in the Strange Situation (a standardized assessment of attachment, described further in chapter 9). However, Randolph specifically states that the four categories have nothing to do with the Strange Situation classifications and that she employs these names only because she cannot think of any others to use. In a later publication, Randolph (2001) did provide some alternative names for the suggested subtypes. She also suggested a test of physical movement as the absolute criterion for diagnosis of attachment disorders; children who could not obey instructions for movements such as crawling backward were said to suffer from the emotional disorder.

Randolph provides behavioral descriptions on which her subtypes appear to be based. Children in the avoidant subtype are said to avoid close contact and friendship, to want others' approval but to have a compulsive need to do what they themselves want, and to be very argumentative. Children in the anxious subtype are worried about their behavior and try to be what others expect them to be. (How this can be congruent with emotional aloofness is not explained.) Children who are categorized as ambivalent are described as aggressive, destructive, cruel to other children and to animals, involved in fire-setting, and inclined to make false accusations of abuse. Children classified in the fourth category, disorganized AD, are said to be psychotic and neurologically impaired, odd, disorganized, moody, and changeable, with peculiar speech patterns but usually no hallucinations or delusions. From Randolph's report, it would appear that Randolph herself categorized the children she studied as well as collecting the RADQ scores she reports as highly correlated with the categories. No independent validation of the categorization is reported in the test manual, nor is there any mention of an attempt at blind scoring based on others' descriptions of the children.

Prevalence

Using agreed-upon diagnostic categories, researchers can estimate how often a problem is found in the general population. This is an important research step from a practical point of view, because knowledge of the prevalence of a disorder helps determine whether an emotional problem should be given high priority, either in scientific study or in expenditures for intervention.

Attachment therapists estimate an extremely high frequency of occurrence of attachment disorders. One Internet source (www.attachmentexperts.com) gives the following estimate and rationale: "Research has shown that up to 80% of high risk families ... create severe attachment disorders in their children. Since there are one million substantiated cases of serious abuse and neglect in the U.S. each year, the statistics indicate that there are 800,000 children with severe attachment disorder coming to the attention of the child welfare system each year." This would mean, of course, that in a ten-year period, there would be 8 million new cases of a serious mental illness in a U.S. population of less than 300 million people, causing some obvious problems, especially in schools. Also, the words "up to 80%" indicate that the actual proportion could be down to 1% or even less. Not all forms of abuse and neglect are equally likely to cause attachment disorders, so the one-million figure is not relevant. (Note also that 80% seems to be something of a magic number for attachment therapists and occurs often in their written and videotaped material.)

The prevalence of attachment disorders is difficult to estimate, because diagnostic categories remain somewhat uncertain and because there is no requirement to report a diagnosis to the Centers for Disease Control for record-keeping. We might make a very rough guess about the frequency of serious attachment problems by making a comparison to the prevalence of autism, a serious emotional disturbance first apparent in early childhood and beginning at about the same age as attachment disorders. A high estimate of the prevalence of autism would be about 1–2 per 1000 people; this would imply from 300,000 to 600,000 autistic people of all ages in the United States population at any time. The attachment therapists suggest that there are many more new cases of attachment disorder each year than there are of both newly and previously diagnosed cases of autism. This seems highly unlikely.

Looking at the Outcome: Attempts to See Whether Attachment Therapy Works

There are no reports of research on the effectiveness of attachment therapy that meet the requirements of the APA task force. There have been no reported studies using randomized trials, where children have an equal chance of being placed in a group that receives attachment therapy or in some type of comparison group.

In all fairness, however, we must recognize the preliminary research steps that usually precede the type of work called Class I in the evidence-based care approach. That there have been no randomized trials does not necessarily mean no efforts for empirical validation have been made. We need to examine these efforts and assess their quality.

Class III Evidence

Evidence at the Class III level involves qualitative, descriptive work such as case studies or reports on a series of similar cases. A good case study is an extremely challenging task rather than the simple matter it is often assumed to be. (A poor case study is a lot easier, of course.) Because attachment therapy has been going on in some form for more than 30 years, we might expect some careful descriptions to have occurred.

In fact, no such studies seem to be in existence, although there are plenty of anecdotes. In a paper published in a German journal, Robert Zaslow (1982) gave brief descriptions of his use of restraint techniques with a girl diagnosed as schizophrenic and another who was a patient at the Colorado School for the

Blind. Each is described as recovering very rapidly, and few details are given. In a more recent publication, Foster Cline (1992) presented a number of vignettes that appear to be part of a case history, but on close inspection these turn out to be taken without clear attribution from a case reported by the hypnotherapist Milton Erickson (1962).

Not only are we without case reports from attachment therapy, but even the published descriptions of the current therapeutic techniques are vague and general. (The older descriptions by Zaslow are quite detailed.) Chapter 3 of this book seems to give the most detailed description in print, and this was made possible only by the videotape shown at the Watkins-Ponder trial.

Class II Evidence: The Ohio Study

Several quasi-experimental studies have focused on the outcome of attachment therapy. The first of these, a before-and-after study by Virginia Lester (1997), is a modest effort but is commendable for its straightforwardness, its attempt to use valid outcome measures, and its sensible interpretation of the results. Participating in this study were 12 adoptive families of children being treated at the Attachment and Bonding Center of Ohio. Ten of the children received intensive treatment with holding and other techniques, with daily 3-hour sessions over a period of weeks, and two others received holding treatment and parent counseling. The children ranged in age from 4 to 15 years.

The children's parents responded to the Devereux Scale of Mental Disorders (Naglieri, LeBuffe, & Pfeiffer, 1994), a published scale with evidence of reliability, as well as to the Beech Brook Attachment Disorder Checklist, an instrument in the process of development at the time of the study. The Beech Brook scale was described as using groups of items relevant to positive attachment and others relevant to negative attachment.

The parents responded to the two questionnaires on four occasions: (a) before the children's initial assessments, (b) at the time of the initial assessments, (c) after the assessments but before therapy sessions began, and (d) at least four weeks after the beginning of therapy. The researcher reported average scores at these four times but gave no statistical analysis of differences among them. She reported improvement in all scores, but noted that in two comparisons the greatest improvement in the parents' reports occurred before therapy actually began.

Lester offered for her findings the reasonable interpretation that the parents may have felt better after talking to supportive people and thus have evaluated the children more positively. We may note another possible reason for the improvement in scores. Problems, whether physical or emotional, do not remain at the same level at all times. They show the natural variability discussed earlier in this chapter, worsening at times and improving spontaneously at others. Parents are likely to seek treatment for a child when a behavior problem seems to be getting worse; if it seems to be getting better, they hope for the best and wait to see what will happen. When a parent looks for help, then, the problem may already be at the point where there is nowhere to go but up. And, of course, if treatment begins at once, the coming spontaneous improvement is attributed to the treatment rather than to natural variation. The assumption of attachment therapists that attachment disorders never change without treatment is especially encouraging to this interpretation.

Two Class II Studies from the Attachment Center at Evergreen

Two studies of the Class II level are reported on the Website of the Attachment Center at Evergreen, Colorado, as well as in other forms. One of these also exists in the form of a dissertation and as a journal publication (Myeroff, Mertlich, & Gross, 1999). These were more elaborate quasi-experiments than Lester's study (described in the previous section). Both used the Achenbach Child Behavior Checklist (Achenbach, 1991) as an outcome measure, although the two sets of data are not entirely comparable because one of the studies did not use all the scales of the checklist.

The first of these studies, conducted by staff at the Attachment Center at Evergreen (apparently under the direction of Elizabeth Randolph), was a before-and-after study using data from 25 children 9–12 years of age who received a two-week intensive treatment and then remained for long-term therapy for a time between 3 months and several years. Twelve of the children remained at the center for at least one year.

The Website report indicates mean scores on the eight subscales of the checklist but presents no measure of variability, an essential measure for understanding the data. The statistical analysis is described as a simple analysis of variance; this would not be the appropriate approach when the parents responded to the questionnaire more than once, and it is not at all clear what comparisons were made. There was only one subscale on which no significant improvement was reported, and five of the subscales were said to show highly significant improvement over a 12-month period.

The problem with interpreting this study, of course, is that there is no standard of comparison. Without data from a group of children who did not receive treatment, it is impossible to know how much of the reported improvement was due to maturation or other factors.

The second study, conducted by Robin Myeroff, looked at assessments of 23 children ranging in age from 4 to 14 years. These children's parents had contacted the Attachment Center at Evergreen seeking therapy for their adopted children, whom they believed to have attachment disorders. One group, incorrectly described by Myeroff as the experimental group, was 12 children who were brought to Evergreen for treatment; the comparison group was 11 children whose parents did not bring them to Evergreen. (Because these groups were self-selected rather than randomly assigned to groups, this is a quasi-experiment, not a Class I study, and the term "experiment" does not apply.) The failure of families to bring the child for treatment was said to be unrelated to the condition of either child or parent, and the two groups were described as similar in age, gender, ethnic background, family income, and pre-adoption placements. Whether they were also matched on their initial checklist scores was not mentioned, although this may be the condition referred to.

Both groups of parents completed the checklist twice, the second time after a four-week interval. For the group that received treatment, a two-week intensive occurred midway between the two data collections. The Website report of this study did not indicate the nature of the statistical analysis but noted a significant decrease in aggression and delinquency scores from the pre-treatment to the post-treatment measure for the treated children, with no significant changes in the parents' reports on the non-treatment group.

The Myeroff study is a step forward because of its attempt to provide a comparison group. However, the researchers failed to address two issues. First, as was the case for the first study, there is a serious question about the validity of the outcome measure. If parents' reports are treated as just what they are— parents' opinions—their use is legitimate, but if they are treated as direct and valid measures of the children's actual condition, they may be a good deal less legitimate. Once again we run into the attachment therapy problem of regarding parental responses as the critical measure, without the need for independent validation.

Even more importantly, though, the Myeroff study did not deal with the differences between the families that determined whether or not the children were brought for treatment. Although we can only speculate on what these differences were, we do know that families that make different treatment choices do so most of the time because of other real differences among them, although chance occurrences may also play a role. For example, families with one or two children may be able to make different choices than those with many children, and those where the marriage functions well may make different choices than those with shaky marital relationships. Types of jobs may help to determine whether travel is possible; physical illness or educational needs of siblings all influence decisions. And all of these factors may have serious impacts on relationships within the family and on the development of adopted children. Randomized trials would make it possible to average out the effects of all these factors. In the absence of randomized trials, we would at least expect to see researchers give some analysis of the role these factors play in differences between quasi-experimental groups.

One more point about the Myeroff work may be made by referring to the Lester study, described earlier in this chapter. Keeping in mind that the measures used focus on the parents' assessments of the children, we should consider whether these measures are influenced by success in bringing the children for treatment versus failure to manage this. All the parents, or at least one per family, presumably felt that treatment at Evergreen would be beneficial. One group thus achieved what they assumed was a beneficial situation, while the other group was disappointed in its attempts—with potential effects on attitudes and evaluations in general.

In addition, the two sets of parents had different experiences over at least the next month. The parents who brought their children for treatment experienced travel and change. They went through a period of at least two weeks without having to take much responsibility for the children whom they had reported to be so difficult to live with. They were given praise and support by the center staff. Some stayed in the area and had a vacation from everyday life. The non-treatment group stayed at home, went to work, cared for the children, and remained in the situation that had led them to seek help; in addition, they had to cope with the factors that had made their attendance at Evergreen impossible. It is not surprising that the first group had a temporary improvement of their view on many aspects of life (including the children) and the second group's view remained the same or even worsened.

CONCLUSION

The conclusion we are forced to draw from these studies is that there is no empirical validation for attachment therapy. There are no Class I studies, and the Class II studies are too weak even to imply the effectiveness of the treatment. It is not usually possible for scientific method to demonstrate that an effect does not exist. However, combining the evidence about AT's efficacy with the deaths associated with the treatment, we have a far stronger argument against the practice than can be presented for it.

REFERENCES

Achenbach, T. (1991). *Manual for the Child Behavior Checklist and 1991 Profile.* Burlington, VT: University of Vermont Press.

Beutler, L., & Harwood, T. M. (2001). Antiscientific attitudes: What happens when scientists are antiscientific? *Journal of Clinical Psychology, 57,* 43–51.

Chambless, D., & Hollon, S. (1998). Defining empirically supported therapies. *Journal of Consulting and Clinical Psychology, 66,* 7–18.

Cline, F. (1992). *Hope for high risk and rage filled children.* Evergreen, CO: EC Publications.

Dawes, R. (1994). *House of cards: Psychology and psychotherapy built upon myth.* New York: Free Press.

Erickson, M. (1962). The identification of a secure reality. *Family Process, 1*(2), 294–303.

Flyvbjerg, B. (2001). *Making social science matter.* Cambridge: Cambridge University Press.

Gottfried, M., & Wolfe, B. (1998). Toward a more clinically valid approach to therapy research. *Journal of Consulting and Clinical Psychology, 66,* 143–150.

Hanson, R., & Spratt, E. (2000). Reactive Attachment Disorder in children: What we know about the disorder and implications for treatment. *Child Maltreatment,* 5(2), 137–151.

Lester, V. (1997). *Behavior change as reported by caregivers of children receiving holding therapy.* Retrieved August 4, 2000, from http//:www.attach.org/lester.htm.

Myeroff, R. (1996). *Comparative effectiveness of attachment therapy with the special needs adoptive population.* Unpublished dissertation, Union Institute, Ohio.

Myeroff, R., Mertlich, G., & Gross, G. (1999). Comparative effectiveness of holding therapy with aggressive children. *Child Psychiatry and Human Development,* 29(4), 303–313.

Naglieri, J. A., LeBuffe, P. A., & Pfeiffer, S. I. (1994). *Devereux Scale of Mental Disorders.* San Antonio, TX: The Psychological Corporation.

Patrick, P., Mozzoni, M., & Patrick, S. (2000). Evidence-based care and the single-subject design. *Infants and Young Children, 13*(1), 60–73.

Randolph, E. (2000). *Manual for the Randolph Attachment Disorder Questionnaire* (3rd ed.). Evergreen, CO: The Attachment Center Press.

Randolph, E. (2001). *Broken hearts; wounded minds.* Evergreen, CO: RFR Publications.

Unterwager, R., & Wakefield, H. (1990). *The real world of child interrogations.* Springfield, IL: C. C. Thomas.

Weisz, J., Weiss, B., Han, S., Granger, D., & Morton, T. (1995). Effects of psychotherapy with children and adolescents revisited: A meta-analysis of treatment outcome studies. *Psychological Bulletin, 117,* 387–403.

Zaslow, R. (1982). [The psychopathology of human aggression in the framework of attachment therapy ...]. *Zeitschrift fur klinische Psychologie und Psychotherapie, 30*(2), 162–180.

Zaslow, R., & Menta, M.(1975). *The psychology of the Z-process: Attachment and activity.* San Jose, CA: San Jose State University Press.

Chapter 8

The Deceivers and the Deceived:
Factors That Made Attachment Therapy
Acceptable to Parents and to Practitioners

A brutally frank title for this chapter might be "When the Charlatans Met the Suckers." However name-calling might relieve our feelings, though, such a title far oversimplifies the problem. The AT practitioners Connell Watkins and Julie Ponder claimed to believe in their own work, and they may well have done so. They were apparently sold some new snake oil by an itinerant rebirthing instructor. Jeane Newmaker, too, seems to have been a "true believer," if only in the need to remake Candace in a different image.

At least three relatively competent adults, each with some type of professional training, thus bought into a set of ideas and practices that many would reject solely on the basis of common sense. The three were joined in this by staff from some North Carolina child protective services agencies and by the insurance company that may have paid some of the fees. Watkins and Ponder, of course, stood to benefit financially by AT practice, but the others did not.

Some who have become familiar with the facts of the Candace Newmaker case have been eager to analyze the personalities of the central adult characters. Superficially, they do seem to share the very personality they postulated as evidence of attachment disorder: manipulative, controlling, cruel, emotionally cold. But we do not have anything like adequate information for such a discussion of these people. Their courtroom appearances and testimony and their actions in the many videotaped records of Candace's treatment give us very little more than the equivalent of gossip over the backyard fence.

Even if we had wonderful insights into these personalities, we would have only one of the many factors that formed the pattern leading to Candace's death. This chapter examines a number of factors that may have gone into that pattern. We look at some facts that could have encouraged the AT practitioners to carry on with their techniques, such as the present use of the Internet and the past history of violent and intrusive treatments in the United States. We also explore the acceptance of AT by parents, looking at some possibly relevant personality characteristics and parental styles, at the effect on parents of AT as opposed to normal family therapy, and at the influence of beliefs about adoption. We examine some common errors of thinking and logic that may have confused both practitioners and parents. Finally, we discuss some national and world events that may have facilitated the acceptance of AT.

THE PRACTICE AND THE PRACTITIONERS

Watkins and Ponder did not make a random error in selecting the treatment that caused Candace Newmaker's death. They were part of a loosely knit group of practitioners who shared activities and a systematically organized set of beliefs. A fringe subculture supported them in their alienation from the work of conventionally trained psychotherapists. In this loose group were a number of people with genuine advanced degrees from accredited institutions, a number of others whose claims on their résumés did not bear verification, and still others with a history of malpractice complaints and suspended licenses. In a field where a measure of success is publication in a peer-reviewed professional journal, most of these people had self-published through local printers or newsletter-like clinic journals.

Shadow Professionals

Fringe psychotherapists, whether practitioners of AT or other approaches, have a tendency to mimic the actions of genuine professionals without actually doing what the professionals do. They produce written material that sounds important to the lay reader. They acquire diplomas and board certifications in large numbers from organizations that seem to exist for no other purpose. They describe themselves as experts. They are especially fond of providing checklists to support the diagnosis that is their specialty. (One practicing exorcist uses both a checklist for demonic possession and an informed-consent document in case of trouble [Wagner, 2000].) These people provide only the shadow of treatment, not the substance given by the genuine professional therapist.

"Shadow professionals" such as AT practitioners often have professional degrees, but their training in fringe practices does not come from accredited institutions. Such practices are not taught in academic settings but in informal workshops, seminars, or apprenticeships of the kind Julie Ponder was doing with Connell Watkins. Ponder's knowledge of rebirthing techniques was acquired even more informally when the California practitioner Douglas Gosney passed through town. The appeal of these informal training approaches is obvious. They are cheap, they are quick, and they do not require preparation, letters of recommendation, or the Graduate Record Examination. The verbal and quantitative skills demanded by accredited graduate work are absent. Shadow professionals like these aspects, but the downside is all too obvious to the rest of us.

The Influence of the Internet

The Internet is an extraordinary source of information, without which the authors of this book would have needed many more years to learn about AT. However, it has provided the shadow professionals with an immensely enhanced power to reach potential customers. The average Internet user does not have the scholarly or professional background to tell shadow from substance and responds positively to the "proof by assertion" characteristic of many Websites.

As we discuss elsewhere in this book, the First Amendment protects communication of ideas, whether the statements are correct or not. It does not protect deliberate fraud, but such deception is remarkably difficult to prove and punish. As a result, claims about AT made on the Internet cannot easily be fought except by contradictory statements of fact. More than 80 separate Internet sites are presently at work either advocating or offering AT, and very few offer competing information.

The Internet also provides nationwide support groups for AT advocates. Living in an isolated town no longer prevents parents from telling each other that AT and the associated therapeutic parenting are the only treatments for their children no matter what is said by disapproving neighbors or ignorant psychologists and social workers.

Internet sources present a dilemma for genuine clinicians. Parents may discover AT on the Internet and come in to demand a referral. They do not want a discussion or explanations, and they make this clear. The therapist who wishes to keep the door open for further contact may feel forced to do as asked, rather than to alienate the family completely.

The History of Intrusive Therapies

AT practitioners did not invent most of the ideas they hold or the techniques they use. On the contrary, similar concepts go back many decades in the United States, making them vaguely familiar to professionals and parents alike and thus facilitating their acceptance. Some of the more recent background of AT was discussed in chapter 3.

Intrusive confrontational therapies can undoubtedly be traced back to the shamans who used bears' heads and rattles to try to shock the spirit of a disturbed person back to good sense. Exorcists had (and have) techniques for scaring away demons that include physical restraint of the "possessed." Franz Mesmer, the eighteenth-century hypnotherapist, used physical touch to bring on a convulsive reaction, and his patients felt better temporarily. But none of these "therapists" had much of a systematic theoretical foundation for their efforts.

Wilhelm Reich

For an organized, systematic intellectual ancestor of AT, we need to look at the 1930s and 1940s when the psychoanalytically-trained German Wilhelm Reich was active in the United States. Reich died in prison as a result of his refusal to stop selling his orgone box, a treatment for cancer and almost everything else. But Reich was actually most interested in the treatment of psychologically based problems, which he believed resulted from disturbance of a pulsatory cycle of tension and relaxation (Sharaf, 1983).

Reich believed that poor early emotional experiences led people to develop "character armor" that limited emotional and sexual expressiveness. This phenomenon had a physical side, indicated by stiffness and tension in various body areas, notably the eyes and chest.

Reich felt that character armor could be caused by prenatal experiences, even by the mother's armor existing during pregnancy. Painful birth experiences could also result in armoring of chest and eyes, with resulting distortions of emotional and perceptual life. A mother's hostile or unresponsive look could create armor, as well.

Reich suggested breaking down the armor by having a practitioner press his thumbs hard into the patient's chest, provoking the patient to tears or rage. Child patients were tickled, restrained physically, and kept in constant eye contact until anger and crying occurred.

It seems that the AT apple has not fallen far from the Reichian tree. In both views, emotional problems are caused by the personality and actions of the mother, both before and after birth. A cycle of need and gratification is the foundation for emotional life. Prolonged eye contact is a source of emotional change, as are physical restraint and pain, culminating in rage and tears.

Is AT solely a Reichian approach, then? No, it probably should not be seen that way, although the connection is a strong one. Physical restraint has been advocated by other American therapists, in addition to people such as Cline and Zaslow who were mentioned in chapters 2 and 3. Milton Erickson (1962), a well-known American hypnotherapist of the 1960s (and not to be confused with Erik Erikson), reported advising a mother to sit with all her weight on her disobedient 8-year-old son, giving him nothing to eat or drink while she held him down for many hours. Erickson felt that this treatment, combined with later withholding of preferred food, caused a dramatic improvement in the child's behavior.

The Self-help Tradition

When we think of people seeking help, our first assumption may be that they go to someone who has some claims of professional expertise at helping others. But we need to remember that the mental health movement in the United States has for almost a century emphasized self-help. From the days of Clifford

Beers' popular book, *A Mind That Found Itself* (1907/1981), we have accepted the idea that the responsibility for mental health must be in the individual. Professional therapists have emphasized the idea that they cannot cure mental illness unless the patient really wants to be cured. Bookstores have specialized self-help sections that provide advice on healing through every means from diet to meditation. Self-help's appeal may be based on the traditional American values of independence and autonomy.

Self-help seems to take on different implications when parents apply techniques to children. By law and custom, parents can exercise their rights to make decisions about their children in much the same way the adults can make decisions about themselves. We argue that treating yourself and treating your children are not the same thing. If you make a mistake in treating yourself, only you will suffer. A mistake in treating a child can cause the child to suffer. Nevertheless, if parents have to give their consent to certain medical procedures before they can be carried out, it does seem logical that no one can forbid the parent to use procedures that are legal and do not require a license. When we combine these factors with another American tradition—the belief that parents have a right to rear their children as they please—it is hard to argue against parents who apply self-help techniques to their children. Only an actual injury to the child gives grounds for legal recourse.

AT fits into the self-help tradition in several ways, permitting and encouraging parents to become participants in therapy. The child's diagnosis is often based entirely on the mother's opinion. Some AT practitioners have trained parents to do holding at home. Most have parents participate in some treatment sessions with their children. Parenting advice is dispensed, recommending such techniques as withholding food, putting alarms on bedroom doors, and requiring strong sitting at length. Attachment disorder support groups recommend these techniques to each other. They also discuss the medications prescribed for children and recommend getting the pediatrician to prescribe particular drugs. Some suggest the use of various over-the-counter medicines, singly and in combination, in ways they have experimented with.

THE CUSTOMERS: FACTORS THAT MAKE PARENTS ACCEPT AT

As we noted earlier, it is impossible to accurately diagnose or even describe personality problems that might have characterized Connell Watkins, Julie Ponder, or Jeane Newmaker. We simply do not have enough information about them, and any statements we make are speculative. In an earlier chapter we discussed the possibility of Narcissistic Personality Disorder as a factor in Jeane Newmaker's responses to Candace and to the AT philosophy, but it seems that with the available evidence we could not legitimately consider everyone connected with AT as narcissists. It would be of greater interest to find nonpathological characteristics of parents who become involved in AT. Such characteristics would have more explanatory power than the relatively unusual pathology does. In the following section we look at some normal but different ways in which adults respond to children to see how these might connect with enthusiasm for AT.

Parenting Styles and Personality Styles

Parents who systematically mistreat their children do not usually do so randomly or unpredictably. Their inappropriate parenting behavior is an integrated part of their personalities and makes sense in terms of the personality as a whole, or at least in terms of the general parenting style. In this section, we discuss personality and parenting issues relevant to the use of AT.

Munchausen by Proxy?

People hearing about Jeane Newmaker for the first time sometimes categorize her actions as "Munchausen (or factitious disorder) by proxy." This classification, named for the tall-tale-telling Baron Munchausen, refers to a situation involving a child's apparent physical illness in which the child's symptoms are actually being caused by secret actions of the parent. For example, the mother of a hospitalized child could prick her own finger to add blood to the child's urine sample and create the appearance of serious illness. More dangerously, a parent could hold a pillow over a child's face until he stopped breathing and then scream for a nurse and claim breathing had halted spontaneously. These Munchausen by proxy parents seem to thrive on the sympathy and attention they receive as they wring their hands helplessly over the sick child. Their tall tales are rewarded by compassion from others.

Could Jeane Newmaker be considered a case of psychiatric Munchausen by proxy in a way parallel to the parent who creates physical symptoms? Although she seems to have been pleased by the sympathy and support she received in Colorado, it is hard to see exactly what she might have done to produce symptoms in Candace. In fact, of course, she did not have to produce any, because according to AT beliefs the mother's report about the child is the most reliable possible information (see chapter 7). The therapists did not assess Candace's symptoms (in fact, her initial diagnosis was done over the telephone) but relied on the mother's statements. If Munchausen by proxy can include simple misstatements of fact, Jeane Newmaker may fit the description; otherwise, she does not.

The Authoritarian Personality

A more general personality concept, rather than a diagnosis, may provide a better description of Jeane Newmaker, at least as she appeared in her courtroom testimony. Newmaker's self-presentation was strongly reminiscent of the pattern called authoritarian personality. This concept, much discussed after World War II, fell out of use as the political climate changed but may be helpful to us. It is a statement about character rather than pathology and, as we will see, provides a remarkably accurate portrait of Jeane Newmaker.

A person with a high level of authoritarianism sees human beings in terms of strength and weakness rather than in more subtle or complex ways. He or she is simultaneously ready to lord over weaker persons and to obey those who are stronger. As one writer has described the authoritarian personality, the term

characterizes the basically weak and dependent individual who has sacrificed his capacity for genuine experience of self and others in order to maintain a facade of precarious order and safety. In the type case, he confronts with a facade of spurious strength a world in which rigidly stereotyped categories are substituted for the affectionate and individualized experience of which he is incapable. Such a person ... lacks self-awareness and shuns intraception. His judgements are governed by a punitive conventional moralism, reflecting external standards in which he remains insecure since he has failed to make them really his own. His relations with others depend on considerations of power, success, and adjustment, in which people figure as means rather than ends ... In his world, the good, the powerful, and the in-group stand in fundamental opposition to the immoral, the weak, the out-group. For all that he seeks to align himself with the former, his underlying feelings of weakness and self-contempt commit him to a constant and embittered struggle to prove to himself and others that he really belongs to the strong and good. (Smith, 1950, p. 776)

Jeane Newmaker's actions seem to fit this description. Weeping on the witness stand, she defended herself by saying she had never concealed anything from "the experts" or failed to cooperate with them, thus aligning herself with those she saw as powerful and, therefore, good. Her relationship with Candace seems to have stressed putting up a good appearance—the horses and dogs, the mother-and-daughter trips, the lessons, and finally the therapy that a good adoptive mother should provide. When questioned about whether she herself had been advised to seek therapy, Jeane Newmaker invariably responded as if the question involved seeking advice about Candace, not counseling for herself. This, and her failure to respond to Candace's muffled pleas and later silence in the fatal session, seem to indicate a lack of self-awareness, blanking out her reading of her own internal response to potential danger.

The entire philosophy of AT reflects authoritarianism. The more intense the distress of the weak, immoral patient, the more it is to be ignored. The weak must always be watched, because their cunning skill at manipulation gives them a paradoxical power. The child's true self-awareness must be flooded out by accusations of hate and hostility. Rigid stereotyping defines the child's diagnosis and determines that all children are to receive the same treatment. When similar views of the world are embraced by an individual such as Jeane Newmaker, that person is probably easily convinced of the value of AT.

Parenting Style

When the term "parenting style" is used, the reference is to the parent's attitudes and expectations rather than to specific techniques of nurturing or of discipline. Two parents might act in similar ways, but if they did so for different reasons they would be evaluated as having different parenting styles—although parents with one style may be less likely to behave in a particular way than parents with another style. A parent's attitudes are partly determined by personality components such as authoritarianism, but they are also derived from the individual's ways of solving problems and knowledge of child development. There have been many attempts to describe and categorize parents' styles, but we can look further at one that seems especially relevant to AT issues: Newberger's (1983) approach, described in chapter 4.

In the approach we will use, parents' styles are categorized in a range from simpler to more complex levels. In the most primitive style, the *egoistic* level, the parent's ways of dealing with the child are determined by the parent's own needs and feelings, not the child's. Typically, a parent at this level might say that she gave a child no breakfast because "I wasn't hungry." Egoistic parents tend to be inconsistent because they enforce rules only when in the mood. They may encourage undesirable behavior when they feel cheerful and think it's funny or even punish "good" behavior when they're irritable and depressed.

At the next level, the *conventional* level, the parent is less controlled by mood and impulse and behaves more consistently. The conventional parent has a set of rules for dealing with children and applies these across the board, in the same way for all children and situations, without regard to outcome. Rules are followed because they are "the rules" or "the right way." The parent is not concerned with having a beneficial impact on the child's development and behavior but with the parent's assessment of himself or herself as a person who does the right thing in the right way.

Two levels of parenting styles are more complex than the conventional style. At the *individualistic* level, the parent tries to use different approaches for different children, with the hope of fine-tuning good techniques for each individual. The focus is on achieving the best outcome for each child. At the *analytical* level, the parent considers his or her own impact on the child's behavior and realizes that parental moods, wishes, or worries may influence the outcome of discipline and training techniques. Compared to the egoistic and conventional styles, these higher levels of parenting style are likely to have better outcomes for family functioning because they allow for individual differences among children and dynamic change in a parent.

Jeane Newmaker and other proponents of AT approaches can hardly be considered to be at either the individualistic or the analytical level. Newmaker's view seems to have been focused on the right thing to do rather than on the outcome of her actions.

The appropriate category for Newmaker's parenting style seems to have been either egoistic or conventional, but it does not seem accurate to describe her as egoistic in the most basic sense. We do not have evidence that she failed to feed Candace unless she herself was hungry or even that she behaved inconsistently as her mood changed. However, Jeane Newmaker did concentrate in some ways on making Candace more like her adoptive mother. She had Candace instructed as a Roman Catholic, in spite of the fact that a 5-year-old child would have had some sense of her birth family's quite different religious orientation. When Candace's family name was changed on her birth certificate at the time of her adoption, she was also given Jeane Newmaker's middle name in place of the middle name her birth mother had given her. These acts may imply a conventional parenting style in which rules were followed without consideration of their effect on a particular child.

We can consider the idea of parental style as it applies to AT as well as to describe Jeane Newmaker. AT and therapeutic foster parenting seem to have an overwhelmingly egoistic approach. The parent's comfort, convenience, and happiness are treated as the critical standards for the child's behavior. The child's own expressed needs are treated as insignificant or even as deliberate deceptions directed at a power grab. The child is to obey at once, in a manner described as "right the first time," "fast and snappy," "Mom and Dad's way." Children are to be especially solicitous of the mother, giving her back rubs and foot rubs and waiting on her as if they were her caregivers.

Other evidence of the egoistic level of therapeutic foster parenting comes from the recommendation that parents should be as unpredictable and arbitrary as possible. Nancy Thomas's writings (Thomas, 2000) for parents suggest that hugs should be given only when a parent feels like it, not at the child's request. Brita St. Clair (1999), Candace's therapeutic foster mother and Watkins's assistant, wrote a pamphlet describing how to "drive your kids sane" with unpredictable and bizarre behavior toward them. That adults must have complete control and authority is the egoistic principle on which much of this practice is based.

Some aspects of AT can also be regarded as part of a conventional style. Techniques such as strong sitting and withholding of food are applied to all children in all circumstances. AT practitioners ignore therapists' usual cautions about the effect of physically intrusive techniques on sexually abused children. The possibility that a child is in genuine physical distress is denied. In the mode of conventional parenting, AT practitioners stress the importance of their right actions over the potential impact of the action on the child.

Parental Control

For a final way of thinking about parental characteristics that encourage use of AT, it may be useful to consider the degree of *control* parents consider suitable. Psychologists such as Brian K. Barber have studied parents' use of both behavioral control of children and psychological control. Psychological control entails attempts to influence children's thinking and emotional processes. It has been described as "a rather insidious type of control that potentially inhibits or intrudes upon psychological development through manipulation and exploitation of the parent-child bond ..., negative, affect-laden expressions and criticisms, ... and excessive personal control" such as possessiveness and protectiveness (Barber, 1996, p. 3297). Barber has noted that such parental control is "a consistently negative and inhibiting experience for children" (1996, p. 3314).

AT clearly employs constant psychological control and does so consistently and deliberately, not as a quick fix for annoying behavior but with the stated intention of altering the child's thinking and influencing emotional processes. In Barber's terms, the parent and the AT practitioner intentionally constrain, invalidate, and manipulate the child's psychological experiences. Some specific actions, common to AT and to the controlling families Barber studied, are interfering with the child's talking, asking leading questions ("You hate your mother, don't you?"), ignoring the child's comments, discounting or misinterpreting a feeling the child expresses, questioning the child's loyalty to the family, and shifting between caring and attacking expressions.

Controlling parenting may seem undesirable to both professionals and many parents, but it has a historical tradition. As we see later in this chapter, some religious traditions assume that a parent's real task is control. But this view overlaps both religious and secular philosophies. In describing child care in the early Israeli *kibbutzim,* for example, Bruno Bettelheim (1969) noted that the settlers were advised by pediatricians simply to spoon food back into a baby's mouth if it had been vomited. Similarly, toilet training involving laxatives and suppositories was at one time a popular approach.

Beliefs and Thought Processes

So far we have been talking about feelings and emotional attitudes that might attract a person to AT as a philosophy or practice. However, people's decisions are not entirely about emotion but include what they know—or, perhaps more accurately, what they think they know. We refer in an early part of this book to the evidence that parents commonly know very little about early emotional development but have systematic erroneous beliefs on the subject. Many well-educated individuals, sometimes even those employed in social services careers, have incorrect beliefs about human beings in the context of which AT seems like a sensible approach.

Catharsis

Many otherwise sophisticated persons still subscribe to the idea of *catharsis,* an ancient belief about negative emotions such as anger. Catharsis assumes that anger builds like a head of steam until it is released through physical and verbal expression. According to this notion, unreleased anger causes problems as excessive steam pressure in a boiler would do. Unblocked anger results in problems such as physical symptoms and the inability to experience positive feelings toward others.

The ancient Greek dramatists designed their plays to cause vicarious emotional experience in the spectators and thus to drain off bad feelings of rage and sadness. Many—perhaps most—modern Americans share this belief and use it to support the continuation of spectacles such as boxing. They are also willing customers for devices such as sponge-rubber paddles for pretend fighting or pillows to punch to release rage.

However, modern psychological research by Carol Tavris (1989) and others shows that the Greeks did not know it all in this case. Work such as Tavris's has demonstrated that actions expressing rage actually make people feel angry longer than if they bottle up their feelings. Although expression of anger can be useful as a communication to other people, it does not destroy the anger any more than laughter destroys joy or kisses destroy love.

AT is based on the ancient catharsis concept. Its advocates assume that anger once stimulated in an abandoned or maltreated child must be released and expressed or it will hang on and block the growth of affectionate feelings. The child who does not spontaneously express rage must have it triggered by physical and psychological pain. Parents or practitioners who believe in catharsis and the venting of rage are likely to feel that AT makes sense, whereas those who reject the catharsis concept would logically also reject the basic principles of AT.

Attachment and Adoption

The belief that biological relationships play a strong role in emotional attachment is common in the United States today. A surprising number of foster parents questioned at a conference about child care expressed their belief that a child's emotional attachment to adults occurs at the time of birth or even before birth. An older college student in a class taught by one of the authors was convinced that genetic relationships between mother and child determined their emotional relationship. When people have such beliefs, they are likely to consider adoption a truly momentous event involving serious emotional trauma. Contrary to all the research that demonstrates excellent development for children adopted in infancy, they anticipate serious problems for all adopted children, just as AT advocates claim.

As writers such as Irving Leon (2002) have pointed out, the belief that adoption causes persistent feelings of loss is not only contradicted by research, it is also not shared by many other societies. In Hawaiian traditional culture, for example, attachments between children and parents were considered to result from care and association. Today, according to Leon, more than 25% of Hawaiian families include nonbiological children, and generally these families do not stress grief or a sense of abandonment as a feature of their relationships. People with belief systems of this type are probably less likely to consider AT reasonable.

Common Cognitive Errors

We have discussed the roles of feelings and of information in making AT seem acceptable or otherwise to parents and practitioners. There is another factor that we need to examine: *cognitive errors,* the mistakes in thinking that plague most of us and can cause confusion when we try to think through facts and make important decisions.

The mistakes we make in solving problems frequently have to do with *cause-and-effect* relationships. Students in college courses often have to struggle to overcome their tendency to believe that one thing must have caused another if they occur close together in time and place. Until an individual masters this concept, he or she is likely to assume that a correlation between two things—such as high divorce rates and the availability of child pornography—means that one must have made the other one happen. In many cases, however, it is some third or fourth or fifth factor that is the actual cause of the first two. One needs to have a genuine understanding of such cause-and-effect concepts before grasping how research should be designed, and most nonresearchers get little practice in thinking about such issues. (As we saw in chapter 7, it appears that even AT advocates who report research have not had sufficient practice.) Most parents have had little involvement in this kind of thought and are thus easily confused about the logic of AT claims and explanations.

Probability is another difficult but important concept. Much scientific reasoning is based on the proportion of times events occur, but errors are very common when people are asked to reason about probability. For example, in chapter 7 we noted the claim of AT advocates that up to 80% of children in certain circumstances develop attachment disorders. Such an estimate, of course, could mean anything from 0% to 80%; what is up to 80% could also be down to 10%, or 1%, or 0%. But, like hopeful shoppers who assume that up to 75% off means their much-wanted shoes will cost only 25% of their original price, we easily assume that up to 80% means the same as 80%. The advertiser or AT advocate did not misstate the facts, but we manage to misstate them to ourselves. This is an especially troublesome problem for people trying to understand research evidence, because the statistical significance of research findings is stated in terms of probabilities that events could occur by chance alone.

Another common *logical error* makes people's critical analysis of AT more difficult. This mistake, termed *affirming the consequent* by logicians, has been called the *dependent variable error* by psychologists who study the development of problem-solving in children (Demetriou et al., 1993). People make the dependent variable error when they assume that if A causes B, it must be equally true that B causes A. AT writers start on their way to the dependent variable error with the simple observation that young children are more likely to make prolonged eye contact with people they feel attached to than with strangers. From this they conclude that attachment causes eye contact to occur (although, as we noted earlier, the two could simply be correlated). Then comes the leap to the dependent variable error: if attachment causes eye contact, eye contact must also cause attachment. Thus a lack of attachment can be corrected by prolonged eye contact, forced by parent or therapist.

Similarly, if children who have formed an attachment are likely to be more compliant and obedient than those who have not, AT advocates conclude that attachment causes obedience. In turn, in the mode of the dependent variable error, obedience must cause attachment. Repeated experiences of forced compliance, the foundation of AT practice, must then cause attachment to occur. Of course, parents who are struggling with decisions about their children are probably even less likely to detect these deeply embedded logical errors in AT than an unconcerned observer.

Cognitive Dissonance and AT

Cognitive dissonance may be a factor in AT advocates' thinking. In this phenomenon, people's opinions alter because of new information that is uncomfortably dissonant (in disagreement with) their existing knowledge and beliefs. These changes of opinion have an internal logic, but they do not necessarily go in the direction we would intuitively guess. For example, members of end-of the-world cults, disappointed of the final conflagration on the predicted day, may become more strongly convinced than ever that the prediction is true. They may argue that God has changed the day to give the world another chance because He was so pleased with the cult's efforts. These people experience dissonance between beliefs they have. They know they have quit their jobs and given away all their possessions, and they "know" the world is coming to an end; these two facts together make sense for a virtuous, intelligent person. But what if they have given up everything when the world is *not* coming to an end? The conclusion is logically one of two things. Perhaps they are not virtuous, intelligent people, but fools—a belief that is uncomfortably dissonant with their view of themselves. More acceptably, they may conclude that there has been a postponement, a belief that is not dissonant with the observed facts or with their views of themselves. The mechanism of cognitive dissonance helps the cultists achieve the more acceptable, second solution.

How does cognitive dissonance apply to AT? We can list some ideas and thoughts that the therapists may have had while they conducted the rebirthing exercise with Candace. They were aware that other rebirthed children had emerged from their wrap in less than 10 minutes. They had told each other how resistant Candace was, and they had undoubtedly read the work of other AT advocates who described children as vomiting and complaining that they were dying during treatment. They had discussed whether Candace had been dissociating, a term under which some AT practitioners seem to include stopping breathing. They believed that Candace could cunningly manipulate them and that they must force Candace to comply to treat her successfully. To decide to release her from the wrap would have been dissonant with these thoughts and with their beliefs in themselves as expert professionals; a simpler escape from the discomfort of dissonance was to perceive what they were doing as a normal, safe process. For Connell Watkins, particularly, a change of plan would have been uncomfortably at odds with the reputation for toughness and decision she had cultivated.

There was distinct dissonance for AT advocates when the therapy on which they had pinned their hopes culminated in the unquestionable death of the patient. AT was supposed by the therapists to be good for children, not harmful. The therapists thought of themselves as good, intelligent people, not vicious fools. How could good people, applying a beneficial technique, find that their patient is dead? The dissonance among these ideas would motivate the practitioners to find a belief that makes sense of it all and removes the dissonance: that the child was already sick and the death in no way associated with the treatment. (An even more extreme solution to dissonance was apparent in the explanation suggested by some support groups who claimed that Candace had died because she wanted to, to cause trouble for Watkins and Ponder.)

No Proof Needed

To conclude our discussion of cognitive issues, we need to consider how rarely people are convinced by anything other than *individual experience*. The vividness of personal experience should not, but does, far outweigh pages of statistical summaries. Even another person's experience, if described in detail, strikes us as more meaningful than bare numbers without human faces, though we actually do a worse job of dealing with abstractions such as probabilities when we have more information about the people involved. Thus, a single, well-told story about an interesting family with an adopted child successfully treated by AT would probably influence most parents far more than all the arguments and analysis marshaled in this book. Nor are professionals free of an unfortunate tendency to be swayed by personal experience. Recently, the director of a public school project expressed her scorn about the need for empirical support for a teaching technique: "I don't need proof," she said (Hershenson, 2000).

Religious Beliefs and Connections

It would be quite incorrect to claim that some particular religious group has a special affinity for AT. Nevertheless, it is true that AT shares some principles and values with religious thinking that goes back to America's colonial days.

For parents who subscribe to similar beliefs, AT must seem to present a familiar and welcome perspective.

The basic belief shared by AT and some religious groups has to do with sin and its *redemption through obedience.* According to this view, Adam's error, the original sin shared by all humanity since the days of Eden, was disobedience to God. Human beings who refused submission and obedience would not be cleansed of the sin they carried from their birth but would go on becoming more depraved in this life, as well as being damned for eternity. Only submission and obedience to God (and possibly to other authorities as well) could restore the soul to a state of grace, permit the living of a moral life, and of course offer salvation in the afterlife. Jesus, according to this view, redeemed mankind by reenacting (recapitulating, to use the technical term) Adam's actions but making everything right by obeying where Adam had disobeyed.

Does something seem to be missing here? AT proponents do try to make the child obedient to the parents, not to God, so the connection may not seem quite obvious. For early American Protestants, however, the parents were seen as God's officers and disobeying them would be the same as disobedience to God. Disobedient children might expect an unpleasant early death, followed by Hell. The child's obedience to the parents was not just a convenience, but the essential first step toward salvation. Whatever methods could produce obedience were thus much to be desired.

In Peter Slater's discussion of early American religious views of child-rearing, he describes a number of practices we can readily link with AT and therapeutic foster parenting. Shutting a two-year-old in a closet until he promised to behave, withholding food and affection, and depriving the child of desirable toys and activities were used to make children compliant. These methods are hardly unique, but they were accompanied by standards of performance that AT shares. Slater (1970) quotes an eighteenth-century autobiography as saying that children's "obedience must be exact, prompt, and cheerful." "Mind your mother; quick! No crying! Look pleasant!" Mothers were seen as central figures in the family.

As Slater points out, however, even the most hellfire-and-brimstone New England Protestants advocated kindness and gentleness as major components of child-rearing. Harsh requirements for obedience and submissiveness were only one theme in that religious view of children, and it would be foolish to picture Connell Watkins as the spiritual heiress of Cotton Mather.

Some American religious groups have made a point of intrusive, controlling parenting in ways that might make AT seem almost mainstream to parents. One example is the Babywise program, designed by a clergyman and a pediatrician and for some time marketed through various church organizations. The Babywise authors recommended that the child should obey "according to the character of true obedience—immediately, completely, without challenge, and without complaint" (Ezzo & Bucknam, 1995, p. 87). The obedient child in question is what the authors call a pretoddler, a word they use to

describe an infant from 5 to 15 months of age. To achieve obedience, one recommended method is to squeeze or swat the child's hand or thigh hard
enough to cause discomfort in response to misbehavior such as dropping food
while eating or placing messy hands in the hair. The authors anticipated the
reluctance of parents to enforce obedience in this way but declare it necessary
to "train the heart."

There is a curious overlap between the AT philosophy and some beliefs connected with exorcism. Not all religious groups believe in possession by demons
or in the power of exorcism to get rid of any that are in residence—nor do AT
practitioners necessarily share such beliefs. However, it is notable that some
exorcists consider rejection by parents to be a possible cause of demonic possession. One has written that adopted children "frequently become very rebel-
lious and difficult to handle. I have usually been led to cast out a spirit of
abandonment residing in adopted kids. They need to pray to forgive their parents for giving them away" (Wagner, 2000, pp. 120–121). The same writer discussed "spirits of trauma, violence, panic and the like" entering when a birth is
difficult or complicated. Lack of early contact with the mother was suggested as
an entry point for "spirits of abandonment, isolation and loneliness." It is hard
to decide whether what we have here is a religious belief that influences the
writer's beliefs about psychology or the influence of popular psychology on
statements of religious concern.

Parents' Experiences with AT

Parents' beliefs, thought processes, and religious views can all affect their acceptance or rejection of AT. Once they have accepted AT practices, however, or
even had preliminary talks with practitioners, they have personal experiences
that need to be considered. These personal experiences can assure their continuing commitment to AT.

Rewards of the AT Experience: Support for Parents

Welcoming and emotional support of parents seem to be a specialty of AT
practitioners. Mothers, especially, are treated as both the expert on and the
emotional focus of the child's life. They are spoken of as "awesome Moms" and
almost by definition considered to be doing their best at a difficult job. Adoptive
mothers are regularly contrasted favorably with the evil, abusive, abandoning
birth mothers whose ill effects on the child have created a dangerous and
frightening situation. It is the child who is to be treated to correct what has
happened.

The AT view of the mother is in sharp contrast with that of child or family
psychotherapy. In standard practice, a family-systems perspective examines the
roles of all family members, including the mother, in establishing or correcting

problems. Every family member is thought of as influencing everyone else. Undesirable influences on a child may come from anyone in the family, however virtuous and blameless that person may otherwise be, and there may be a need to alter the beliefs and actions of one or more people to treat the child. This perspective includes the mother as an influential member of the system, of course, and considers that she too may have to change so the child's symptoms can improve.

Reading the messages posted by Internet AT support group members shows the fury and contempt with which some mothers respond to the idea that they may need to change in any way. (And, as we saw earlier, Jeane Newmaker did not seem even to understand questions related to this idea.) Fulminations against "experts" are common among these messages and seem often to be touched off by suggestions that a mother could try another approach or could be making a mistake. One such mother, who claimed that her adopted daughter was severely disturbed, insisted on pursuing a second adoption and expressed rage over her caseworker's concern that the two children would be too much for the mother. This mother attributed the caseworker's judgment to an excessive affection for the first adopted child.

Rewards of AT: Respite Care

AT practitioners recommend that parents have holidays from caring for their AT-treated children, who remain in respite care with an outside caregiver while the parents have a break. Respite care is not unusual in the lives of children with severe handicapping conditions such as cerebral palsy, but it is much less common in the case of mental illness, especially if the behavioral symptoms are not dangerous ones. It seems especially odd for practitioners to advise separation when the problem is thought to be connected with attachment. Therapeutic foster parents, too, are to have respite help, but those respite workers are not to make eye contact with the child or provide preferred foods for fear that their actions will make the child attach to the respite caregiver.

CHANGING TIMES, CHANGING LIVES: NATIONAL AND WORLD EVENTS RELEVANT TO AT ACCEPTANCE

The factors we have already discussed provide some explanation for the strange eagerness with which some parents accept AT. But when we look at the recent past, we see what appears to be proliferation of the practice. An increasing number of Internet sites advertise AT, and they do so in increasingly organized and deceptively professional ways, using terms such as evidence-based and posting nationwide schedules of lectures and workshops. Have events created a more fertile field for AT?

National Events: Internet and Television

There is no question that increased access to the Internet has been a windfall for fringe therapies of all kinds. People living in rural areas, who may have little contact with anyone except neighbors, can now easily find information—or disinformation—on any topic. In addition, that information will be in whatever form its author wanted; no publisher has had the chance to reject it, and no editor has checked its accuracy. Advances in technology have thus potentially stimulated retreats in critical thinking about fringe therapies.

Some television and radio programs have offered AT as an exciting "story," and few if any have taken a critical approach. For example, the television program *Law and Order* used a story line involving a child's death during rebirthing, using phrases that were recognizable from the Watkins-Ponder trial, but altered the ending so the child died from an allergic reaction rather than from the treatment. The message seemed to be that AT was strange and suspicious but not essentially harmful to children.

More egregiously, National Public Radio presented a program on attachment therapy that had been purchased from a non-NPR source. This program offered sound bites from both advocates and opponents of AT but never stated that a real difference of opinion exists between the AT advocates and serious professionals such as Charles Zeanah and Beverly James. Zeanah and James were not aware that their contributions were to be edited into a format that minimized the differences of viewpoint. The contributions of the AT group were given maximum impact on listeners by the inclusion of personal anecdotes and vivid stories. The comments taken from Zeanah and James were general and abstract rather than detailed and concrete. The overall impact of the program was thus supportive of AT in spite of the inclusion of opposing voices and did not reflect the views of the majority of the professional community.

National Events: Deinstitutionalization

For much of the twentieth century in the United States, severely handicapped or mentally ill individuals were most commonly placed in institutional care. In the case of children, such placement could occur soon after birth and might be based on illegitimacy or fears of hereditary problems rather than evident handicapping conditions. It was the rare (and, usually, the wealthy) family that cared for a handicapped relative at home.

By about 1970, however, opinions about institutional care were changing. There were revelations about cruel treatment of inmates and much publicity from documentary films such as Joseph Wiseman's "Titicut Follies." Evidence was accumulating that institutional life caused even further deterioration in those who began life with handicaps. Concern increased about the civil rights of oppressed groups, in and out of institutions. And, of course, there were questions about the cost of institutional care to society, naturally followed by discussion of cheaper ways to deal with the institutionalized population.

The result of these events was a move toward *deinstitutionalization* and community-based care for all but the most fragile or potentially dangerous mentally ill patients. Perhaps the most conspicuous outcome of deinstitutionalization has been an enormous increase in homelessness, as mentally ill persons have drifted into living on the streets. A less conspicuous but significant effect has involved new roles for the foster care system. Special-needs children form a growing proportion of children in foster care as their birth families fail to function or become homeless themselves.

Deinstitutionalization has thus placed a novel burden on the foster care system. In the past, foster parents might do a successful job if they simply offered the kinds of care every child obviously needs. Today foster parents may be asked to deal with children whose special needs would strain the resources of highly qualified professionals and whose needs range from heart monitors to suctioning of breathing tubes to supervision of medication for depression. Adoptive parents, too, may be asked to learn to deal with special-needs children who once would have been labeled unadoptable.

Finally, we see foster and adoptive families taking larger numbers of children than were usually cared for by one family in the past. Increased employment of women and other factors have reduced the number of foster homes available and increased the demands made on the individuals who are willing to take on this work.

Thus we now have foster parents trying to care for large groups of children, many of whom are medically and emotionally fragile and who may have extensive histories of new placements and new separations. It is not surprising that these well-meaning adults are easily persuaded to become involved in fringe treatments. They are probably right in thinking that the rest of us have no idea what they are going through. No wonder they reject our suggestions in favor of a proffered miracle.

National Change: Medical Intervention

As we have noted elsewhere, AT purports to treat emotional problems its practitioners attribute to early pain and suffering. Although it is not at all clear how pain in early life affects emotional development—if it does so at all—effective modern medical interventions for infants can certainly be accompanied by repeated pain and distress. Compared to past situations, today's living children are more likely to have been saved medically from life-threatening conditions and to have experienced suffering in the course of the treatment that saved them. This is true in spite of the fact that medical professionals are more aware than they used to be of the need to manage infants' pain appropriately (Mercer, 1998).

The fear and anxiety of parents with a sick baby are not readily conquered, even when the baby recovers and thrives. The agony and guilt of failing to protect the child from distress may color the parents' feelings for years into the future. Such parents may constantly anticipate serious problems from the child who used to be sick and to search for ways to avoid or cure them.

The AT philosophy offers an acknowledgment of the parents' fears and a method that claims to cure the problems that the parent is sure must be there. As medical interventions become more common and more dramatic without assuaging parents' worries, more customers for AT may be created.

National Events: The Homeschooling Movement

Educating your children at home has always been an American option, but in the past was most often chosen for children in poor health or families living in remote areas. Children whose intellectual precocity challenged the public schools might also be homeschooled. Public schools in the past regularly asked homeschooling parents to provide evidence of their own education and of their curricular plans.

Today homeschooling has become associated with hot-button issues about religious beliefs. Children are often schooled at home to avoid contact with ideas such as evolution rather than to provide a more convenient or intellectually superior education. As a result, more children are kept out of school, and fewer parents are asked to provide an educational plan. Such a request from the schools could be interpreted as an interference with the parents' freedom to practice their own religion.

What connection can we make between the homeschooling movement and AT? Obviously, the claim of a direct relationship would be bizarre and unsubstantiated. Many homeschoolers find AT repugnant, and many children receiving AT attend public or private schools. Nonetheless, one set of ideas may influence acceptance of the other. For example, the idea that unusual child-rearing approaches may have a religious basis has a tendency to inhibit criticism. Children's infrequent school attendance, common in therapeutic foster parenting, may receive less investigation if schooling is seen as an aspect of the parents' religious choices. Complete nonattendance may never be questioned by a school district if a religious motive is present or implied.

Although some families have excellent homeschooling plans and good reasons (religious or otherwise) for following this educational approach, many families and children would benefit more from school participation. Involvement in school decreases the social isolation that is well known as a factor in child abuse. Both parents and children receive feedback from others in the school setting, reminding them when their family's practices diverge too far from community standards. Finally, schools act as gatekeepers to community resources, report evidence of abusive treatment to authorities, and can provide informal help to stabilize a family in a minor crisis. School attendance can thus diminish parents' motivation to accept fringe treatments such as AT.

National Change: Fear of Violence

Violent acts by children and adolescents have not increased in frequency in recent years, but people think they have and are frightened. With each report of an isolated violent act such as the Columbine killings, newspaper and television reports encourage the belief that the nation is on the brink of an insurrection of children, and their audience accepts this idea. In reality, mental illness and associated violence among the young are no more common than in the past, although easy access to firearms increases the chances of multiple deaths in one incident.

Fear of youthful violence provides a significant motivation for acceptance of AT. Advocates of this practice put constant stress on the desire of young attachment-disordered children to commit bloodcurdling violence such as tearing the heads off puppies. Early experiences of separation are claimed to be predictors that the children will grow up to be serial killers like Ted Bundy, a favorite example of AT advocates. AT is offered as the only possible prevention of these horrible anticipated acts.

World Events: Adoption from Other Countries

The adoption situation in the United States has also changed in ways that have facilitated acceptance of AT. Years ago, many infants were available for adoption solely because their unmarried mothers had "gotten in trouble" and wanted to evade the disgrace of unwed parenthood. These children often had reasonable prenatal care, and the mothers had little access to drugs or alcohol in the "homes" where they spent their pregnancies. The mothers unquestioningly gave up their parental rights and tried to keep this chapter of their lives a secret one. Unmarried fathers were not asked their opinions, nor was termination of their rights considered necessary.

After the early 1970s, teenage girls became far less likely to allow their babies to be adopted. About equal numbers chose abortion or attempted to rear the babies themselves, and only about 5% elected adoption soon after the birth. This did not mean that the larger group of babies necessarily stayed with their mothers permanently, however. Negligence and abusive treatment led to many later foster placements. Termination of parental rights often did not take place until the children were too old to appeal to adoptive parents, who might not in any case want the challenge of a child from a destructive background.

Potential adoptive parents thus found themselves with few healthy babies available in the United States. Some parents and some caseworkers were also concerned with the racial match between adoptive family and child. The process of terminating parental rights became more complex and began to include the rights of unmarried fathers. Open adoption, with the preservation of some relationship between birth parent and child, was a solution for some families but a serious problem for others.

The geopolitical changes of the late 1980s and early 1990s brought an unexpected alteration in the availability of adoptive children (Rutter, 2002). Orphanages in Eastern Europe were opened up to North American adoptive families, who were excited to find this source of young children whose parents were neither legally nor emotionally in the picture. Not long afterward, as the Chinese instituted their "one child" policy, there were countless opportunities to adopt Chinese baby girls, at least for families with the resources to travel to China.

Positive though these events may have been, any thinking person would be likely to consider the sad and frightening aspects of these adoptees' histories. The Eastern European orphanages made distressing news stories as reporters revealed the dismal neglect and sometimes brutal abuse the children had experienced. Little food, little cleanliness, little attention, little or no medical care: these had been the stories of their young lives. Parents could not help wondering what had been the impact of these horrors on their children's emotional development. They asked themselves whether their families could deal with the potential outcome.

The formation of adoption support groups such as the Association for Treatment and Training of Attachment in Children (ATTACh) presented potential adoptive parents with a solution for their worries. However bad the orphan's early experience and however serious the birth mother's prenatal grief or rejection of the fetus, AT could remove the child's rage and make him a normal, loving, obedient, true child of the adoptive family. For some adoptive parents, planning how to create an attachment became as important as going through the legal steps for adoption. Practitioners such as Ronald Federici made a specialty of foreign adoptions. Unfortunately for some of the orphans, however, these efforts did not solve all the family's problems—as witness the 2-year-old Russian child David Polreis whose adoptive mother claimed he had beaten himself to death with a wooden spoon.

CONCLUSION

This chapter has offered discussion of many factors, intrapersonal, social, and even political, that explain some aspects of parents' and therapists' enthusiasm for AT. We have not attempted to explain their acceptance as a result of their own psychopathology, tempting as it may be to ascribe the choice of this practice to pathological motives. It seems only sensible to avoid the temptation to diagnose when in fact we know little of these people's inner lives. It also seems constructive to examine how parents' misguided decisions and advocates' choice of techniques are caused by factors we might be able to control. Above all, it is critical to base our examination of the AT phenomenon on the understanding that complicated events have complicated causes. No single factor can explain the similar actions of thousands of people over many years and many miles.

REFERENCES

Barber, B. K. (1996). Parental psychological control: Revisiting a neglected construct. *Child Development, 67,* 3296–3319.

Beers, C. W. (1907/1981). *A mind that found itself.* Pittsburgh, PA: University of Pittsburgh Press.

Bettelheim, B. (1969). *Children of the dream.* New York: Macmillan.

Demetriou, A., Efklides, A., Papadaki, M., Papantoniou, G., & Economou, A. (1993). Structure and development of causal-experimental thought from early adolescence to youth. *Developmental Psychology, 29,* 480–497.

Erickson, M. H. (1962). The identification of a secure reality. *Family Process, 1*(2), 294–303.

Ezzo, G., & Bucknam, R. (1995). *On becoming babywise. Book Two: Parenting your pretoddler, five to fifteen months.* Sisters, OR: Multnomah Books.

Hershenson, R. (2000, August 6). Debating the Mozart theory. *New York Times Education Life Section,* pp. 22–23.

Leon, I. (2002). Adoption losses: Naturally occurring or socially constructed? *Child Development, 73*(2), 652–663.

Mercer, J. (1998). *Infant development: A multidisciplinary introduction.* Pacific Grove, CA: Brooks/Cole.

Newberger, C. (1983). Stages of parental understanding in child abuse and neglect. In V. Sasserath (Ed.), *Minimizing high-risk parenting.* Skillman, NJ: Johnson & Johnson.

Rutter, M. (2002). Nature, nurture, and development: From evangelism through science toward policy and practice. *Child Development, 73,* 1–21.

Sharaf, M. (1983). *Fury on earth: A biography of Wilhelm Reich.* New York: St. Martin's Press.

Slater, P. G. (1970). *Child rearing during the early national period.* Unpublished doctoral dissertation, University of California, Berkeley, CA.

Smith, M. B. (1950). [Review of the book *The authoritarian personality.*] *Journal of Abnormal and Social Psychology, 45,* 775–779.

St. Clair, B. (1999). *99 ways to drive your child sane.* Glenwood Springs, CO: Families by Design.

Tavris, C. (1989). *Anger: The misunderstood emotion.* New York: Simon & Schuster.

Thomas, N. L. (2000). Parenting children with attachment disorders. In Levy, T. M. (Ed.), *Handbook of attachment interventions.* San Diego, CA: Academic Press.

Wagner, D. M. (2000). *How to cast out demons.* Ventura, CA: Renew.

Chapter 9

The Law and the Child: How Our Legal System
Affected Candace Newmaker's Life and Death

If Candace Newmaker had been born into a functional family, she could easily have reached driver's license age without ever being aware of the law's potential impact on her. She would have been the subject of legal requirements such as mandatory school attendance, but these would have involved actions desired by her family rather than resisted or forced upon them. Candace might even have been little affected by the law if her family had been equally dysfunctional but more affluent so that social services agencies did not notice their problems.

As a child and a grandchild of foster children, however, Candace was born to be monitored by the legal system. In ways both general and specific, the law determined major events such as termination of her parents' rights to Candace's custody. Law as well as custom gave her adoptive mother the right to make decisions about medical and other treatment for Candace.

The laws in question were intended to protect Candace, but they did not succeed. This chapter discusses some relevant laws and notes the trouble they have in dealing with difficult, complex family situations. We examine the idea of children's rights and see how they may conflict with parents' rights. We examine the process by which Candace's birth mother's parental rights were terminated, freeing the child for legal adoption.

We discuss the principle called "the best interests of the child" and see the role played by attachment concepts in child placement decisions. Finally, we look at present and developing guidelines related to Candace's treatment experience: laws about child abuse, new views of physical restraint of children, and the protection the First Amendment gives to AT claims on the Internet and elsewhere.

CHILDREN'S RIGHTS AND PARENTS' RIGHTS

Did Candace Newmaker have the right not to be killed by Connell Watkins and Julie Ponder? Yes, she did, but Jeane Newmaker also had the right to seek medical or other treatment for Candace as she chose, and Candace did not have the right to refuse the treatment as an adult might have done. The rights of child and of parent are of quite different natures and may well come into conflict.

Children's Rights

Children do not have rights or obligations in the sense that adults do. Children have certain very basic rights, such as the right not to be killed, but they cannot own property by themselves or vote in elections or decide not to go to school; we depend on their parents to make the decisions for them and in their best interests. Depending on the state they live in and their exact age, minors may be able to marry or to have an abortion with or without their parents' permission, but generally these are considered to be matters that an adult should decide. If under 18, children do not have obligations such as jury duty or military service any more than they have certain legal rights. However, views on children's rights are in the process of change, and many countries (not yet including the United States) have voted to ratify the United Nations Convention on the Rights of Children, a document that clearly states the rights of the young not to be tortured or kept apart from their families.

If children do not have rights in the usual sense, are there any guarantees that society gives them? Yes, there are, because particular adults have obligations toward particular children. Parents have obligations to provide food, shelter, and medical care for their children and to make sure they receive a minimum level of education. These obligations are enforced by laws about abuse and neglect of children. Parents who fail in their obligations may be punished by fines or imprisonment and in some cases by legal termination of parental rights.

The Desire for Parenthood: The Great Motivator

Why is termination of parental rights a punishment? Surely we might think that an adult who has neglected or abused a child would be happy to be relieved of his or her obligations. On the whole, however, people are not happy about such an event. They want to maintain their connection with their child, however badly they have mistreated that child. The law takes this motivation into account and uses it to make as sure as possible that children are cared for. Most people value the status associated with parenthood and will work to achieve and maintain it. Like the abused child who still is attached to the parent, the abusing or neglectful parent still wants both the child and the idea of parenthood.

The issue of parental involvement touches on both attractive and unattractive aspects of human nature. If human beings have any instinctive tendencies to care for their offspring, these seem to be weak and easily distorted by unfavorable circumstances. Human beings are far from consistent in their attitudes toward their children; we might even say ambivalence is the essence of parental love. Our feelings about parenthood imply at least as much for our opinions of ourselves as they do for our treatment of our children. The fact that there is a child is a public confirmation of the parent's role as an adult. But a person whose children have been legally taken away has been judged as unfit and undesirable in a very public fashion. In addition, a parent is almost by definition a member of a social network, not a complete misfit or isolate. Termination of parental rights may recast the parent as a loner who lacks even basic relationships.

Even parents who rarely see their children tend to resist vehemently any attempts to free the children for adoption. To accept this would mean to accept the judgment that they will never be capable of making a home. For all these reasons, parents usually want to maintain relationships with their children, even when they must be forced by law to carry out their parental obligations.

The common parental motivations that make even bad parents resist termination of their rights were among the reasons Jeane Newmaker wanted to adopt a child when it seemed unlikely that she would become a parent otherwise. She had similar motives for keeping custody of Candace and seeking treatment for her rather than disrupting the adoption, in spite of the distress she apparently experienced in living with Candace (see chapter 1).

The Law and Parents' Obligations: The Public Interest at Work

Children's access to the care they need depends on their parents' many and contradictory motives and sometimes on the enforcement of parental obligations by law, as discussed in the previous section. But where do those laws come from? Why does the wider society concern itself with children rather than leaving them to the parents' good or ill treatment? A major reason is that the state has interests in what happens to children. These interests can be different for different societies. Some groups at some times have a special interest in producing as many children as possible, when the population has been decimated by war or disease. Such societies may forbid abortion or even contraception because of the overriding concern with population increase, even though such laws interfere with the private interests of citizens.

In modern industrialized societies, however, the interest of the state is not usually in simple population increase but in children as potentially valuable citizens. The state has an interest in growing citizens who are healthy and productive because of their long-term value to the whole society; its interest in maintaining the lives of those who are seriously handicapped exists but is based on different motives. As a result of their interest in children as potentially productive citizens, modern industrialized countries have laws intended to improve the chances that children will grow up mentally and physically healthy. If physical abuse is thought to harm children's development, industrialized countries tend to forbid or at least limit it. If poor emotional development characterizes children who later become unproductive citizens, the state requires parents to fulfill their obligations by seeking mental health treatment when it is needed. Above all, modern industrialized societies provide free public education for children and demand that parents make their children attend school and receive any treatment needed to facilitate education.

The interests of the state played a powerful role in shaping Candace's life. Her parents' rights were terminated because Candace was not expected to become a productive citizen under their care. Her adoption by Jeane Newmaker was expected to increase her chances of living a law-abiding, constructive life. Her adoptive mother was expected to carry out her obligations for Candace's physical and mental health and for her education in ways that would best assure the child's healthy development into a responsible adult.

Parents' Rights versus Children's Rights

Our discussion of the rights of children needs to be placed in the context of the rights of parents. When a society structures laws in terms of individual rights, certain issues are bound to arise. One is that different persons may be seen as having different sets of rights, either at all times or under different circumstances. For example, a woman may claim her right to abortion during early pregnancy, but at another time in her life may claim redress against someone whose actions caused her to abort a different pregnancy against her wishes.

A second issue is that there may be conflicts between rights. If a child's possible rights are honored, the result may be that the parent's rights are not, and vice versa. Similarly, if parents were to claim all rights of decision-making about their children without any legal constraints, other citizens might find that the resulting adolescents interfered with many people's enjoyment of their own rights, contrary to the public interest.

The concept of rights almost guarantees that no one will get everything they think they should have. Nevertheless, the idea of rights has a long history in Europe and the Americas, and many of our laws affecting children have emerged from related concepts such as parents' property rights. Whether the laws should continue upon this foundation is an arguable point.

Property Rights

Many laws about the rights of parents to make decisions for their children have come historically out of property rights. For European families of title and property, children were needed to keep the rights to a title and to keep property together. (And, however peculiar these motives may seem to the untitled American, they were strong ones.) Parents had rights to make decisions about children because the children's health, education, and conduct were relevant to the parents' own property and social position.

For lower-status as well as aristocratic families, the children's labor and other achievements were relevant to the parents' rights to their own property. Children began to work at early ages; if they received wages from employers, these belonged to their parents, who had a right to make the decisions that would add to their property. Even among the wealthy, an attractive, well-conducted son or daughter could "marry money" that would be settled on the maintenance of an estate or payment of debts—the plot of many a Victorian novel. Decisions made in rearing these children were connected to the parents' right to their property. When adoption laws and procedures became formalized, they were based largely on existing laws about the conveyance of property.

Rights and Relationships

The relationships between parents and children have obviously changed since the days when children added to property. Today, parents in industrialized societies feel they have a right to make decisions about their children, but they usually do not see those rights as connected to property. Except for services such as baby-sitting younger brothers and sisters, children are more likely to subtract from than to add to their parents' property holdings. Parental rights and parent-child relationships are perceived as involving personal feelings and attitudes about the self and others rather than the transmission of goods and social status. For good or ill, Jeane Newmaker's adoption of Candace was not intended to increase her affluence. Instead, the adoptive mother's goal seems to have been to create an affectionate relationship that she could enjoy.

Are Parents' Rights a Myth?

Laws and opinions about parents' rights are still in the process of change. One author, Philip Montague, has argued that parental rights are a myth and should not be considered as central to relationships between parents and children (2000). He has pointed out a number of cases where parents' exercise of their rights was detrimental to their children. The withholding of medical care from children because of parental religious beliefs is a typical situation.

In examining issues about parents' rights, Montague noted that not all human rights are of the same nature (2000). Rights can be categorized as liberty rights or as claims rights. Liberty rights involve acts that a person is free to carry out, that other people should not prevent, but that no one else is obliged to facilitate. The liberty right exists simply because no law forbids the person to carry out the act. A parent, for instance, has a liberty right to put pink clothes on a baby boy or blue on a girl or to decorate a bedroom with Little Bo-Peeps, football players, or nothing at all. Jeane Newmaker had a liberty right to apply to adopt a child.

Claim rights, on the other hand, are rights that imply other people's obligations to make sure the right can be enjoyed. If a parent has a claim right to make choices about a child's sex education, society is obliged to support that right by providing punishment for people who hand out pornographic material on the playground. Jeane Newmaker, like other parents, had a claim right to choose her child's religious education; anyone who interfered with her decision to rear Candace as a Roman Catholic could have been ordered to stop, even though the change from the birth family's religion would not ordinarily be considered good practice in adoption of an older child. Parental claim rights seem to be more closely associated with actions that we think influence children's development than liberty rights are; in other words, parental claim rights have something to do with the rights children would have if they had rights in the way adult citizens do.

Ordinarily, when we talk about people having rights, we mean they are entitled to something that will do them good. Parental rights seem to be different because they are so intertwined with obligations to carry out acts whose direct good is to the children. Any real rights parents have seem to be connected to choosing how to carry out their obligations; they do not have much choice about whether they do carry them out.

Termination of Parents' Rights

Logically, we can conclude that parental rights do not exist in the same sense as a right to privacy or a right not to be killed. However, American and European laws are written as if parental rights are like other types of rights. Under certain circumstances, people can lose many types of rights through legal action, and parental rights too may be terminated. In Candace Newmaker's case, her birth parents' rights were legally terminated to make it possible for her to be adopted.

The idea of parents' rights generally assumes that there is only one set of parents' rights per child. A mother cannot have her rights terminated and her child adopted by another woman who is married to a man other than the child's father unless the child's father's rights are also terminated. Two people cannot split a set of parents' rights unless they are now married, were married when they had the child, or in some way were both recognized at some time as having parental rights to a particular child.

Like many other aspects of family law in the United States, parental rights are shaped by state laws. For this reason, a complete discussion of rules about termination of parental rights would be too extensive for this book. Even a single state's guidelines tend to show swings of the pendulum back and forth from aggressive termination of parental rights to the opposite extreme of stress on family preservation. As a result, our comments must come with the warning that rapid changes can occur.

Issues about termination of parental rights most often occur when a child is already in the custody of the state's child protective services agency and generally in foster care placement (Gilberti & Schulzinger, 2000). This situation usually exists because the child appears to have been neglected, abused, or abandoned. What the parents actually did or failed to do may vary greatly from case to case. No simple list of neglectful or abusive acts is possible, because the effect of most parental actions depends on the child's age and other circumstances; to leave a newborn infant alone in a house for two hours is a very different matter from leaving a 12-year-old at home for the same period. The age of the child thus helps determine whether an action will be considered neglectful or abusive. It is probably also the case that poor, uneducated, or handicapped parents are more likely to have their children taken into custody following events such as unexplained injury or complaints of the children being left alone.

Of course, not all parents whose children are placed in foster care will later have their parental rights terminated. Many work hard and successfully to maintain their visiting relationship with the child and to correct the situation that caused the initial problem. Their families are often reunited.

Once the child has been placed in foster care, however, new or old circumstances may well lead to the termination of the parents' rights. Generally, this action depends on clear evidence that certain events have occurred *and* the judgment that termination of parental rights will be in the best interests of the child—an important concept that is discussed in the next section.

A wide variety of actions can result in termination of parental rights. In Texas, for example, these can range from violent acts such as murder or sexual assault, through less serious but relevant behaviors such as possession of child pornography, to causing the failure of the child to be enrolled in school.

What if a parent decides voluntarily to give up his or her rights? This is a momentous decision, and any change of mind would have serious consequences for the child and for an adoptive family. States try to regulate these decisions by limiting the times when they can be made (for instance, relinquishment may be formalized only after the child is born) and by setting varying time limits on how long the parent has to reconsider the matter. This can lead to an extremely confusing situation for adoptive parents if a child is being adopted in a state that allows a shorter time for reconsideration than the state where the birth mother lives.

Mental Illness and Parents' Rights

Parental mental illness can be an issue in the termination of parents' rights. Not all parents who are mentally ill have their rights terminated for that reason, although their mental illness may cause dangerous actions that can trigger loss of their rights. Under the Texas code, for instance, termination because of mental illness can occur only if the mental illness actually interferes with the care of the child and if it will interfere with the parent's future ability to perform such care.

In Candace Newmaker's case, there were many elements that would make termination of parental rights likely, but one unusual feature involved the contribution of mental illness to the decision. Under North Carolina law, a diagnosis of mental illness in childhood was necessary for continued services to age 18 for people whose violent behavior was considered to be related to emotional disturbance. As a result of a 1980 class-action lawsuit involving a teenager called "Willie M.," the state had created the requirement of this specific diagnosis, one that was often considered humiliating by its recipients. Candace Newmaker's birth mother, Angela Elmore, had received the Willie M. diagnosis as a child and was still eligible for services when she gave birth to her first child and then became pregnant with Candace. Social services workers were aware of this and may have been especially attentive to her performance as a mother; her history of explosive anger would certainly alert anyone to the possibility of child abuse, although there seems to have been no suggestion that she was so seriously disturbed that she could not care for her children (Crowder & Lowe, 2000).

THE BEST INTERESTS OF THE CHILD

If children have no clear rights other than basic considerations such as the right not to be killed, and if the existence of parents' rights is at best arguable, what foundation do we have for legal decisions about children? For fair and consistent decision-making, some principles need to be applied, but they cannot involve rigid rules because children and families can differ so greatly—especially in the United States, where there are remarkable regional and cultural differences.

The guiding principle of *the best interests of the child* was proposed about 30 years ago and has become a major basis for judicial decisions about children. The authors of several books outlining this principle (most recently, Goldstein, Solnit, Goldstein, & Freud, 1996) presented it as a way of making decisions, not as a clearly stated goal for the child's life. Considering that all possible real-world decisions about a child are likely to have their negative as well as their positive aspects, the authors suggest that the least detrimental alternative should be sought and that this should be done in the least detrimental way.

The Least Detrimental Alternative

The least detrimental alternative for a given child would be the choice that would interfere least with the child's development. Such a choice might have certain great advantages, but if those accompanied great disadvantages to development they could not be considered to be in the child's best interests. For example, the choice between placements for a child might involve one rather average parent who would provide an ordinary life. The other option might be a brilliant, talented, well-connected adult who would provide the best opportunities for travel and education but would also enlist the child in the making of pornographic films. In this (one hopes) imaginary scenario, the great advantages of placement with the second adult are outweighed by the serious detrimental effects. The first adult would provide a situation that was not especially advantageous but was clearly the least detrimental to the child's development.

The Least Detrimental Method

An important point of the best-interests principle is the idea of using the least detrimental *method* to discover the least detrimental decision. This approach stresses the timing of an investigation and of decision-making as it appears from the child's point of view. The time required to make a determination has a different meaning for a child than it does for an adult, and the younger the child, the greater the impact of a long wait. One or two years' wait for a decision is high-speed work in the judicial system, but for a toddler or preschooler it is an eternity. The least detrimental way of finding the least detrimental alternative needs to be quick as well as careful.

The question of speed may be especially important when it is possible that the parent has committed criminal acts that would lead to termination of parental rights. The parent's right to a thorough investigation of the matter may well conflict with the quick decision-making that would be in the child's best interests. For example, in one case, a woman who had adopted her stepdaughter and had a second child with her husband was accused of abusive treatment and starvation of the stepdaughter, who was placed in foster care. Child protective services personnel also took the other child, a healthy, well-cared-for infant of just under a year, and placed her with the same foster family as her half sister. A year-and-a-half later, both parents were convicted of abuse of the older child, and their parental rights to both children were terminated. By this time, both girls were doing well, and the younger appeared to have formed an attachment to the foster family, who wanted to adopt the two. The outcome seems to have been good for the girls, but we should consider what would have happened if the parents had not been convicted, their parental rights had not been terminated, and they had asked for the children to be returned to them, as would be their right. The lengthy period of time before the matter went to trial would still have been enough for the baby to adjust to the separation and form a new attachment—and now she would have been asked to do the same again, experience a loss, and come to terms with a woman who (although actually her mother) was to all intents and purposes a stranger.

The Child's View of Investigation

Particular ways of investigating may also work to the child's developmental disadvantage. Having a child appear in court to identify an abuser may be traumatic. A robed judge or police on duty in a courtroom can be frightening to a child already sensitized by previous experiences.

Investigations can be both inaccurate and traumatic to children when they ignore the discomfort with strangers that is part of good mental health in early childhood. For example, if a preschooler is placed in a foster home, part of the decision to reunite the family may be based on observation of parent and child together during a supervised visit. This is a good idea in itself, but it is all too common for the child to have to deal with many strange people and places before, during, and after the visit. An unfamiliar driver is likely to come in an unfamiliar car to take the child to an unfamiliar office, where an unfamiliar social worker takes him or her to an unfamiliar room. There, the child meets the mother or father, who probably feels and acts differently than usual because there is an observer and the stakes are very high. After the meeting is over, strangers again return the child to the foster home. This procedure is not only distressing in itself but can hardly be said to give a good assessment of either the parent's or the child's ordinary interactions. It is questionable whether this kind of investigation can accurately identify the least detrimental alternative for the child.

THE IDEA OF PSYCHOLOGICAL PARENTING

Many decisions based on the principle of the best interests of the child have employed the concept of "psychological parenting" or "bonding." Jurists using these concepts borrow from psychological theory the idea that the important emotional connection between children and their parents comes from mutual experience, not from their biological relationship. They also make use of the idea that separating a child from familiar, emotionally connected adults causes trauma and undesirable developmental consequences.

Terms and Meanings

As is discussed in a number of places in this book, emotional attachment is an important topic in the study of child development and as such uses a specialized vocabulary. Technical terms used by psychologists discussing emotional development do not necessarily carry the same meaning they would have for specialists in other disciplines. The term "attachment," as used by psychologists, is roughly equivalent to the term bonding used in legal circles. The legal term psychological parenting refers roughly to the experiences children have that cause them to form an attachment to familiar adults. (Neither bonding nor psychological parenting is generally used in a technical sense in professional psychology today.)

The Idea of Development

In addition to an altered vocabulary, the law has adopted a number of ideas about attachment from psychological work and used them in the search for the best interests of the child—at least, it has done so up to a point. The great difference between legal and psychological thinking on these issues is a matter of a developmental orientation. Developmental psychologists are concerned with the ways a child's environment and experiences can affect the person the child grows up to be, but they also consider the child's maturation. Maturational changes are developments that occur because of genetic determinants rather than because of experiences. Because the child goes through the processes of maturation as a part of development, he or she is constantly changing into a somewhat different being. That different being reacts differently to experiences than the person the child used to be. To state this in terms characteristic of psychology, there is an interaction between maturation and experience. How events affect a child depends on how mature the child is at the time (as well as on other, individual factors).

The process of attachment is deeply influenced by maturation. There is a period of time in early life when attachment is easily created. Not long afterward, there is a time when separation from familiar people is especially painful and harmful to development. In middle and later childhood, loss of familiar people is distressing but the long-term impact is not as great as it is for the younger child. If legal decisions were to follow developmental psychology, the guidelines of the best interests of the child would consider psychological parenting in ways that change systematically with the child's age. Examining child placement decisions, we see that judges often make very different assumptions about the role of attachment for children at different ages—but they do not do so in a systematic way.

When Are Custody Decisions Made?

What are the circumstances under which judges have to make decisions like these? One example would be a custody decision in divorce, where both parents may seek physical custody of a child or where there may be disagreements about the visitation privileges one parent will have. Another example is a child who has been with a foster family for several years, perhaps since soon after birth; the foster parents want to adopt the child, but a biological parent wants to be reunited with his or her child. There have also been cases when a biological father did not know of the pregnancy or birth, but upon finding out about it later wants extensive contact with the child, who may have been adopted. Yet another situation might concern a stepfather who has not legally adopted his stepchildren but whose wife, their mother, has died; the stepfather has no parental rights to the children even if he has lived with and reared them for many years. In recent years, cases of second-parent adoption or visitation rights have occurred when a lesbian couple has separated following a period of co-parenting children to whom one of them gave birth. Finally, the termination of parental rights following child abuse or neglect might involve a decision taking into account the child's very possible attachment to the abusive parent.

Expert Custody Recommendations

When psychological parenting is being considered as part of the determination of the best interests of a child, judges may seek expert testimony about attachment. This may be presented in terms of a "bonding assessment" (although, once again, the term bonding is rarely used in psychological research today). A bonding assessment or attachment assessment is a statement about the emotional attachment between child and parent and is probably based on some systematic observation by the expert (Gardner, 1999).

Usually, however, the materials presented in these statements are both less and more than the name implies. They often do not involve much information that is directly related to attachment. They do involve information on other topics, such as the parents' attitudes and knowledge about their children or their values and morals. Such assessments might more accurately be called custody recommendations than bonding assessments. They are attempts to predict the circumstances in which the child's best future developmental interests will be served, basing the prediction on information from the past and the present.

There are systematic approaches to the measurement of a child's attachment to an adult, and these are frequently used in research on emotional development or on parent-child relations. However, these approaches are not very useful in providing information for a judge to use, although it would be possible to do the systematic work that would make them useful.

Can Psychological Research Be Applied?

The first problem about application of attachment research to practical custody decisions is that the best-developed test of attachment was designed to work with 12-month-old children, not with older children or younger babies. Children at different stages of development do not behave in the same ways, and the behavior of an older or younger child cannot be compared meaningfully to data about 12-month-olds.

Second, the best-developed test of attachment is unwieldy and time-consuming rather than a quick checklist approach. This test, called the "Strange Situation," puts the parent and child into an unfamiliar playroom and exposes the child to a series of brief, harmless changes, evaluating the child's behavior as it indicates the relationship with the parent.

There is extensive research involving the Strange Situation, and the test could become the basis of legal decisions about certain children (Teti & Nakagawa, 1990). However, most of the work has concentrated on children within a narrow age range. We cannot necessarily jump logically from 12-month-olds to 3-year-olds, and certainly not to still older children. (Some attachment therapy literature does try to make this leap, but it is inappropriate both clinically and legally.)

The Nature of Assessments

We can conclude that there are many reasons why the Strange Situation should not be used in assessment for custody or parental rights decisions—and, of course, it is not normally used. What other information can we use, then? What facts are the bases of expert custody recommendations?

Custody recommendations that use terms such as bonding or attachment are sometimes extremely general. They may be based on one or two observations of a parent and child together, sometimes focusing simply on whether the parent behaves appropriately and the two seem happy together. Other custody recommendations (e.g., Gardner, 1999) are based on past history, particularly on who the primary caretaker was during the child's early years. Consideration may also be given to the fact that older children's needs are affected by many factors other than the primary emotional relationships.

Some assessments look at parenting capacity in the form of knowledge of effective child-rearing techniques. They may consider various measurements of parenting style and favor some styles over others. The parent's value system and moral choices may be discussed, as may the parent's availability to the child (for example, a predictable or unpredictable work schedule), involvement in education, and commitment to good health care. As children get older, factors such as acquaintance with the child's friends become more important, and so does the child's own stated preference, especially if the child gives good reasons to support it.

One recent idea is that placement decisions should consider "reciprocal connectedness," interactions between parent and child that change as the child matures but always indicates the feelings the two have for each other (Arredondo & Edwards, 2000). An observation of an adult with a very young child might take into account eye contact and affectionate touching, but an observation at a later age might emphasize events when the adult tries to teach the child and the child tries to learn from the adult. For an adolescent, reciprocal connectedness might be shown by the extent to which the parent and child cooperate in setting controls, limits, and boundaries.

No Assessments for Candace

What do these ideas have to do with Candace Newmaker's life? Did anyone ever assess her possible circumstances or make a custody recommendation based on evidence? No, assessment occurred only in the most sketchy way for Candace, as is the case for thousands of children like her. This was not because anyone was careless or particularly because funds were short, but because there were not many options open.

First, Candace's birth mother's parental rights were terminated after her children were removed from the home by social services staff workers. The details behind the removal are confidential information, of course, but relatives provided some background to the news media. As we noted elsewhere, the birth mother had been classified as a Willie M. child, receiving services because of a diagnosis of mental illness, and social services staff were aware of this fact. Fights between the parents attracted police attention. There was a report of possible abuse causing scrapes across Candace's sister's back, though her mother explained that the child had fallen out of the trailer through a loose door. The birth parents took the children and moved out of the county while this incident was under investigation, a decision that prompted the authorities to take custody of all three children when they were found. Although the children were placed in foster care at that time, Candace was later returned to her mother and counseling services were provided, suggesting that someone was thinking the family could be reunited successfully. But a quarrel between Candace's mother and grandmother soon culminated in another foster placement when one took the car and the other could not pick up Candace at her Head Start program. This series of incidents led social services workers to decide that continued life with the birth mother was not an acceptable option for Candace. The birth parents' rights were judicially terminated, freeing Candace for adoption.

Limited Options

Two factors in Candace's life set further limits on her options at this time and made it still less useful to do formal assessments or custody recommendations. First, at age 5, she was old in the eyes of most potential adoptive parents. On the whole, adoptive parents want infants. They want to replicate "natural" parenthood as much as possible, and they prefer not to have to deal with the results of other people's child-rearing mistakes. They may be more or less sophisticated about attachment issues and realize the importance of good early relationships. A small number of potential adoptive parents begin by thinking they want an older child whose "messy" stage is past, but many of these become more realistic about the nature of a parent's job. In any case, not many potential adoptive parents are looking for a child as old as Candace was at this time.

A second limiting factor was Candace's background of instability and poverty. In many families, relatively young grandparents like Candace's would have stepped forward to provide kinship care for the children. This might have concluded with their formal adoption of Candace and the others or with the children's being reunited with their mother. But these grandparents had few resources, and they had responsibility for an elderly great-grandmother. They felt they must take all three children or none at all and decided on none because they did not feel equal to the task. The grandmother herself had spent her childhood shuttling between foster homes and had given her own daughter up to foster care at an early age; it would not be surprising if she felt overwhelmed at the idea of dealing with the three young siblings. She may have considered foster care undesirable but not shockingly unfamiliar as an alternative to the birth family.

Under these limiting circumstances, there would be little concern about attachment issues. There is no point in assessing attachment unless the information helps decide among choices. Descriptions of Candace's behavior when she was taken from her birth mother suggest that there was an attachment there, which is what we would expect from their history of life together when Candace was 6 months to 24 months old—the time at which she was most ready to make an attachment. The 18-year-old birth mother, however incompetent or negligent she might have been at times, apparently planned the pregnancy and tried to read aloud and listen to classical music while she was pregnant. She seems to have been fascinated by this plump second child of hers, perhaps more so because she had given up her first baby for adoption. Emotional attachment is a robust process, and the fact that her mother was young, poor, unstable, and possibly abusive would not have prevented attachment in Candace's case.

No one, of course, would have expected Candace to have formed an attachment to her potential adoptive mother, Jeane Newmaker, at the time their relationship was formalized. Not only was Candace too old for the usual process of emotional attachment, but their time together had been limited to visits, one or two for a few days at Jeane Newmaker's house, and not sufficient for attachment even in a much younger child.

Assessing the Adoptive Parent

The major concern after Candace was legally available for adoption would have been not attachment but Jeane Newmaker's application to an adoption agency and the state Department of Social Services home study or preplacement assessment. The application to the agency would have included a discussion of Newmaker's family background and present situation, as well as information about the kind of child she wanted to adopt. The home study would have included discussions with a social worker. The potential adoptive parent might also be asked to take special preparation classes, directed at developing the skills needed for parenting a child who had experienced losses. (Candace was certainly such a child, but it is not known whether Jeane Newmaker took the classes.)

After the Adoption

Once the adoption was approved, the need for assessment would have diminished but not disappeared. Under North Carolina law, the child would have to be in the adoptive home for three to six months before the process could be completed. During this supervisory period, a social services worker would make regular visits to the home to offer support and, presumably, to note any occurrences that would suggest that the adoption should not proceed. The decree of adoption at the end of the supervisory period was followed by the issuing of a new birth certificate with the child's new name.

Especially when an older child is adopted, post-adoption services and continuing assessments of progress may be very helpful in preventing disruption of the adoption. Candace and Jeane Newmaker sought counseling services, although it would appear that the focus was always on treating the child rather than assessing the adoptive relationship.

The North Carolina Department of Social Services has one guideline that does not seem to have been considered in Candace Newmaker's post-adoption treatment, however. The Department suggests that even when parents' rights have been terminated, children who have an emotional bond to the birth parents should be helped to stay in contact with them. Continuing assessment would have been needed to monitor this process. AT treatment, of course, was not concerned with continued contact but with facilitating Candace's anger and hatred for her birth mother in order to create love for her adoptive mother. This treatment did not have the goal of maintaining Candace's familial relationships, as the department's policy would appear to recommend.

THE TREATMENT AND THE LAW

We have seen that legal procedures and considerations shaped many of Candace's life experiences. Our society's beliefs about Candace's rights and needs and about those of her parents laid out part of her future life story before she was even conceived. But what about the treatment she received at the hands of Watkins and Ponder? Did the law make their actions more, or less, likely than they might otherwise have been? Were there laws or guidelines that were even relevant to the bizarre events and ideas that culminated in Candace's death?

Colorado Law

At the time Candace died there were no Colorado laws forbidding the use of restraint by unlicensed therapists. When the legislature subsequently passed Candace's Law, they still did not specifically prohibit holding therapy, attachment therapy, or any similar practices with other names. Candace's Law forbids "reenactment of the birthing process through therapy techniques that involve any restraint that creates a situation in which a patient may suffer physical injury or death." The law makes a second offense a felony punishable by up to a year's imprisonment and a $100,000 fine. This law is likely to be read as applying to rebirthing only. Holding as a technique of treatment may result in some bruises but probably nothing sufficient to be judged as genuine physical injury when it is performed by a therapist. The emotional effects of holding therapy and of therapeutic foster parenting (see chapter 3) are not covered in any way by Candace's Law.

Child Abuse Laws

Watkins and Ponder were charged with abusive treatment as a result of Candace's death. It was the fact of the death that essentially defined the treatment as abusive. But was the treatment she received definable as abusive by its nature, without consideration of her death?

This question does not have an easy answer. Different states' laws define child abuse very differently. States are under some pressure from the Federal government to shape their definitions in particular ways, however.

Under Federal laws about reporting abuse and neglect—the Child Abuse Prevention and Treatment Act (CAPTA)—states that wish to receive related Federal grant money must have certain minimum standards in their definitions. According to CAPTA, child abuse and neglect refers to any recent act or failure to act by a parent or caregiver that results in imminent danger of serious harm or actual death, serious physical or emotional harm, sexual abuse, or exploitation. But even using the CAPTA minimum standards, states may define child abuse and neglect as a single concept or may have different definitions for physical abuse, sexual abuse, emotional abuse, and neglect. Sometimes neglect even includes mild forms of physical assault, but it usually refers to deprivation of adequate food, shelter, or medical care unless this results from financial inadequacy.

Because Candace's treatment culminated in her death, it seems simple enough to conclude that the treatment would be considered child abuse under CAPTA guidelines. But there is a logical problem here. The AT practitioners claimed that no child had previously died or been injured under the circumstances of the treatment. Although they admitted that Candace's rebirthing session went on far longer than any others they had done, they maintained throughout their testimony that they did not expect her to die and interpreted her pleas as part of the therapeutic process. Part of their defense was the claim that Candace died of some cause unrelated to the treatment, and this stance was maintained even though the evidence did not show any other reason for her death. Generally the intention of the adult would be taken into account in a situation like this, and Watkins and Ponder did not intend to cause death. If we are to argue that Watkins and Ponder's treatment was abusive, we may have to base that argument on their failure to act in a situation where common sense would say injury was likely. According to the therapists' own argument, the fault was not inherent in the treatment but resulted from their mismanagement, culpable or otherwise.

Emotional Abuse

Did Watkins and Ponder's treatment of Candace involve emotional abuse? We might look at this question under the CAPTA guideline about emotional harm, but this is not easy to demonstrate or even to examine in this case. Candace lived for only a few days after the commencement of the treatment, so there was little enough time for her to show the effects of emotional injury. According to courtroom testimony, there was some concern that Candace was beginning to show signs of dissociation, an emotional absence or failure of contact with others, that were apparently not present or noticed before the trip to Colorado. If Candace had lived and had shown later emotional disturbance, it would not necessarily have been easy to show that her problems were the result of Watkins and Ponder's treatment. After all, a child is presumably in therapy because there is emotional disturbance already present, and developmental change might create a worsening of symptoms even in the absence of bad experiences.

Emotional abuse has been considered difficult to define as well as to detect, but some suggestions have been made by James Garbarino (1998) and others about possible components of emotionally abusive treatment. Not all forms of emotional abuse would include all the suggested components.

One such component, *rejecting,* is the adult's refusal to acknowledge that the child has worth or that his needs are legitimate. As we saw in the description of Candace's treatment in chapter 3, rejecting was an important part of the rebirthing session, as Candace's pleas for release were deliberately ignored and treated as ploys for resisting emotional change. While Candace was presumably dying, Watkins spoke of how miserable the child made everyone around her, a clear rejection of the idea that she had any value for others.

A second component of emotional abuse, *isolating,* is a matter of exclusion from normal social experiences and can include keeping the child restricted to a room. Candace was limited to very brief interactions with her adoptive mother and was kept isolated much of the time while with the therapeutic foster mother.

Another possible component of emotional abuse is *terrorizing,* which is, of course, a major part of attachment therapy and is intended to produce the expression of rage. Candace was persistently threatened with abandonment and institutionalization, and the physical intrusions that are part of AT were also implied threats of more serious assaults. *Verbal assault* is an aspect of emotional abuse that was very much present during Candace's treatment sessions. She was addressed as a "twerp" and a "liar" and accused of wanting her mother to die; questions she asked were met with ridicule and humiliating sarcasm.

Although one or two of the components suggested as parts of emotional abuse were absent in Candace's situation, there were enough present for us to conclude that emotional abuse occurred. Whether they were sufficient to do actual harm to her mental health is something we cannot know.

Laws About Physical Restraint of Children

Do developing laws and policies provide some hope that the future will see better control over the use of fringe treatments such as AT? Will a Candace of the year 2010 receive better protection against her mother's misguided efforts or another therapist's mistaken acceptance of concepts without validity? One way to answer these questions is to look at recent changes in laws about related practices, such as the physical restraint of children during psychiatric treatment.

Even before Candace's death, there was a marked increase in public concern about the use of restraint of any type in psychiatric settings. Too many deaths had been associated with physical restraint. Advocacy groups such as the National Alliance for the Mentally Ill were already working toward the establishment of guidelines for the use of either physical restraint or seclusion during psychiatric treatment. More recently, the focus of concern came to be on the use of restraint in response to children's behavior in residential treatment centers. Physical restraint may sometimes be deemed necessary for the assurance of a child's or staff member's physical safety, but questions arose about its use for punishment.

In 2001, the Federal agency then called the Health Care Financing Administration released regulations that covered the use of physical restraint and seclusion with persons under 21 receiving inpatient psychiatric services under the Medicaid program. (These regulations, even if they had been in existence, would not have affected Candace Newmaker's treatment, because private insurance rather than Medicaid paid her fees.)

Under the new guidelines, children in residential psychiatric treatment are to be free from the use of restraint as "a means of coercion, discipline, convenience or retaliation" (*Federal Register*, 2000). We may assume that restraint as a means of treatment was omitted by the framers of these guidelines not because it was considered acceptable but because it was thought too inappropriate even to need mentioning.

The Federal Register guidelines on the use of restraint accept it only as an emergency response to situations where physical safety is an immediate concern. Any needed restraint must employ the smallest possible level of restriction. A trained practitioner must assess the condition of the restrained patient after one hour and must do this face-to-face. (If this had been done in Candace's case, she might still have been resuscitated.) Ongoing training and documentation of the use of restraint are required under these guidelines.

The Federal Register guidelines could provide an excellent model for legislation restricting AT, and they were suggested as such during discussion of legislation in Utah. However, as of this juncture, the model has not been extended to situations outside residential treatment centers or outside Medicaid funding.

THE FIRST AMENDMENT AND REGULATION OF ADVERTISING

In thinking about regulation of fringe therapies, we usually give first consideration to state legislation and Federal funding guidelines as the most obvious forms of control. In the case of treatments such as AT, however, there are also some relevant constitutional concerns. The First Amendment guarantees freedom of speech and prevents the suppression of information, even of ideas that are the potential cause of dangerous actions.

The guarantees of the First Amendment do not take into account that the basic concepts of AT are without validation. AT advocates are protected by the First Amendment from attempts to prevent them from making claims of validity. The First Amendment does not protect deliberately misleading or fraudulent statements such as a cry of "Fire!" in a crowded theater by a person who knows there is no fire—but we cannot show that AT advocates are intentionally misleading people. Fortunately, the First Amendment is equally protective of the rights of the authors of this book to argue against AT. Our true cry of "Fire!" cannot be suppressed either.

Like so many aspects of the United States Constitution, the First Amendment's meaning has been elaborated by court decisions. These have made it clear that commercial speech must be protected by the First Amendment unless its restriction affects an important governmental interest. As a result, the more than 80 Internet sites offering or advocating AT are protected by the First Amendment against regulation.

When representations about fringe treatments such as AT are deliberately deceptive, however, the advocates may be charged with fraud. The First Amendment does not protect them, but they often do not need much help in escaping punishment. For AT advocates to be found guilty of fraudulent practices, it would be necessary to show empirical evidence that their claims are actually false. That is, it is not enough to show that there is no evidence that the claims are true.

This is a point on which legal and scientific thinking styles are virtually irreconcilable. Scientific hypothesis-testing culminates in a statement of the probability that an event would occur by chance alone, not that a statement is true in the absolute sense. Hypothesis-testing work can similarly state only that there is a large probability that an event could have occurred just by chance, not that a statement is false. Science can only rarely show evidence that a statement is false, and this can be accomplished only if we can show a very small probability of the incorrectness of an incompatible, mutually exclusive statement. In most cases there are many possible hypotheses or "statements" that attempt to explain an event—not just a single, clearly incompatible pair of alternatives.

Even if it were possible to provide evidence that a treatment claim is false and known to be so by its promoters, a successful charge of fraud would have to show that the deliberately false claim was the cause of harm that occurred. In the case of Candace Newmaker's death, the videotaped evidence showed her alive at the beginning of the rebirthing treatment, recorded her sounds of distress during the period of restraint, and showed her dead when unwrapped. The jury accepted this as evidence that the treatment caused the death, in spite of defense attorneys' arguments that she died of some other cause. Without the videotape, however, it might have been very difficult to establish a direct causal link between the two events. This would be true of much scientific evidence unless it involved actual experimental control over the treatment. It would thus be difficult indeed to make a charge of fraud stick.

WHO IS AN EXPERT?

A final issue to be considered in this chapter is the role of the "expert" in the legal world. Our system allows for expert witnesses to give their opinions to jurors or judges when a trial hinges on technical knowledge. In the Watkins-Ponder trial, several witnesses were called, including a police forensics expert who described the analysis of physical evidence such as the sheet Candace had been wrapped in. Expert witnesses were also called to give their opinions of the events that brought about Candace's death.

What made these people experts? The answer to this question is in the process of change, like many other factors we have discussed in this book. The traditional view under federal law—and the one applied in Colorado—was that acceptable expert witnesses on matters of scientific evidence were people who passed the Frye test. In other words, they were in compliance with earlier Supreme Court standards, because they had the credentials that showed their expertise in the relevant area, and the opinion they gave was one generally accepted by the scientific community.

Federal courts (but not necessarily individual states' courts) changed their definition of expert witnesses following an important Supreme Court decision in 1993. This decision, in the case of *Daubert v. Merrell Dow Pharmaceuticals*, rejected the idea that a well-credentialed witness could simply state an opinion as being that of the scientific community. Instead, the Supreme Court set up some specific criteria that expert evidence had to meet before it could be accepted in court. The Supreme Court required that the evidence be relevant to the issues of the case. It also demanded that the evidence be reliable scientific information as shown by four criteria: it must be based on research whose hypotheses could be rejected on the basis of evidence; it must be based on work that had gone through peer review and been published; the potential rate of error for the method of testing hypotheses must be known; and the method must be generally accepted.

Colorado did not use the Daubert criteria for expert testimony. Indeed, in cases involving AT, this could not easily have been done even if the state had adopted the Daubert standards. There have been no tests of AT using generally accepted methods of hypothesis-testing, so no evidence conforming to the Daubert standards is available for expert witnesses to use.

The expert witnesses at the Watkins-Ponder trial were experts in terms of their credentials, but they were not in a particularly good position to present their opinions as those of the scientific community, as the pre–Daubert Frye standards would require. The great majority of the scientific community had never come across AT before Candace Newmaker's death, and most did not hear of it afterward except as a bizarre and disturbing news story. No analysis of the type done in this book had occurred before.

So, who are the experts? In addition to the Frye version and the Daubert version, we may have to find another version: witnesses testifying in fringe areas where there is no acceptable scientific evidence and the matter is so obscure that finding even a self-proclaimed expert is difficult. In the Watkins-Ponder case, the expert witnesses for the prosecution may have contributed to the conviction, but with more genuinely expert testimony a longer sentence might be possible, with a potentially greater deterrent effect.

CONCLUSION

Our discussion of legal issues shows the extreme complexity of regulation of treatments such as AT. Although there may be some progress in regulation of physical restraint for psychiatric purposes, it is slow indeed. First Amendment guarantees make it necessary for us to restrict the practice directly rather than restricting information about it, even if the information is deliberate disinformation (Kennedy et al., 2002). State legislation may be the simplest and most effective approach. We will see next what progress is being made in this area.

ACKNOWLEDGMENT

The authors thank Sheila Suess Kennedy, Esq., for her review of this chapter.

REFERENCES

Arredondo, D. E., & Edwards, L. P. (2000). Attachment, bonding, and reciprocal connectedness. *Journal of the Center for Families, Children, and the Courts, 146,* 109–127.

Crowder, C., & Lowe, P. (2000, October 29).Her name was Candace. *Denver Rocky Mountain News*, pp. 1A, 1M-7M, 9M-12M.

Federal Register (2000, May 22), *66*(99), 28110–28117.

Garbarino, J. (1998). Psychological maltreatment is not an ancillary issue. *Brown University Child and Adolescent Behavior Letter, 14*(8), 2–4.

Gardner, R. (1999). Guidelines for assessing parental preference in child-custody disputes. *Journal of Divorce & Remarriage, 30*(1–2), 1–9.

Gilberti, M., & Schulzinger, R. (2000). *Relinquishing custody: The tragic result of failure to meet children's mental health needs.* Washington, D.C.: Bazelon Center for Mental Health Law.

Goldstein, J., Solnit, A., Goldstein, S., & Freud, A. (1996). *The best interest of the child: The least detrimental alternative.* New York: Free Press.

Kennedy, S. S., Mercer, J., Mohr, W., & Huffine, C. (2002) Snake oil, ethics, and the First Amendment: What's a profession to do? *American Journal of Orthopsychiatry, 72*(1), 5–15.

Montague, P. (2000). The myth of parental rights. *Social Theory and Practice, 26* (1), 47–68.

Teti, D., & Nakagawa, M. (1990). Assessing attachment in infancy: The strange situation and alternate systems. In E. Gibbs & D. Teti (Eds.), *Interdisciplinary assessment of infants.* Baltimore: P. H. Brookes.

Conclusion

Lawsuits and Legislation: Where Do We Go from Here?

Many readers do not finish a book if they disagree strongly with it. If you are still reading, you probably share the serious concerns about AT that have been expressed in this book. You may even be thinking about what can be done to regulate these practices or to prohibit them altogether. However, you might still wonder whether it is a good idea to regulate AT or any other treatment. The children's deaths we have mentioned were few and unintentional. Many more children are killed each day riding in cars without seatbelts. And there are plenty of other bizarre child-rearing practices, some directly harmful.

Why do we propose to regulate AT or any other unvalidated treatment? We can give some good reasons for this, with both general and specific arguments. Our reasoning here does not depend on the possibility of death or injury but on other factors more likely to affect large numbers of children. In addition, we need to consider factors that have gradual rather than dramatic ill effects on children so that existing laws about neglect and abuse do not become relevant until a long period of harm has already occurred.

REASONS FOR REGULATION

When families become involved with unvalidated treatments, they may become less likely to seek suitable help when it is needed. When people see that an action is not doing any good, they are likely to escalate it rather than to try a different approach. (This is one reason why physical punishment may turn imperceptibly to abuse.) Although unvalidated treatments are sometimes called complementary to conventional techniques, the former easily become the single approach a family uses—and this may occur whether or not a family thinks the unvalidated approach is working.

Unvalidated treatments such as AT use up family resources, both of time and of money. Parents who are committed to a form of treatment may put so much energy into it—driving to distant therapists, going through home exercises every day—that other, more beneficial family activities lose their place on the schedule. For example, in the "therapeutic parenting" associated with AT, parents may have to spend hours each day monitoring and timing strong sitting. Other children in the family, as well as the one identified as the client, suffer from the parent's preoccupation and lack of free time.

Unvalidated treatments can have a negative effect on schooling. Part of this results simply from the time they require; looking back at Jeane Newmaker's trips to High Point with Candace, we wonder how the child ever had time to do her homework. In some versions of therapeutic parenting (foster, or otherwise), school is spoken of as a right, not a privilege. Children may not be allowed to attend school, or arrangements may be made for them to "take a hike" and go home if a teacher feels they are not cooperating.

AT in particular is associated with the unhealthy use of food as a manipulative device. Foods may be limited to less palatable basics such as peanut butter or oatmeal for months at a time. One 7-year-old, whose adoptive mother was apparently following therapeutic-parenting principles, was found eating from a garbage can at school; at home, she was required to hold weights over her head before meals, and if she did not manage to hold them long enough, she was not fed.

Finally, the practice of AT makes it easier for other dangerous treatments to seem acceptable. For example, some wilderness therapy camps seem to follow principles like those of AT; Foster Cline, the AT apologist, made this connection himself. The deaths that have occurred in such camps have resulted from the use of physical restraint. Illnesses and injuries have resulted from the principle that a child's apparent distress is simply a symptom of his or her resistance to authority.

LAWSUITS

There seem to be a number of reasons to discourage the use of AT, even if its physical safety for children could be guaranteed. But how can AT be discouraged? It would be relatively simple if we could invoke the protection of existing laws. As we saw in chapter 9, though, the protection of the First Amendment and the difficulty of proving fraud make this a difficult approach.

Criminal Cases

Under our present laws, it is extremely difficult to bring a successful criminal case against AT therapists unless some serious physical harm has already been done to a child. If Candace Newmaker had only been battered and bruised, there might well have been no clear case against Watkins and Ponder. Physical injuries, unless very severe, would probably heal without being documented; even if injuries were noticed by authorities, few prosecutors would be aware that a pattern of treatment such as AT could be responsible. Relative to AT, we are in a period like the one that preceded the identification of battered-child syndrome when physicians and prosecutors easily accepted explanations of children's injuries as accidental. We need a clear description of a sort of "AT child syndrome," including physical injuries, nutritional problems, and social and educational deficits.

Psychological injury resulting from AT would be almost impossible to demonstrate. The children involved are already considered to be emotionally disturbed, and the records available about their conditions are primarily those kept by the AT practitioners. It seems likely that the very experience of AT is traumatic, especially to children who have previously experienced abuse. To provide evidence for this statement would be a difficult matter, however, involving detailed clinical work both before and after the AT treatment. This would not be a practical possibility unless a well-trained clinician were able to "go underground" and spy in an AT treatment center.

Civil Suits

In many ways, it seems that a *civil* suit brought against AT practitioners would be more effective than criminal charges. Civil suits are decided on a less stringent basis than criminal cases (in terms of the preponderance of evidence rather than a certainty "beyond a reasonable doubt"). A jury that hesitates to send a therapist to prison might be more willing to assess financial damages.

There has been one civil case against a practitioner of AT (who used the older term "rage reduction therapy"). In 1989, Jeannie Warren, then 15 years old, was committed by her mother to a Fort Worth, Texas, psychiatric hospital. In the next 14 months, Jeannie went through about 25 restraint sessions, one lasting 5 hours. A nurse at the hospital documented bruises on the girl and later testified in court. Seven years after her treatment, Jeannie Warren sued the psychiatrist responsible, Dr. Robert Gross, who was ordered to pay over $8 million in damages. Not surprisingly, Gross skipped town, and Warren received nothing (Cohen, 1996).

There are other problems in civil suits against AT practitioners, in addition to the possibility that a therapist may skip or simply be unable to pay. Normally, we would expect a parent to bring a suit on behalf of an injured child who is too young to start the legal process on her own. But in these AT cases, the child's natural advocate and protector—the parent—has sought and approved the treatment. Unless adult guardians change their minds or claim they failed to understand the nature of AT, it seems unlikely they will bring legal objections against actions they previously condoned.

What about children bringing suits after they are grown up? Some young adults appear to be considering this possibility, but so far none of them have taken any specific steps. They would not, of course, have the support and guidance of their parents as many other people in their 20s might have. Their experiences with AT may well have undermined their self-confidence and their trust in our legal system. Their lives have not helped these young people achieve good earning capacities, and they may be afraid of the financial obligations a lawsuit could lead to. Finally, these AT victims have had limited educations and may have difficulty addressing authorities. The very injuries that require redress make it difficult for them to ask the law to help them.

The Federal False Claims Act

It can be difficult under our legal system for a private citizen to sue for fraud and win. The Federal government takes a dim view of its being defrauded, however, and has created laws that make it much easier to prove someone has committed fraud in their dealings with government. If AT practitioners were successfully to sell their services and have them paid for through Federal funding, it is possible they could be severely fined under these laws.

Qui tam provisions are legal guidelines that allow private citizens to bring complaints on behalf of the government, much as they can for themselves. These provisions have gone through several stages in the United States. The Federal False Claims Act of 1863 was passed to deal with fraudulent sales of worthless supplies to the Union Army during the Civil War. It included both criminal and civil penalties. One important feature was that the law allowed the whistleblower who reported the fraud to collect a proportion of the damages.

In 1943, Congress amended the False Claims Act, narrowing its use greatly and reducing the whistleblower's share of damages. The result was that very few such suits were brought for some years. The 1943 changes were reversed in 1986 with a new set of amendments. Today, suits under the False Claims Act are far more frequent, easier to bring, and easier to prove than they were. The time limits for bringing such a case are longer, the damages have increased to triple the amount of which the government was defrauded, and the defendant must pay the whistleblower's legal fees if found responsible for fraud.

The problem with applying the Federal False Claims Act to AT remains the demonstration of *intent* to defraud. If a practitioner truly believes, against all evidence, that AT is an efficacious treatment, and if he or she manages to sell services to the Federal government, it is unlikely that fraud can be proved.

If the Federal False Claims Act can be used against AT, it will probably be in cases that involve misrepresentation of diagnoses or of services provided. And, of course, the Act applies only to cases where payment comes from Federal funds. Services paid for by Medicaid would qualify, but not those paid for by private insurance. Monitoring of the Internet postings of AT parents' support groups suggests that practitioners are very careful not to get involved with Medicaid.

LEGISLATION

The difficulties of using existing legislation to fight AT suggest that new legislation may be our most effective approach to regulation. There have been some efforts along this line, but they have run into roadblocks.

Writing a Bill

Good bills are hard to write and hard to get passed by legislatures. Suppose, for example, that we wanted to write a bill that would apply, at the state level, rules based on the Federal Register guidelines on restraint and seclusion of children. The language we used would have to take into account situations where children are briefly but appropriately and legitimately restrained. Young children, especially, are often physically slowed down or stopped by caregivers, even carried away kicking and screaming to take a nap or have their diapers changed. Caregivers may use this kind of restraint with good humor and good judgment, but they do use it, and a bill that ignored this fact would make criminals of people who are doing their jobs properly.

One of the problems of a bill to regulate AT is the need to consider the intent of the practitioner. We do not want to prevent caregivers from using restraint for comfort, to ensure physical safety, or even as a way of communicating with young or developmentally delayed children. Physical contact and restraint—even types that can inadvertently cause pain—have a place in child care.

What we do want in a bill to regulate AT is the prevention of restraint used with the purpose of reaching a therapeutic goal with the assumption that either emotional attachment or simple obedience will result from restraint techniques. Unfortunately, many of the actions of AT—even grabbing the child's face or telling her to kick—could conceivably occur in acceptable contexts. Only a few specific acts, such as telling the child to shout distressing statements, are unlikely to occur in any situation other than AT treatment.

Perhaps it is this difficulty with questions of intent that has made drafts of anti-AT bills stress specific actions. Preliminary discussions of these bills, and some of the bills themselves, have stressed rebirthing rather than more typical AT techniques. It is fairly easy to describe the steps in rebirthing, and no ordinary child-care functions use any of them. Unfortunately, rebirthing is a red herring in spite of its causal role in Candace Newmaker's death, for it is an infrequent part of AT. Practitioners of AT could easily continue their usual practices if prohibited from using rebirthing.

Getting Public Support for a Bill

Policy- and law-making in the United States depend on bringing together heterogeneous groups and conflicting interests. A common and effective way to do this is through the use of a *condensational symbol* (Merrick, 1992), an image—usually of a person—that provokes pity, admiration, tenderness, concern, and perhaps relief that we do not share that person's less fortunate characteristics. The emotions elicited by the image are then used to fuel support for legislation or policy decisions.

Use of a condensational symbol depends on the availability of a good "poster child." Often these actually are children, attractive, brave, uncomplaining, cheerful, and with handicaps that frighten the rest of us just enough. The contrast between the child's handicap and his or her attractiveness seems essential.

It is hard to find a person to be an adequate poster child for mental illness unless we take some of the liberties with reality seen in the film *A Beautiful Mind.* The mentally ill are not only reminders of our fears about our own sanity but often frankly unattractive and annoying when we meet them. Mentally ill children are even more likely to attract hostility rather than sympathy, as people often feel that "a good spanking" would straighten them out. To find a poster child who triggers sympathy for mistreatment of the mentally ill is especially complicated and difficult.

AT Poster Children

Candace Newmaker's life was used as a condensational symbol to garner support for Candace's Law, a Colorado law banning rebirthing. Her grotesque death did not make her a very appealing poster child, however, and it is doubtful that other AT victims would be much better. It is far too easy for AT practitioners to blame these children for their own suffering. Nancy Thomas, the advocate of therapeutic foster parenting, has stated that we know parents are doing well with an attachment-disordered child if that child still has his head, arms, and legs on. The claims of AT practitioners that the children will grow up to be serial killers are likely to negate any genuine charm they have.

Living potential AT poster children who have recently had the treatment are likely to be thin, ill-kempt, and frightened-looking. (Thomas also advised that the children wear dark glasses in public so their sad looks will not attract attention and sympathy.) If they are older teenagers or young adults, they are likely to be gauche and to present themselves poorly as a result of their experiences. The poster child approach doesn't play well as a way to rally support for a bill opposing AT.

Opponents to Bills

Other factors work against the chances of passing good legislation to regulate AT. It is generally correct to say that the opponents of an anti-AT bill would be well organized but the advocates less so. Some professional groups almost automatically lobby against any regulation relevant to their practices. They are naturally concerned about control exerted by nonprofessionals who do not know much about their work. (When we realize how little members of the helping professions have known about AT, we can also see why they might dismiss this particular regulatory attempt as unnecessary.)

There is, of course, a genuine pro-AT lobby made up of groups such as AT-TACh and representing AT practitioners and advocates. These people have every reason to fight regulatory legislation. As we pointed out in chapter 2, they have hired a public relations firm that claims expertise in regulatory and public-affairs matters.

LEGISLATION IN PROGRESS

We have noted elsewhere the difficulties of legislation that could prevent or at least regulate the use of coercive restraint techniques such as AT. Fortunately, some legislators and activists are already working on writing and passing suitable legislation; unfortunately, they are encountering many obstacles. In this section, we discuss events in this frustrating process.

The Colorado Legislation

Candace Newmaker's death was a powerful impetus for changes in Colorado law. However disorderly the United States may sometimes seem, citizens' first response to distressing events is often that "there oughta be a law" against what has happened.

A Proposal for Regulation

In Colorado, the first proposal for legislation, following Candace's death in 2000, had to do with regulation of individuals practicing psychotherapy. Colorado had at one time had regulatory legislation, but more than a decade before Candace's death this had been altered to a simple requirement for registration with the state. More recently, unlicensed psychotherapists had also been asked to attend a yearly workshop about legal issues. After Candace's death, Coloradoans asked whether a return to state regulation could prevent the use of harmful treatments. The answer to this question would probably have been "no" in practice, but political pressures from unlicensed therapists ensured that no Colorado politician took an interest in the proposal for regulation.

The Bill Banning Rebirthing

Candace's catechism teacher seems to have made the first suggestion for an alternative proposal. He suggested a bill that he called Candace's Law, making use of the dead child as a condensational symbol to focus interest and support. This bill was to outlaw rebirthing or any restraining therapy. With the encouragement of two of the authors of this book, then-freshman state legislator Debbie Stafford (herself a registered but unlicensed counselor) introduced a bill to prohibit rebirthing, calling it Candace's Law. If this legislation passed, therapists would be prohibited from "using or recommending rebirthing as a therapeutic treatment." According to this bill, "'Rebirthing' means the reenactment of the birth process through psychodrama techniques, including, but not limited to, physical restraint creating a situation in which a patient may suffocate."

The potential loopholes and difficulties with this language soon became apparent. The bill was altered so that rebirthing was defined as "the reenactment of the birthing process through any therapy techniques that involve any restraint that creates a situation in which a patient may suffer physical injury or death." Additional language in the new draft provided that parental consent to such procedures could not be given on behalf of a child. This bill was passed unanimously and signed by the governor of Colorado in a ceremony attended by Candace's birth grandmother and her husband in April 2001—about a year after Candace's death and in the last week of the Watkins-Ponder trial.

Pressure for Revision

The passage of Candace's Law has not been the end of this story. For those who are concerned about regulating AT, of course, the bill does not go nearly far enough. For various practitioners of unvalidated treatments, it goes much too far. The latter group expressed concern to Rep. Stafford and asked for revisions of the bill that would limit it to situations of serious physical injury or death. The face-off between supporters and opponents of the bill's current language ended without introduction of a revised bill that, if passed, would for all intents and purposes have repealed Candace's Law.

The Danger of the AT Belief System

However, Candace's Law as it stands presents little difficulty for AT practitioners, who use rebirthing far less frequently than other restraint techniques. Although Candace's Law is a step in the right direction, to attempt a ban on rebirthing is to distract attention from the real issues. Rebirthing may be a senseless ritual, but it is dangerous only in combination with the beliefs and attitudes characteristic of the AT philosophy. Candace Newmaker could have survived her experience; she was alive after 10, 20, perhaps even 40 minutes of pressure and restraint. What killed her was the belief system of the therapists: that the child's pleas could not be accepted as genuine, that she could perform the action demanded if she were not resisting, and that her resistance must be met with redoubled physical and emotional pressure. Without these beliefs, the AT practitioners would soon have realized that Candace was in real trouble and would have released her.

Utah: Efforts at Legislation

The emphasis of this book on Candace Newmaker's AT treatment in Colorado may have obscured the fact that such practices exist in other states as well. Utah, too, had an AT poster child, Krystal Tibbets, who died at the age of 3 in 1996. Krystal stopped breathing while her adoptive father lay on her, apparently following the advice of an AT practitioner, Larry van Bloem, and an agency-ordered condition for adoption.

Concerned citizens, including Jon Barney, a young activist whose friend had been subjected to AT, and Alan Misbach, a social worker who had seen holding done on children, approached Utah legislator Mike Thompson about legislation. In 2002, Thompson proposed a bill that would apply existing Utah laws about the use of restraints in medicine to parallel situations in mental health treatment.

Political pressure to hold up this bill came from a number of sources: Nancy Thomas, the therapeutic parenting advocate from Colorado; the leader of the conservative Utah Eagle Forum, who was concerned that the bill compromised parental rights; and, of course, AT practitioners in the state. The Thompson bill succeeded in passing the legislature's lower house, but a threat to filibuster and prevent passage of the state budget prevented a vote in the upper house, delaying the anti-restraint legislation for a year. As this is written in January 2003, work on this legislation is once again active in Utah.

Other States

Legislation to regulate restraint is being discussed in some other states too. Legislators in North Carolina are working on an anti-rebirthing bill that would have all the flaws discussed earlier with respect to control of AT. New Jersey has had several bills proposed to deal with the use of physical restraint in schools for handicapped children but has not yet focused on its "therapeutic" uses.

What Would Make Good Anti-AT Legislation?

A bill that would actually control the use of physical restraint in psychotherapy would probably be difficult to pass, for reasons outlined earlier in this chapter and throughout this book. The need to compromise on legislation is one of the realities of life. Nevertheless, we might do well to consider the ideal proposal, the position from which we might have to retreat to find sufficient support to pass a bill.

Scientific Evidence

One approach, suggested by psychologist-lawyer Christopher Barden (an expert witness for the prosecution at the Watkins-Ponder trial) is to require by law that all mental health treatments meet the criteria for scientific evidence we discussed in earlier chapters. This is an admirable goal and one that would have benefits far beyond the regulation of AT. However, the fact that the restraint in question is done to children makes this solution less viable, even if we had sufficient evidence about all treatments.

Legitimate Restraint

As we noted earlier, physical restraint is used in children's everyday lives as well as in AT sessions. Physical restraint of children is practiced in many legitimate situations, especially with young children or with children who are developmentally delayed or emotionally disturbed. Such restraint may be part of physical care procedures or may be an attempt to keep the child or another person safe. The length of restraint may be short or long, and the extent can range from a hand on the shoulder for slowing a running child to a full-scale "takedown." Children may be restrained by their parents, teachers, day care providers, school crossing guards, nurses, or mental health professionals. We expect these people to use restraint appropriately, but we cannot take away their freedom to use restraint when it is necessary.

Intentions

We are thus faced with a problem much like that inherent in defining child abuse: the issue is not so much what people do as their intention in doing it. A parent who accidentally injures a child is not guilty of child abuse; a teacher who stops a running child is not using restraint in the way that concerns us.

But how can we tell what the person's intention is? In normal life, we do a good job of this as we exercise the "theory of mind" we developed as children. If we want to understand someone's intention, we look at a variety of factors: events right before the action, the actor's facial expression, and what the person says before, during, and after the act. In the case of deliberate restraint intended as therapy, only one of those—the events just before the action—seems very helpful for an understanding of the holder's plans and intentions. Restraint used legitimately generally follows specific types of events: the young child raises her hand to grab a toy, the developmentally delayed child is running toward the top of the stairs, the emotionally disturbed child has a cigarette lighter.

Restraint used intentionally as therapy does not occur under these triggering circumstances. It is planned without much regard for concurrent events. An appointment may even have been made for the holding session.

Documentation of Restraint

We may propose, then, that legislation to regulate AT could focus on the circumstances under which restraint occurs. To save the time and energy of professionals who work with children, we might consider only incidents where restraint lasts more than 5 minutes. (A need for brief restraint can arise often in a child's normal day, but AT holding sessions usually last much longer.) For restraint incidents longer than 5 minutes, our bill would require documentation of the circumstances just preceding the restraint, as well as the length of the restraint. The restraint records kept by any practitioner (including teachers and child-care workers) would need to be maintained systematically and available on request for inspection by an appropriate agency. The law would include penalties for more than a minimum of inappropriate restraint, as well as for falsification or mishandling of records.

"Documentation" is a word that can be worrisome to busy professionals, but it can be done very quickly by means of a checklist or other prepared form. Documentation of events in a child's day outside the home can be an extremely positive step toward quality care and treatment. The National Association for the Education of Young Children considers such record-keeping a part of high-quality early-childhood programs, and there are parallels for older children with physical, cognitive, or emotional handicaps. Documentation of the reasons for restraint can also be helpful for mental health workers and other professionals in the event of accusations of abusive treatment.

Beyond Documentation

There are a number of problems in this proposal. One is that it would be easy for parents who really wanted restraint to find individual therapists, working in their homes, whose very existence would be unnoticed by any agency. Documentation would be a concern only for large AT enterprises such as those that advertise on the Internet.

Requiring and assessing documentation may be only a partial solution to the use of restraint for therapy and for other reasons as well. The Colorado and North Carolina AT practitioners and many others would be susceptible to this type of control, but other holding proponents instruct parents rather than themselves carrying out restraint. The Utah practitioner Larry van Bloem seems to have been one of these, and he had no direct responsibility for Krystal Tibbets's death but had advised her adoptive father about restraint. Psychiatrist Martha Welch and her student Bryan Post take similar approaches, as does Ronald Federici.

To pass or enforce a law requiring parents to document restraint would be an impossibility. Not only would groups such as the Eagle Forum resist this fiercely as a compromise of parental rights, but the job of assessing compliance would be beyond state social services agencies even if they gave up all other tasks.

Passage of appropriate legislation will be dependent on good *professional* and *public education*, as will persuasion of parents to avoid inappropriate restraint. Professional organizations need to use care in their approval of continuing professional education courses. Mental health professionals need to learn both about advances in their fields and about fringe treatments, so they can be a source of accurate information for their clients. Parents whose information comes from the Internet and the mass media are at risk of being drawn into unvalidated treatments, even if those treatments are illegal. Without serious efforts for education, we can expect to hear about more Candaces, more Krystals, and more Davids.

UPDATE

Between the completion of the major portion of this book and the point when it is about to go to press, a number of incidents have shown that the AT problem is an ongoing one.

On the positive side, the American Psychiatric Association issued a policy statement rejecting treatments that involve coercive restraint. Less positively, their press release on this statement stressed rebirthing as the important issue and seriously underplayed the more frequently used types of physical restraint.

Representative Sue Myrick of North Carolina introduced a proposal for a Congressional statement condemning rebirthing. Her proposal did not mention other types of coercive restraint, and her office did not respond to suggestions for change. Unfortunately, the proposed statement as it stood as of this writing was a potential red herring, although undoubtedly well meant. AT practitioners, who rarely use rebirthing in any case and who seem quite frightened about it now, can point to the failure to mention other AT techniques as a form of support. "When people were considering these treatments, they rejected rebirthing; had they wished to reject our other techniques, they would have done so at the same time" might be the claim of AT advocates.

AT Internet support groups continue to flourish and to accept the AT belief system. One recent discussion in such a group involved ways in which an adult could bite a child without leaving tell-tale marks (biting the finger was advised). Deliberate failure to feed children was also a topic of discussion. The case of a girl with frequent nosebleeds was treated as if the child were at fault, and pouring vinegar up her nose was offered as a remedy.

An AT organization has placed on the Internet a letter for the parents of RADishes to give to their children's teachers. This letter advises teachers to disbelieve whatever the child says and to give no sympathy for any complaints or failures. The teacher is also to insist on eye contact, a procedure that might be especially disturbing to minority children. The authors of this book are preparing mailings to education associations in the hope of countering this disinformation.

Finally, and most disturbingly, 4-year-old Cassandra Killpack of Springville, Utah, died in June 2002 under circumstances suggestive of AT treatment. According to reports in the *Salt Lake Tribune* (Broughton, 2002), Cassandra had been treated by therapists at the Cascade Center for Family Growth in Orem, Utah, an organization that has favored coercive restraint in the past. The Cascade Center was searched by police a few days after Cassandra's death. The investigation is still in progress and little information has been released, but according to newspaper reports Cassandra died as a result of brain swelling resulting when she was forced to drink quantities of water as a paradoxical treatment and consequence after she disobediently took a drink without asking.

REFERENCES

Broughton, A. (2002, June 13). Therapy center searched in probe of girl's death. *Salt Lake Tribune*. Retrieved June 13, 2002, from http://www.sltrib.com/2002/jun/06132002/utah/745060.htm.

Cohen, E. (1996, October 24). Rage reduction therapy: Help or abuse? *US News*. Retrieved October 30, 2001, from http://www.cnn.com/US/9610/24/rage.reduction.therapy/.

Merrick, J. (1992). Conflict, compromise, and symbolism. In A. Caplan, R. Blank, & J. Merrick (Eds.), *Compelled compassion*. Totawa, NJ: Humana Press.

Polanco, M. (2001, May 10). Jury sentences Liberty Hill pair to 2 years in jail. *Austin American-Statesman*, B6.

Bibliography of Materials Relevant to Attachment Therapy

Current materials posted on the Internet may be found at the Websites of such groups as the Heal the Heart Foundation, ATTACh, and the Attachment Center at Evergreen, as well as those of attachment disorder support groups such as one found through the Marymount University Website.

Allen, J. A. (1976, December). The identification and treatment of "difficult" babies. *Canadian Nurse,* 11–16.

Allred, D., & Keck, G. (1996, spring/summer). The evolution of attachment therapy. *Attachments* (Newsletter of the Attachment Center at Evergreen). Retrieved July 18, 2000, from http://www.attachmentcenter.org/evolve.htm.

Anderson, J. (1990). Holding Therapy: A way of helping unattached children. In P. Grabe (Ed.), *Adoption resources for mental health professionals.* New Brunswick, NJ: Transaction Publishers.

Association for Treatment and Training in the Attachment of Children. (1999). ATTACh: Basic assumptions. Retrieved July 18, 2000, from http://www.attach.org.

Bath, H. (1994). The physical restraint of children: Is it therapeutic? *American Journal of Orthopsychiatry,* 64(1), 40–49.

Berliner, L. (2002). Why caregivers turn to "attachment therapy" and what we can do that is better. *APSAC Advisor,* 14(4), 8–10.

Bowers, K. (2000, July 27). Suffer the children. *Westword.* Retrieved July 27, 2000, from http://www.westword.com/issues/2000–07–27/feature.html.

Broughton, A. (2002, June 13). Therapy center searched in probe of girl's death. *Salt Lake Tribune.* Retrieved June 13, 2002, from http://www.sltrib.com/2002/jun/06132002/utah/745060.htm.

Buenning, W. (2000). Attachment and bonding. Part III. *Chosen Child,* 2(4). Retrieved July 21, 2000, from http://members.aol.com/RADchina/buenning.

Cline, F. W. (1979). *What shall we do with this kid? Understanding and treating the disturbed child.* Evergreen, CO: EC publications.

Cline, F. W. (1992). *Hope for high risk and rage filled children.* Evergreen, CO: EC Publications.

Cline, F. W. (1994). *Toward an understanding of the essentials of bonding theory and attachment therapy.* Retrieved November 15, 2000, from http://www.netw.com/fostercline/understandingbonding.html.

Cohen, E. (1996, Oct. 24). Rage reduction therapy: Help or abuse? *US News.* Retrieved July 10, 2000, from http://www.cnn.com/US/9610/24/rage.reduction.therapy/.

Crowder, C. (2000, May 19). Therapist has long ties to "holding" treatment. *Rocky Mountain News.* Retrieved July 21, 2000, from http://insidedenver.com/news/0519gsid2.shtml.

Crowder, C. (2000, July 29). Prosecutors add charges for rebirthing therapist. *Rocky Mountain News.* Retrieved July 29, 2000, from http://www.insidedenver.com/news/0729char).shtml.

Deam, J. (2000, June 4). Controversial therapy worked, patient said. *Denver Post,* p. x. Retrieved June 10, 2000, from http://www.insidedenver.com/news.

DeAngelis, T. (1997). When children don't bond with parents. *American Psychological Association Monitor.* Retrieved June 10, 2000, from http://www.apa.org/monitor/jun97/disorder.html

Delaney, R. J., & Kunstal, F. R. (1993). *Troubled transplants: Unconventional strategies for helping disturbed foster and adoptive children.* Fort Collins, CO: Horsehead Press.

Drisko, J. (1981). Therapeutic use of physical restraint. *Child Care Quarterly, 10,* 318–328.

Emerson, W. R. (1996). The vulnerable prenate. *Pre- and Perinatal Psychology Journal, 10*(3), 125–142.

Erickson, M. H. (1962). The identification of a secure reality. *Family Process, 1*(2). 294–303.

Fahlberg, V. I. (Ed.). (1990). *Residential treatment: A tapestry of many therapies.* Indianapolis, IN: Perspectives Press.

Federici, R. S. (1998). *Help for the hopeless child.* Alexandria, VA: Dr. Ronald S. Federici and Associates.

Friedman, R. (1970). A "rage-reduction" diagnostic technique with young children. *Child Psychiatry and Human Development, 1,* 112–125.

Friedman, R., Dreizen, K., Harris, L., Schoen, P., & Shulman, P. (1978). Parent power: A holding technique in the treatment of omnipotent children. *International Journal of Family Therapy, 6,* 66–73.

Friedrich, W.N. (2002). Introduction to holding therapy: Part I. *APSAC Advisor,* 14(3), 2–3.

Friedrich, W.N. (2002). Introduction to the Special Issue: Part 2. *APSAC Advisor,* 14(4), 2.

Friedrich, W.N. (2002). Points of breakdown in the provision of services to severely disturbed foster and adoptive children. *APSAC Advisor,* 14(3), 11–13.

Hage, D. (1997). Holding therapy: Harmful?—or rather beneficial! *Roots and Wings Adoption Magazine, 9*(1), 46–49. Retrieved June 15, 2000, from http://debrahage.com/pwp.

Hanson, R.E. (2002). Reactive Attachment Disorder: What do we really know about this diagnosis? *APSAC Advisor,* 14(4), 10–12.

Hanson, R. F., & Spratt, E. G. (2000). Reactive Attachment Disorder: What we know about the disorder and implications for treatment. *Child Maltreatment, 5*(2), 137–146.

Helding, C., & Cline, F. W. (n.d.). *Choosing to use confrontive therapies with attachment disordered children.* Retrieved July 11, 2000, from http://cathyhelding.com.

Horn, M. (1997) A dead child, a troubling defense. *US News Online.* Retrieved July 21, 2000, from http://www.usnews/issue/940714atta.htm.

Howe, D., & Fearnley, S. (1999). Disorders of attachment and attachment therapy. *Adoption and Fostering, 23*(2), 19–30.

Hughes, D. A. (1999). Adopting children with attachment problems. *Child Welfare, 78*(5), 541–561.

Hunt, J. (n.d.). *The dangers of holding therapy.* Retrieved August 16, 2000, from http://www.naturalchild.com/jan_hunt/holding_therapy.html.

Janov, A. (1970). *The primal scream.* New York: Dell.

Jernberg, A. M. (1990). Attachment enhancing for adopted children. In P. Grabe (Ed.), *Adoption resources for mental health professionals.* New Brunswick, NJ: Transaction Publishers.

Keck, G. C., & Kupecky, R. M. (1998). *Adopting the hurt child: Hope for families with special-needs kids.* Colorado Springs, CO: NavPress Publishing Group.

Kennedy, S. S., Mercer, J., Mohr, W., & Huffine, C. (2002). Snake oil, ethics, and the First Amendment. *American Journal of Orthopsychiatry, 72* (1), 5–15.

Konia, C. (1996). Orgone therapy: The application of functional thinking in medical practice. Part XVI: Children and adolescents. *Journal of Orgonomy, 29.* Retrieved December 1, 2000, from http://www.orgonomy.org/articles_022.html.

Krenner, M. (1999). *Ein Erklarungsmodell zur "Festhaltetherapie" nach Jirina Prekop.* Retrieved October 25, 2000, from http://www.uni-wuerzberg.de/gbpaed/mixed/work/mkrenner/.html.

Lester, V. S. (1997). *Behavior change as reported by caregivers of children receiving holding therapy.* Retrieved August 4, 2000, from http://www.attach/lester.htm.

Levy, T. M. (2000). Attachment disorder and the adoptive family. In T. M. Levy (Ed.), *Handbook of attachment interventions.* San Diego, CA: Academic Press.

Levy, T. M., & Orlans, M. (1998). *Attachment, trauma, and healing.* Washington, DC: Child Welfare League of America.

Levy, T. M., & Orlans, M. (1999). Kids who kill. *The Forensic Examiner,* March–April, 19–24.

Levy, T. M., & Orlans, M. (2000). Attachment disorders as an antecedent to violence and antisocial patterns in children. In T. M. Levy (Ed.), *Handbook of attachment interventions.* San Diego, CA: Academic Press.

McKelvey, C. A. (Ed.).(1995). *Give them roots, then let them fly.* Evergreen, CO: The Attachment Center at Evergreen.

Magid, K., & McKelvey, C. A. (1987). *High risk: Children without a conscience.* New York: Bantam.

Martinez v. Abbott. (1997). Unpublished report of Minnesota Court of Appeals. Retrieved August 5, 2000, from http://www.finance-commerce.com/cort/opinions/970829/C89766.htm.

Mercer, J. (2001). "Attachment therapy" using deliberate restraint: An object lesson on the identification of unvalidated treatments. *Journal of Child and Adolescent Psychiatric Nursing, 14*(3), 105–114.

Mercer, J. (2002). Attachment therapy. In Shermer, M. (Ed.), *Skeptic's encyclopedia of pseudoscience.* Santa Barbara, CA: ABC-CLIO.

Mercer, J. (2002). Attachment therapy: A treatment without empirical support. *Scientific Review of Mental Health Practice, 1(2),* 9–16.

Mercer, J. (2002). Child psychotherapy involving physical restraint: Techniques used in four approaches. *Child and Adolescent Social Work Journal, 19(4)*, 303–314.

Mercer, J. (in press). Violent therapies: The rationale behind a potentially harmful child psychotherapy and its acceptance by parents. *Scientific Review of Mental Health Practice.*

Moss, K. G. (n.d.). *What is attachment?* Retrieved July 5, 2000, from http://www.attach.org.

Myeroff, R. L. (1997). Comparative effectiveness of attachment therapy with the special needs adoptive population. Unpublished dissertation. Cincinnati, OH: The Union Institute.

Myeroff, R. L., Mertlich, G., & Gross, G. (1999). Comparative effectiveness of holding therapy with aggressive children. *Child Psychiatry and Human Development, 29(4)*, 303–313.

New Hampshire Executive Council. (1999). *Minutes, Item #85A.* Retrieved August 19, 2000, from http://www.state.nh.us/council/min092899.html.

Oreskovich, R. (2002). Educating about "holding therapy": Comments from a child welfare administrator. *APSAC Advisor, 14(4)*, 7.

Randolph, E. (1997). *Attachment therapy does work!* Retrieved January 20, 2001, from http://www.attachmentcenter.org/articles/article015.htm.

Randolph, E. (2000). *Manual for the Randolph Attachment Disorder Questionnaire.* Evergreen, CO: The Attachment Center Press.

Randolph, E. (2001). *Broken hearts; wounded minds.* Evergreen, CO: RFR Publications.

Reber, K. (1996). Children at risk for attachment disorder: Assessment, diagnosis, and treatment. *Progress: Family Systems Research and Therapy, 5*, 83–98.

Reich, W. (1945). *Character analysis.* Rangely, ME: Orgone Institute Press.

Rosin, D. (1994). Medical orgone therapy with children. *Journal of Orgonomy, 27.* Retrieved December 1, 2000, from http://www.orgonomy.org/article_095.html.

Rouse, K. (2001, April 22). Rebirthing verdict may curb restraint therapy. *Denver Post.* Retrieved April 22, 2001, from http://www.insidedenver.com/news/0422.

Sainsbury, C. (2000). *Holding therapy: An autistic perspective.* Retrieved August 19, 2000, from http://www.oneworld.org/autism_uk/archive/hold.html.

Saposnek, D. T. (1972). An experimental study of rage-reduction treatment of autistic children. *Child Psychiatry and Human Development, 3*, 50–61.

Schiff, J. L. (1969). Reparenting schizophrenics. *Transactional Analysis Bulletin, 8(31)*, 47–63.

Schiff, J. L. (1970). *All my children.* New York: M. Evans.

Sharaf, M. (1983). *Fury on earth: A biography of Wilhelm Reich.* New York: St. Martin's Press.

Silver, L. B. (1995). Controversial therapies. *Journal of Child Neurology, 10*, 96–100.

Smith, L. (1996, July 12). Full of woe. *Los Angeles Times*, Life & Style Section, p. E1.

Speltz, M.L. (2002). Description, history, and critique of Corrective Attachment Therapy. *APSAC Advisor, 14(3)*, 4–8.

Spoolstra, N. (1997). *Are we prepared for intensive therapy? What is holding anyway?* Retrieved August 10, 2000, from http://www.syix.com/adsg/articles/holding.htm.

Sroufe, L.A., Erickson, M.F., & Friedrich, W.N. (2002). Attachment theory and "attachment therapy." *APSAC Advisor, 14(4)*, 4–6.

St. Clair, B. (1999). *99 ways to drive your child sane.* Glenwood Springs, CO: Families By Design.

Thomas, N. L. (2000). Parenting children with attachment disorders. In Levy, T. M. (Ed.), *Handbook of attachment interventions*. San Diego, CA: Academic Press.

Tinbergen, N., & Tinbergen, E. (1983). *"Autistic" children: New hope for a cure*. Boston: Allen & Unwin.

Verny, T., & Kelly, J. (1981). *The secret life of the unborn child*. New York: Dell.

Verrier, N. N. (1993). *The primal wound*. Baltimore: Gateway Press.

Ward, S. M. (n.d.). *Therapeutic parenting*. Retrieved August 10, 2000, from http://www.hannahandhermama.com/rad/therapeutic.htm.

Welch, M. G. (1983). Retrieval from autism through mother-child holding. In N. Tinbergen and E. Tinbergen, *"Autistic" children: New hope for a cure*. Boston: Allen & Unwin.

Welch, M. G. (1989). *Holding time*. New York: Fireside.

Wilson, S. L. (2001). Attachment disorders: Review and current status. *Journal of Psychology, 135*(1), 37–52.

Woods, K. (1998). The danger of sadomasochism in the reparenting of psychotics. *Transactional Analysis Journal, 28*(1), 48–54.

Zaslow, R. W. (1966). Reversals in children as a function of midline body orientation. *Journal of Educational Psychology, 57*, 133–139.

Zaslow, R. W. (1982). Der Medusa-Komplex. Die Psychopathologie der menschlichen Aggression in Rahmen der Attachment-Theorie, widergespiegelt in Medusa-Mythos, dem Autismus und der Schizophrenie. *Zeitschrift für Klinische Psychologie und Psychotherapie, 30*(2), 162–180.

Zaslow, R. W., & Menta, M. (1975). *The psychology of the Z-process: Attachment and activity*. San Jose, CA: San Jose State University Press.

VIDEOTAPED MATERIAL

Copies of commercial productions are not easily available, but useful:

Buchanan, A. (1997). *Understanding attachment*. Beech Brook Spalding Adoption Program, 3737 Lander Road, Cleveland OH 44124.

48 Hours. (1993). "Afraid of Our Children." Harold Dow, correspondent. CBS, New York. Available at http://store.cbs.com/video.php?itemID=4504.

Prime Time. (2001). "Roots of Rage." Diane Sawyer, correspondent. ABC, New York. Available at http://abcnews.go.com/sections/primetime/2020/primetime010712_twins_feature.html.

Thomas, N. (1998). *The circle of support for Reactive Attachment Disorder*. P.O. Box 2812, Glenwood Springs, CO 81602.

Thomas, N. (1999). *Captive in the classroom*. P.O. Box 2812, Glenwood Springs, CO 81602.

Index

Abandonment, 1, 19, 40
Acting out, 18, 123–25, 142
Adolescence, 102–3
Adopted children, 59, 149–51, 207–8
Adoption, 15–17, 211, 215–17, 224–26
Adoption beliefs, 197–98, 202, 207–8
Adoptive disruption, 20
Alcoholism, 42, 146–47
American Psychiatric Association, 47, 246
American Psychological Association, 8, 164
American Psychological Association task force, 164, 172, 173
Analytical parenting style, 105, 194
Antisocial or borderline personalities, 131
Anxiety, 119, 147
Anxiety disorders, 120, 122
Asphyxiation, 30–32
Association for Treatment and Training of Attachment in Children (ATTACh), 26, 45–47, 50, 208
Attachment and Bonding Center of Ohio, 182
Attachment Center at Evergreen, 43, 44, 178
Attachment Disorder Checklist, 178
Attachment disorders, 24–25, 74, 112–15, 178–79
Attachment theory, 51, 95–100

Attachment therapists. *See* Cline, Foster; Ponder, Julie; Watkins, Connell; Zaslow, Robert
Attachment Therapy (AT): background, 43, 189–90; definition, 2; historical empirical evidence, 177–85; practices, 58–59, 60–71; rationale, 72–80
Attachment Therapy philosophy, 57–59, 61–62, 72–79, 202
Attention Deficit Disorder, 21, 23, 29
Authoritarian personality, 192–93
Autism, 118, 119

Babywise program, 201
Barden, Christopher, 243–44
Barney, Jon, 243
Beheler, Norma, 25–27
Bell, Mary, 132–33
Best interests of the child, 218–20
Bipolar disorder, 29
Birth experiences, 76, 93–94, 202
Birth mother. *See* Elmore, Angela
"Blind" studies, 173–74, 180
Bonding assessment, 222–23
Borolby, John, 74, 98
Bundy, Ted, 207

Candace's Law, 240–42
Case Management, 22–23

Case Studies, 171, 181–82
Catharsis, 75, 196–97
Cause-and-effect thinking, 139, 198–99
Cellular memory, 93
Character armor, 190
Checklists, 25, 170, 178, 179–80
Cherney, Mary Sue, 19, 27
Child abuse, 127–28, 227–28
Child Abuse Prevention and Treatment
    Act, 227–28
Children's rights, 212–17
Civil lawsuits, 237–38
Class I evidence, 170–72
Class II evidence, 170–72, 174–75,
    182–85
Class III evidence, 170–72, 181–82
Cline, Foster, 43
Cognitive-behavioral psychotherapies, 136
Cognitive dissonance, 199–200
Cognitive errors, 198–99
Colorado law, 44, 240, 241–42
Colorado School for the Blind, 43,
    181–82
Columbine High School, 124, 207
Communication, 136, 138
Comparison group, 171, 174, 183
Complementary and alternative medicine
    (CAM), 54–55
Compliance training, 62–63
Compression therapy, 68
Condensational symbol, 239–40
Conduct disorders, 124–27
Continuing professional education, 8–9
Control, 61–62, 195–96, 201
Conventional parenting style, 104,
    194–95
Criminal law, 236–37
Crowder, Carla, 38
Cruelty to animals, 61, 180
Cuddling, 64, 68
Cultural factors, 130–32
Custody decisions, 221–22
Cycle of need and gratification, 95, 96

Daubert decision, 165, 231–32
Daubert v. Merrell Dow Pharmaceuticals,
    231–32
Davis, David, 39, 40

Davis, Mary, 39, 40
Dawes, Robyn, 53
Death certificate, 32
Deinstitutionalization, 204–5
Delinquent behavior, 124–25
Demonization, 61
Dependent variable error, 198–99
Depression, 17, 121–23, 147
Descriptive research, 169–70, 181
Developmental dysfunctions, 116
Developmentally appropriate practice, 138
Dexedrine, 18, 19, 28
Diagnosis of mental illness, 110–13
Discipline techniques, 106–7
Disobedience, 201
Display rules, 41
Divorce, 149–51
Documentation, 244–45
Domestic violence, 39
DSM-IV, 111–12
DSM-V committee, 46–47
Dyadic psychotherapy, 144

Eagle Forum, 243
Educational testing, 21–22
Effexor, 31
Egoistic parenting style, 104, 194–95
Elkind, David, 129
Elmore, Angela Maria, 39–41
Elmore, Candace Tiara. *See* Newmaker,
    Candace Elizabeth
Elmore, Todd Evan, 39–40
Empathy, 99–100, 132, 142, 156–57
Empirical evidence, 165–85
Ethical guidelines, 48–51
Evaluation of treatments. *See*
    Empirical evidence
Evergreen, Colorado, 42–44
Evidence-based care, 164–67
Exorcism, 202
Experts, 222, 231–32
Externalizing affective disorders, 123–25
Eye contact, 58, 68, 75, 118–19, 223
Eye movement desensitization and repro-
    cessing (EMDR), 55

False memory, 164
Falsifiability, 168–69

Family counseling, 137–38, 154
Family reunification, 40
Family systems, 37–38, 40, 137–38
Federal Register, 229–30
Federici, Ronald, 208
Feinberg, Neil, 44
Fire setting, 121
First Amendment issues, 230–31
Floor time, 138
Food, 43, 79
Foster care, 16, 39–41, 217
Fraudulent practices, 230–31
Fringe therapies, 2–5
Froelich, Molly, 19–20
Frye test, 231

"Ghosts in the nursery," 151
Ginsburg, Mai Mai, 17
Goal-corrected partnership, 98
Goble, Bill, 26
Gosney, Douglas, 69
Grandin, Temple, 118
Greenspan, Stanley, 138
Gross, Robert, 237
Guilford Attachment Center, 24–26

Head Start, 40
Holding Therapy.
 Attachment Therapy
Home schooling, 206
Home study, 16
Homework, 21–22
Hughes, Daniel, 157–58

Individual Educational Plan, 22
Individualistic parenting style, 104–5,
    194
Individuals with Disabilities
    Education Act, 23
Infant mental health, 140–41
Infertility, 147
Informal consent, 48–49, 175
Intensive treatment, 26
Intergenerational concerns, 40–41
Internalizing affective disorders,
    121–23
Internal working model, 95, 98–99
Internet, 189

James, Beverly, 120
Joint planning, 99

Koop, Everett, 6

Lachiewicz, Ave, 18, 25
Learning disorder, 21
Legislation, 239–43
Levy, Terry M., 44
Licking, 68
Locus of control, 101–2
Lowe, Peggy, 38

McDaniel, Jack, 64–66, 69–70
Manipulativeness, 61–62
March, John, 18–19
Martinez v. Abbott, 33
Maternal depression, 129, 147
Maturational change, 174
Media influences, 124–25, 204
Mental illness, 109–33
Mentalization, 156
Mesmer, Franz, 189
Meta-analysis, 173
Mind-body connections, 77–79
Misbach, Alan, 243
Munchausen (factitious disorder) by
    proxy, 192
Myeroff, Robin, 183

Narcissism, 148–49
National Alliance for the Mentally Ill, 229
National Association of Social Workers, 8, 50
Newmaker, Candace Elizabeth: adoption,
    15–17; birth family, 38–41; death, 1,
    2, 30–31, 68–71; diagnosis, 17–25;
    treatment, 59–72
Newmaker, Jeane Elizabeth: family back-
    ground, 41–42; personality, 148, 192–93;
    professional training, 42
Newmaker, John, 41–42
Nichols, Todd, 46
Nightmares, 19, 69
North Carolina law, 16, 39, 218
Nurse-practitioner training, 42

Obbema, Diane, 36, 60, 65
Obedience, 97, 100, 120, 201–2

Operationalism, 176
Oppositional Defiant Disorder, 18, 20, 21, 29, 179
Organ transplantation, 30, 31, 35
Orlans, Michael, 43

Pain, 75, 78, 239
Parental awareness, 104–5
Parental rights, 38, 40, 214–15
Parental style, 194–95
Parent-professional relationships, 51
Parent therapy, 154, 155
Pathology report, 31
Patterning, 3, 76
Permanency planning, 145
Personality, 85–87, 93, 115–16, 148–49, 192–94
Pervasive Developmental Disorders, 118–19
Physical contact, 49–50
Physical exercise, 63, 68
Physical punishment, 106, 107, 127
Physical restraint, 5, 25, 29, 30, 59, 65, 68, 70, 229, 230
Physical stimulation, 43, 78, 79, 190
Pickle, Paula, 46
Play, 22, 100–101
Play therapy, 154–55
Polreis, David, 5
Ponder, Julie, 28, 30, 34, 35–36, 45
"Ports of entry" for psychotherapy, 151–52
Post-Traumatic Stress Disorder (PTSD), 19, 120–21
Prenatal life, 58, 92, 93
Preoccupation, 142
Preplacement assessment, 16, 223–25
Prevalence, 180–81
Pro-AT lobby, 241, 243
Probability, 198
Professional training, 53–54
Property rights, 214–15
Prosecution, 34, 236–37
Prozac, 18
Pseudosymmetry, 6–7
Psychodrama, 60
Psychodynamic psychotherapies, 136

Psychological maltreatment, 128, 228
Psychological parenting, 220, 221
Psychosis, 18, 125–26
Psychotherapy, 151–57, 173

Quasi-experiments, 171, 174, 175, 182–85
Qui tam lawsuits, 238

"RADishes," 45, 105
Rage, 59, 66, 72, 74–75, 78, 80, 190
Randolph Attachment Disorder Questionnaire (RADQ) 26, 115, 179–80
Randolph, Elizabeth, 46, 179
Randomized assignment, 172
Reactive Attachment Disorder, 24, 25, 112–14, 178
Rebirthing, 30, 68–71, 76, 239, 241–42, 246
Recapitulation, 75, 77, 201
Reciprocal connectedness, 223
Redemption, from sin, 201
Regulatory disorders, 117
Reich, Wilhelm, 190
Reliability, 172–73
Religious belief, 200–202
Respite care, 203
Risperdal, 19
Ritalin, 17–18
Rutter, Michael, 2, 51

St. Clair, Brita, 28, 45, 60–61
Schizophrenia, 125–26
School experiences, 21–22, 100–102, 206
Screening, 178–79
Sechrest, Lee, 53
Self-concept, 101–2
Self-help, 190–91
Self-regulation, 94–95
Sensitive periods, 91
Sensitivity and responsiveness, 106
Separation, 51, 95
Serial killers, 61
Shadow professionals, 188–89
Shame reactions, 97–98
Sleep, 19
Social class, 41

Social emotions, 97–98
Social referencing, 96
Spaulding, Jean, 17
Stafford, Debbie, 242
Stages of development, 90–91
Standards of practice, 49–50
Statistical analysis, 167–68, 173, 182–84
Stenmark, Kurt, 32
Strange Situation, 222–23
Strong sitting (power sitting), 62–63
Support groups, 47–48, 191, 200
Sweets, 63, 79
Syntonic symptoms, 136
Systems approach, 38, 86, 87–88, 137

Tactile defensiveness, 117
Tantrums, 117, 118
Temperament, 115–16
Tenex, 19
Teshuvah, 76
Therapeutic foster parents, 49, 60–64
Thomas, Nancy, 26, 46, 61–62, 195
Thompson, Mike, 243
Tibbets, Donald, 5, 243
Tibbets, Krystal, 5, 243
Transactional processes, 86
Transductive reasoning, 139
Transference object, 137, 145

Transformational therapies, 80, 136
Traumatic experiences, 120–21

United Nations Convention on the Rights of Children, 10
Unlicensed therapists, 44
Unvalidated treatments, 3–4
Utah legislation, 243

Validation, 164–65
Validity, 172
Van Bloem, Larry, 243
Variability, 167–68
Videotaping, 30, 34
Violent behavior, 207
Vlosky, Mark, 43

Warren, Jeannie, 237
Watkins, Connell, 29–30, 35–36, 43–44, 64–70
Whistleblowers, 238
Wilderness therapy, 9
"Willie M." designation, 39, 40, 218

Zaslow, Robert, 43
Zeanah, Charles, 2
Zero to Three, 5
Zoloft, 19
Z-therapy, 43

About the Authors

JEAN MERCER is a Professor of Psychology at Richard Stockton College. She is also currently President of the New Jersey Association for Infant Mental Health.

LARRY SARNER is an official with the American Association for the Humane Treatment of Children in Therapy, and a past Researcher with the National Council Against Health Fraud.

LINDA ROSA is a Researcher with the National Council Against Health Fraud.

GERARD COSTA is the founding director of the YCS Institute for Infant and Preschool Mental Health. He is a Clinical Assistant Professor in the Department of Psychiatry at the University of Medicine and Dentistry of New Jersey. The New Jersey Child Assault Prevention (CAP) Program selected him as the recipient of the 2003 state award in the category of Mental Health Professional for outstanding work in the prevention of child abuse.